THE LATTER DAYS AT COLDITZ

The Latter Days at Colditz

P. R. Reid

CORONET BOOKS
Hodder Paperbacks Ltd., London

To
Michael, Diana,
Christopher and Christina

Copyright © 1952 by P. R. Reid
First published 1953 by Hodder & Stoughton Ltd.
Coronet Edition 1965
Second Impression 1965
Third Impression 1969
Fourth Impression 1970
Fifth Impression 1972

Printed and bound in Great Britain for
Coronet Books,
Hodder Paperbacks Ltd,
St. Paul's House, Warwick Lane,
London, EC4P 4AH
by Hazell Watson & Viney Ltd,
Aylesbury, Bucks

ISBN 0340 01180 7

ACKNOWLEDGMENTS

My principal collaborators in the work of collecting the material for this book have been Captain "Dick" Howe, M.B.E., M.C., formerly of the Royal Tank Regiment, and Captain "Lulu" Lawton of the Duke of Wellington's. Major Harry Elliott of the Irish Guards has been a close third. Without them this book would not have been written. It is a happy coincidence that Dick and Harry should have been my colleagues on one of the first escapes from a German prison camp in the last war—early in September 1940!

From Holland I have had unstinted, generous help from Captain G. W. T. Dames of the Royal Netherlands Indies Army. I could not have written of the Dutch without him. From France I have had the help of General le Brigant through his well-known work, *Les Indomptables*, the French classic on the fortress prison, and of Père Yves Congar, who has written a memorable epitaph to the Frenchmen who never returned, in his book *Leur Résistance*.

Mr. John K. Lichtblau, the well-known American critic and newspaper correspondent, has helped me to follow up trails in the U.S.A., and Major V. Dluznievski, now living in England, has traced for me many obscure details concerning the remnants of the Polish contingent of Colditz.

Herr Hans Pfeiffer has been my link with Germany, and in a frank, friendly manner has given me the German point of view.

Returning to Britain, I acknowledge with gratitude—and pleasure, because they are still very much alive—the help of many ex-Colditz men: Alan Campbell, who has contributed poetry [1] and notes of his legal battles with the German High Command; Rupert Barry and Peter Storie Pugh for their scrap-books of the war and their notes; Geoffrey Wardle and his wife and children for an enjoyable evening in which the

[1] He has recently published his Colditz poems in *Colditz Cameo* (from the Ditchling Press, Ditchling, Sussex), which I consider to be a highly talented and moving anthology.—P. R. R.

glider was rebuilt in fantasy; Peter Tunstall, Kenneth Lee; Padre Ellison Platt for the use of his sermon and his song; Edmund Hannay and Mike Harvey.

I wish to acknowledge my indebtedness to *The Times* and to the *Sunday Express* for the reproduction of extracts from editions of May 1945, and to the publishers of *Detour*, which contains an interesting series of war reminiscences and much about Colditz. This book has often helped me over questions of history, in particular with regard to the names of officers and to dates of occurrences.

Jack Best sent me the original glider plans and most useful technical notes all the way from Kenya. Lorne Welch and his wife have together rechecked those plans in order to confirm, once more, that the machine could take the air.

Commander and Mrs. Fowler and Wally Hammond lent me their private writings, which I found most helpful and from which I have quoted.

Lastly, to those who criticised the roughs of this book, in particular my wife and Mr. H. R. Chapman, C.B.E., I owe a great deal; and to my wife especially, who slaved through the late and early hours typing the manuscript, I am irrevocably indebted.

I have not exhausted the list of those who have helped to make this story a reality in print. I cannot forget the succulent meals with which Nanny—Miss Freda Back—kept body and soul together during the long sessions. More names spring to mind as I write: General Giebel, Colonel Guy German, Kenneth Lockwood, Roger Madin . . . I ask them all to accept my thanks and only hope that the story will do justice to their efforts.

P. R. REID

PLANS

PROLOGUE

I HAVE often been asked the question: "Why did the Germans put up with so much from the Allied P.O.W.s in Colditz? From the stories told, one is almost sorry for the Germans— the prisoners gave them such a h—— of a time!" In order to answer this question, I wrote—some years after the late war— to the only contact that I could trace among the German personalities of those days. Herr Hans Pfeiffer, the German interpreter at Oflag IVC, Colditz, was, happily, still in the land of the living, safe in the Western Zone of Germany. Colditz, by the way, is in the Eastern Zone, behind the Iron Curtain. Pfeiffer's reply to my letter was written in good English and this is what he said:

> You ask for my impressions of Colditz. I think our treatment of you was correct. Of course it was your *verdammte Pflicht und Schuldigkeit* as officers to escape, if you could, and it was likewise our 'damned duty' to prevent your doing so. That some of you did actually manage to get away under such difficult circumstances could only arouse the admiration of 'your friends the enemy', but I think your own book shows that such a collection of *enfants terribles* as yourselves could not be handled with kid gloves. *Nichts für ungut!*—no offence meant.

The Germans looked upon the prisoners as 'their friends the enemy'. It was a curious friendship, but I can see what Herr Pfeiffer means. It was of the kind that springs from respect; that might easily have sprung up, for instance, between the Desert Rats and Rommel's hardened campaigners, if circumstances had ever presented the opportunity.

Colditz was the prison to which Allied officers were sent after trying to escape from Germany. (Towards the end of the war there was not room in the camp for them all, and some who

7

should have been there never had the dubious honour of residence within its walls!) The initial spark of defiance thus shown in captivity and registered by transfer to Colditz, produced the reaction mentioned by Herr Pfeiffer.

In Colditz itself, however, the spirit of defiance blossomed. In the tropical atmosphere of the prison, where 'the heat' was turned on by the prisoners, this spirit thrived. The germ of admiration planted in the minds of the warders grew to a personal respect as they came into daily contact with men who would stand no bullying and who showed by their actions that the weapons in the warders' hands were not conclusive arguments as to the conduct of affairs in the prison.

The result was a *modus vivendi* 'comparatively' neutral as opposed to hostile. The Colditz prisoners received, on the whole, what might be termed manly treatment.

Pfeiffer apologetically explains that the prisoners could not be handled with kid gloves. What he is referring to are, largely, the conditions over which he and his fellow junior officers had little control; the cramped and stifling life in the camp. The German High Command was so intent on keeping the P.O.W.s inside—with a force of guards outnumbering the prisoners—that excesses in the laying down of prison orders were inevitable. Within these limits, the Germans were almost compelled to use the kid glove.

The prisoners were hostages—that became apparent after a couple of years. If the war was to take a wrong turning for Hitler and his entourage, the prisoners of Colditz would be held up to ransom. Perhaps the emergence of this fact caused the Germans to treat the prisoners warily. A dead hostage is no use at all. Of course he could be replaced—but there would be undesirable repercussions. So, it was worth their while to be tolerant within reason, on the principle that it is better not to tempt fate by baiting a spirited, if not dangerous animal, even though it may be, apparently, securely caged.

Where the Germans failed was in their excess of zeal to keep the P.O.W.s in prison. Their efficiency reached regrettable heights when they refused, during the lengthening years, to re-

8

move sick prisoners and, more particularly, the unfortunate ones who went 'round the bend'. It was inevitable that in the confined atmosphere of Colditz there would be mental suffering among men whose very presence in the camp testified to their deep-seated yearning for freedom. There were several who became mentally unbalanced, even suicidal. They should have been removed. They were a menace to themselves and to the mental balance of their fellow prisoners. They had to be looked after tirelessly. They had to be guarded by men who could sense the danger to themselves, as if they were nursing patients suffering from an infectious disease.

One officer who had delusions and who, thank God, has completely recovered, described his feeling to me recently in this way:

After this failure to escape, I was so disgusted that I took to studying and research. Shortly after D-Day, I got some peculiar delusions—a long story in themselves. I got the impression that we were all drugged and under semi-hypnosis which was the reason the Germans caught every attempt to escape. One day I saw the Castle burning and could see the flames and the smoke and the beams crashing down. Of course, my fellow prisoners got so thoroughly scared that they got Dickie (the doctor) to give me an injection of morphia and put me in a cell.

The desire to escape was paramount among the men of Colditz. They were of all nationalities fighting on the Allied side: Englishmen, Scotsmen and Irishmen from Britain and every corner of the Commonwealth—Canada, Australia, New Zealand and Africa. There were Poles and Yugoslavs, Dutchmen from the Netherlands East Indies as well as from Holland, Frenchmen from the African colonies as well as the mother country and, long before the end, there were Americans too.

Naturally, under conditions in which everybody was trying to escape, there was a serious danger that plans would overlap if not conflict. An Englishman building a tunnel was in danger of meeting a Frenchman digging from another direction!

Each nationality had its Escape Officer; a man placed in

9

charge of escape affairs, who was made aware of the plans of the other nationalities, who prevented congestion along the lines, and initiated an orderly roster with his colleagues. The result often went like this:

Sorry, old chap, a Frenchman (or a Dutchman or an Englishman, etc.) has already registered that plan. You'll have to wait three months when it's due to come off. If it's not blown sky high after that, I'll see you're entered on the list for the next go, by the same route.

The reader can well understand that the position of Escape Officer was a most important and ticklish one. The holder, of necessity, had to have the implicit trust of his fellow officers. It was axiomatic that he was excluded from escaping himself; no little sacrifice for a man who, by his nature and experience—even before his promotion to the post—possessed all the qualifications for making a successful getaway.

While on this point, I am reminded of another which I must place before the reader. Some who have read *The Colditz Story* have said to me: "Surely the remark you made about so much having to be left unsaid was merely intended to intrigue the reader by introducing an air of mystery?"

May I be forgiven for repeating again that much interesting and exciting material has, necessarily, in the conditions of the world to-day, to be omitted. If the reader feels, on occasion, that he would like to know more than he is told, I hope he will remember this point.

Apart from this, there is, nevertheless, enough material to fill another book. I have had to pick and choose. I must, therefore, ask for the indulgence of the reader if, occasionally, I pass lightly over certain events and mention casually characters that have 'gone before'. I cannot hope to achieve the finesse of Sherlock Holmes, who was wont to say cryptically: ". . . You will notice, my dear Watson, a distinct resemblance here, to the case of the Daskerville Diamonds. . . ." I feel sure the reader will understand that, although this story should be sufficient unto itself, it is, at the same time, the second in a series.

It is with deep regret that I have had to sacrifice a 'heroine' on the altar of truth. Neither would it be honest to the fair sex to withhold from them—or the men—the fact that there are no female characters in the story. On page 145 I have done my best. It was the nearest a woman ever approached to the forbidding portals of the Castle. Even so, she wasted no time. I can only lean on a good precedent in order to bolster up my failure to make good the omissions of history. Surely I cannot go far wrong in emulating a drama without a heroine that once held the stages of the world for record breaking runs—none other than *Journey's End*.

With this introduction, may I usher the reader into the auditorium, where the overture is about to begin. . . .

PART I: *1942*

CHAPTER I

OVERTURE

THIS book is the story of a castle in Saxony during those years of the Second World War between November 1942 and April 1945. It covers only a fleeting moment in the history of the Castle as measured by the life-span of hewn stone and oak timbers. There must have been many periods, as the scrolls of the centuries unrolled, when the *tempo* of man's activity within its walls rose to dramatic heights; but, probably, none was more dramatic than the short interval in which this story of human endeavour unfolds itself.

Not that the interval was short for the actors who then walked upon the Colditz stage. It is short in retrospect. The passage of time is registered physically and mechanically in minutes and hours by the clock. A year may sear itself upon the soul of a man so deeply that it becomes a lifetime or it may pass so refreshingly over him that it is gone like a gay summer's day. Man measures time by happiness or sorrow, by tranquillity or torture. The one is past and gone so quickly that it is seldom seized and savoured. The other turns the hours into days and the weeks into years, and can turn man's nature into unrecognisable shapes.

During the period of which I write, Colditz Castle was the *Sonderlager* or *Straflager* of Germany. It was the stronghold where Allied prisoners of war who had dared to break their chains were incarcerated. It was the cage in which were shut the birds that longed to be free, that beat their wings unceasingly against the bars. In such conditions birds do not usually survive long. It says something for the resilient spirit of man that those Allied prisoners, the inveterate escapers, who were sent to Colditz mostly survived the ordeal.

For such men, much more than for others, the hours were days and the weeks were years. They were men of action by nature, and they lived a long time the torture of forced inactivity. They were prisoners expiating no other crime than the unselfish service of their country.

Taking stock of the situation at Colditz in the bleak winter of 1942 entails, first and foremost, taking stock of the escaping situation.

The escape-proof castle of the 1914–18 war had been made to look like a riddled target. Holes had been made everywhere —metaphorically and literally—in its impregnable walls.

By the end of 1942, the British prisoners' contingent had risen to eighty strong. Officers from the three Services and from every country of the Commonwealth, they had all committed offences against Hitler's *Reich*. About ninety per cent. of them had escaped at least once from other camps. There were three padres: the Reverends Ellison Platt, Heard and Hobling, who had made themselves such nuisances elsewhere, clamouring for Christian treatment for their flocks, that the German High Command considered Colditz the only appropriate place for them. Here, at least, their clamours would not penetrate the thick walls of the fortress.

Seventy-three 'officer-attempts' to escape had been registered so far. The term 'officer-attempt' was used in the statistics so as to be able to register each attempt of each officer. Thus, seventy-three officer-attempts does not mean that seventy-three officers out of the eighty tried to escape. That figure was probably nearer forty than eighty, but as several of the forty attempted two or three times they were given their individual totals on the escape record, and the total of the whole column— so to speak—added up to seventy-three. It was not often that a Senior British Officer had an opportunity to escape, but Colonel Guy German was not omitted from an early attempt which would have left the camp devoid of the entire British contingent!

Out of the total recorded, twenty-two officers had succeeded in getting clear of the camp. They were 'gone away', as it was termed. The number included five Dutch officers taking part in British escape attempts. The statistic, however, that the camp was most proud of, and which has never been equalled by any P.O.W. camp in Germany, was the number of successful escapes. Officers' home-runs into neutral or friendly territory totalled no less than eleven out of the twenty-two—fifty per cent.!

The fortunate eleven were: Airey Neave and Tony Luteyn; Bill Fowler and Van Doorninck; the two E.R.A.s, Wally Hammond and Tubby Lister; Brian Paddon; Ronnie Littledale, Billie Stephens, Hank Wardle and the author.

Coming next to the Dutch contingent, which numbered sixty at the end of 1942, the equivalent records were approximately as follows (excluding the Dutchmen above mentioned): officer-attempts about thirty, gone-aways ten and home-runs six.

The French contingent numbered one hundred and fifty, including a batch of fifty Jewish French officers who, with rare exceptions, did not interest themselves in escaping. Frankly, the latter realised that recapture for them meant extermination (in prisoner jargon a 'Klim-tin'), and their lives were probably safer in Colditz than in France.

French officer-attempts numbered somewhere in the region of twenty to thirty—I cannot recollect them more exactly. Gone-aways numbered about ten and home-runs amounted to at least four.

The Polish contingent had left during the year. They had numbered eighty strong, and had been at Colditz from the beginning of the war. They were already there when I arrived in November 1940. They had come from *Sonderlager* of the First World War, Spitzberg and Hohenstein, from where they had registered twelve gone-aways and three home-runs to the Polish Underground. Tragic, indeed, it is to recollect that they had no homeland that they could make for. When they succeeded in breaking out of the Castle they headed for Switzerland, Sweden or France, leaving their homes and loved ones farther than ever behind them. Half a dozen had gone-aways to their credit, but, though some of them reached the Swiss

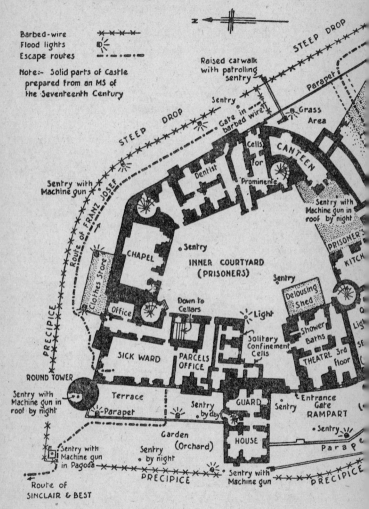

COLDITZ CASTLE
OFLAG IVC 1939-45

Barbed-wire
Flood lights
Escape routes

Note:- Solid parts of Castle prepared from an MS of the Seventeenth Century

STEEP DROP

STEEP DROP

Raised catwalk with patrolling sentry

Parapet

Sentry

Gate in barbed wire

Grass Area

Cells for Prominente

CANTEEN

Dentist

Sentry with Machine gun

Route of FRANZ JOSEF

Sentry

CHAPEL

INNER COURTYARD (PRISONERS)

Sentry with Machine gun in roof by night

PRISONER'S KITCH

Clothes Store

Office

Down to Cellars

Sentry

Delousing Shed

Light

PRECIPICE

SICK WARD

PARCELS OFFICE

Solitary Confinement Cells

Shower Baths

THEATRE 3rd floor

Light

ROUND TOWER

Terrace

Parapet

Sentry by day

GUARD

Sentry

Entrance Gate RAMPART

Sentry with Machine gun in roof by night

Sentry with Machine gun in Pagoda

Sentry by night

Garden (Orchard)

HOUSE

Sentry

Parape

PRECIPICE

Sentry with Machine gun

PRECIPICE

Route of SINCLAIR & BEST

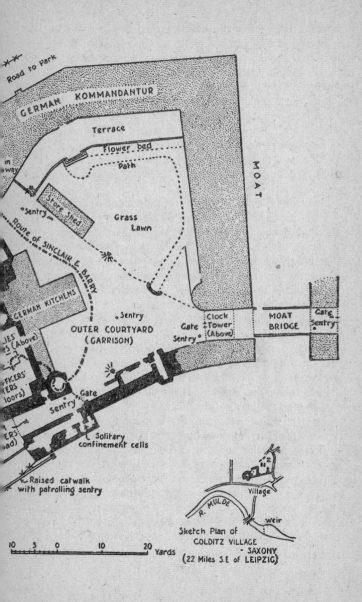

Road to Park

GERMAN KOMMANDANTUR

Terrace

Flower bed

Path

in way

Store Shed

"Sentry"

Route of SINCLAIR E. BARRY

Grass Lawn

MOAT

GERMAN KITCHENS

Sentry

OUTER COURTYARD
(GARRISON)

Clock Tower (Above)

Gate Sentry

MOAT BRIDGE

Gate Sentry

IES
S (Above)

FICERS'
ERS
loors)

Sentry

Gate

ERS'
ad)

Solitary confinement cells

Raised catwalk
with patrolling sentry

Village

R. MULDE

weir

Sketch Plan of
COLDITZ VILLAGE
- SAXONY
(22 Miles S.E of LEIPZIG)

10 5 0   10   20 Yards

frontier, they were caught and the record showed no home-runs to neutral territory from Colditz for this company. Nevertheless, after leaving Colditz, two at least escaped from a camp farther east in Germany and made their way to France and England. They were Felix Jablonowski and Tony Karpf. The former, an international lawyer and university lecturer, has recently gone to America to seek his fortune and a new life; while Karpf, happily married, has settled in Glasgow.

Airey Neave was the first Englishman to reach England from Colditz *via* Switzerland, France and Spain.[1] That was in May 1942. Paddon followed closely at his heels—in time, though by another route—Sweden.

So much for the record up to the autumn of 1942; but what were the prospects for the future? Conditions were undoubtedly becoming more difficult. Within the Castle the roll-calls for prisoners settled down to a regular four *Appells* every day. The times at which the *Appells* occurred were, however, by no means regular. The factory siren which had recently been installed would shriek its warning at odd hours of the day, in the grey light of dawn or in the night hours. The parade started five minutes after the siren's moans had subsided. Our men, wherever they were working at their nefarious activities, had only one compensation. In the deepest shaft or the longest tunnel, the siren could be heard and tools downed at once. Nevertheless, the five minutes tolerance gave little time for sealing entrances and cleaning up. It was always a close thing and wearing on the nerves. The fact that there were four *Appells* every twenty-four hours also broke up the working shifts, impaired efficiency and slowed progress considerably.

It was inevitable, too, that, as time went on, escape routes out of the Castle would become fewer and fewer. The Castle, as already mentioned, presented to the escaper by 1943 the picture of a target riddled with holes, but unfortunately, at this stage, behind every hole stood a sentry. The garrison outnumbered the prisoners. Catwalks had been erected providing an unhindered view into all the nooks and crannies in the battlements.

[1] Neave has written the story in *They Have Their Exits* (a PAN BOOK).

They hung suspended like window-cleaners' cradles; they stood on long poles clinging, sometimes perilously, to walls, like builders' scaffolds supported from narrow ledges in the cliff sides. Wherever a prisoner had escaped, there new and forbidding rolls of concertina wire were stretched. Jerries hung out of skylights with machine-guns beside them surveying roof ridges, slopes and gutters.

Sound detectors were being installed everywhere. The exits through the thinner walls being nearly exhausted, men were digging deeper into the formidably heavy foundations of the older structure of the Castle.

Colditz, like many other ancient buildings, was not one castle but many castles; built and ruined, rebuilt and ruined again by wars and weather, by time and usage. Thus, although some of the senior prisoners' quarters and probably the interior decoration of the Castle chapel was attributable to architects and builders working to the orders of Augustus the Strong, King of Poland and Elector of Saxony from 1694 to 1733, the garrison quarters around the outer courtyard were of eighteenth- and early nineteenth-century design. Returning within the keep, however, most of the architecture and the building construction bore witness to a *Schloss* built in earlier days during the sixteenth century. In these medieval halls and casemates the junior officers lived. When the tunnellers among them began delving downwards, they came upon yet earlier foundations of a castle destroyed, apparently, in the Hussite wars of the fifteenth century. In fact, it can be vouched with assurance that almost as long as man existed in those parts and wished to defend himself against his enemies, he must have built himself an eyrie on the easily defendable, towering rock promontory of Colditz.

The searchlights increased in number, dispelling the last shadow which might shelter a lurking form on its desperate route to freedom.

Then there were the Alsatian dogs. They had not increased in number, as far as was known, but they were worked harder. Patrols, with or without the Alsatians, had become frequent, and were the more dangerous as they became more irregular, touring the Castle at unpredictable intervals of time.

It was also natural that the prisoners and the guards should learn more and more of each others' habits and methods. As the scales were from the first weighted in favour of the guards, they held an advantage which told more heavily as the years passed. The training of sentries for the work at Colditz became more scientific. They were instructed in all the known tricks and wiles of the prisoners; warned again and again of what they might expect; their duty stations changed often to prevent staleness dulling the edge of their preparedness. They toured, regularly, the escapers' museum in the garrison headquarters, carrying away mental pictures of the escaper's art, his tools, his keys, his maps, papers, clothing and his false uniforms, his trap-doors and his camouflage. The prisoners' ingenuity was stretched to limits which only the story in its unfolding can adequately describe.

The prisoners were becoming physically weak. Even the most robust men could not stand up indefinitely to the meagre diet. Albeit that Red Cross food was available, there was never enough. Men were always hungry and could only bloat them-selves with unappetising mealy potatoes and stomach-revolting turnips and swedes. Alternatively they took to their beds for long periods of the day, preserving thereby what little energy their nutrition gave them.

The spirit was unconquered but the flesh was weak. The change in physical condition came imperceptibly and, as each suffered alike, a prisoner did not appreciate the alteration taking place within himself or his companions around him. A form of evolution was going on within the Castle walls and a different kind of human being was coming into existence: a scrawny individual with a skin and bone physique seriously lacking in vitamins. Mentally, the prisoner who kept himself occupied was none the worse for his captivity. On the contrary, in many cases the enforced life of the ascetic sharpened the wits and enlarged the horizon of the mind. The age-old secret of the hermit was manifestly revealed; men's minds and souls were purified by the mortification of the body.

Unfortunately, a man cannot escape from a fortress by mind alone. He has to drag his body with him. Although the escaper's wits were sharpened and his mind as clear as a bell, his body, in 1942, could not perform the feats it did in 1940 unless scourged by the driving force of a powerful will.

So much for conditions within the fortress, but what of the great outside? The huge face of Germany lay for hundreds of miles in all directions around the Castle embedded in the very heart of the *Reich*. To the men incarcerated in the camp the changing circumstances outside were mostly a closed book. Every tit-bit of information gleaned was treasured and recorded for possible exploitation, but so much was unknown. Although the Colditz techniques for the production of false papers were highly skilled, though false identities could be faithfully reproduced which would pass muster under known conditions outside the camp at a given date, these very conditions were altering rapidly for the worse and changes were unpredictable.

The change that was coming over Germany is well illustrated by the two largest breakouts of the war from camps other than Colditz. Jumping ahead in time for a moment, on the night of August 3rd–4th, 1943, sixty-five British officers escaped by tunnel from Oflag VIIB at Eichstätt in Bavaria. It was a beautifully engineered escape, but not one of the officers made the home-run. Apart from the fact that the majority of them were ill equipped both as to civilian clothing and as to identity papers, according to the best standards, they under-estimated the reaction of the Germans to their escape. The latter, during the winter of 1942–3, were beginning to feel the flail of Allied heavy bombing; of our great aircraft sweeps over their territory. They were organising their Home Guard feverishly. It was known as the *Landwacht*. The *Hitler Jugend* was also mobilised, and children of tender age were not excluded from routine duties and from lessons upon how to recognise and how to capture enemy airmen. Thus, it was not a far cry to transfer their activities, at short notice, to the recapture of escaped prisoners. When large numbers escaped together, the organisation required would be no different from that which came into play after a heavy aerial bombardment.

Reports have it that after the Eichstätt escape no fewer than sixty thousand of the *Landwacht* were in action within twenty-four hours searching for the escapers. It was not an escape that paid dividends. Undoubtedly, of course, it gave the Germans 'a packet of trouble'——that was a good thing. It harassed them, and because of that alone it was probably worth while. But it is also argued that it gave the *Landwacht* a good field day—impromptu manœuvres—which made them more efficient later on against our airmen parachuting into Germany and trying hard to evade capture. The escape failed on points of strategy rather than in the tactics of its execution.

Practically the same results were achieved, only with far worse consequences, by another, and the last, large British breakout recorded during World War II. This was the disastrous escape of seventy-six officers from Stalag Luft III. The escape occurred on March 24th, 1944.[1] Three made home-runs. Fifty out of the seventy-six who escaped were murdered by the Gestapo. Such a breakout may have been thought good for morale, but no visible uplift in escaping morale was noticeable according to subsequent accounts.

The mass escape was the ideal form that escaping could take from 1940 up to the end of 1942.

A superb escape and—though it is always a matter of opinion —probably the finest British escape of the whole war is another illustration of the point. It was known as the 'Warburg wire job', and it occurred on August 29th, 1942—within the early period of the war. Forty-three officers escaped, in one minute, over the wire barricades of Warburg prison camp with home-made storming ladders. It would be of interest to establish who provided the inspiration and leadership of this escape. He de-

[1] See *The Great Escape*, by Paul Brickhill.

serves a decoration.[1] David Walker and Pat Campbell-Preston, both of the 1st Battalion the Black Watch, had something to do with it. J. E. Hamilton-Baillie, Royal Engineers, designed the ladders. Again the accoutrement and clothing for the outside part of the attempt was incomplete. Nevertheless, three officers in battle-dress made their way to France and subsequently a home-run to England. It is doubtful if they would have succeeded (in battle-dress) a year later.

By 1943, a regime had come to an end, and even if a great tunnel was built and completed with a good outfall beyond the camp confines, experience—bitter experience—encourages the thought that such a tunnel might have been better employed otherwise than as means for a mass break-out. If a transport plane had been laid on from England at a rendezvous to take the men off—that would have been another matter.

It is only too easy to criticise after the event—and nobody could wish to detract from such magnificent escapes as those above mentioned. This said, there can be no harm in going over an exercise performed, to draw out the lessons for the future, provide food for thought and encourage the fertile imagination. The mind can exercise itself in fields of interest, not to say of entertainment, by posing a few questions. "What might have happened if . . . ?"

What would have happened if ten officers had escaped instead of seventy-six? They would have been very well equipped —for they would have had the equipment of the sixty remaining behind to draw upon to fill any gaps in their own make-up. The most eligible team would be chosen for the attempt, and every advantage would be concentrated in the team to go. Once outside the wire—and once the alarm was given—what might the German reactions be? Ten British officers have escaped. Turn out the local *Landwacht*, say two hundred strong; search the locality; send out descriptions and photos; alert all railway security police and report the escape to Corps Headquarters.

[1] According to recent reliable information, Tom Stallard, then a Major of the Durham Light Infantry, now a Lieutenant-Colonel with the D.S.O. and O.B.E., was responsible.

Now, consider the escape of seventy-six officers. This is serious. It cannot be kept from the General Staff, nor from Himmler, nor even from Hitler, and what is the result. *Landwacht* alerted in their thousands—nearly a hundred against each one, and the consequent chances of escape reduced to about the same ratio; the Gestapo sleuths placed hot on the scent, and the revengeful spirits of the maniac leaders of the country roused to anger; fifty of our finest officers murdered!

If only ten men had moved out, how many might have made home-runs? Judging by Colditz statistics, the number might have been as high as five. It would be reasonable to say two or three.

The discussion does not end there. What is the effect on the morale of those who stay behind; firstly, upon the whole prison contingent amounting to hundreds of officers; secondly upon the sixty-six standing down, who have had a more personal stake in the escape attempt?

Are the hundreds jealous they were not included in the escape? No! They could not be. Are the sixty-six? A few may be, but the majority are more pleased at the result, feeling they have contributed to the achievement. Their enthusiasm is whetted. Encouragement at the sight of success ensues and morale is lifted. 'Nothing succeeds like success' applies forcibly to escaping. What is the reaction of the hundreds to the success of the few? Morale is naturally improved. Quite the contrary is the result when many men go out and they all come back or when a large proportion of them are shot.

One question has been begged throughout. What is the reaction when only ten men go out where seventy-six might have gone and when ten men return? This is when the fur begins to fly, and recrimination, in the confined atmosphere of a crowded camp, quickly takes on the aspects of a revolt. Among the sixty-six feeling, naturally, runs high. Why were they not allowed to 'have a bang at it'? Herein lies the difficulty of decision, and he has a strong character who makes the unpopular decision and sticks to it. The mass break-out is the easier course to adopt. Is it the right one?

By way of a corollary, and a sop to Cerberus, the man who makes the difficult decision can partially insure himself by seeing that the tunnel is properly sealed at entrance and exit after the 'ten' have gone, with a view to a second ten departing after the first hue and cry has died down. The chance of this ever being possible is a minimum, but it provides a safety-valve and parries the worst fomentations aroused by disappointment.

Lastly, the value of a home-run is not to be under-estimated. Airey Neave and Brian Paddon, returning to England in 1942, were among the pioneers, lecturing our forces training at home upon escape techniques as being developed in Colditz at the time. Their advice on the theory and practice of 'evasion' and their encouragement of our thousands flying regularly over enemy territory was an inspiration. They, and those who followed closely after them, helped materially in the success of the 'evasion' campaign which resulted in so many Allied airmen, parachuted from crippled aircraft, returning home safely by devious routes, each with a story of adventure and courage in adversity.

Even the unlucky ones who were captured and thrown into prison camps had some consolation. Their numbers swelled to large proportions from 1942 onwards as our planes, in increasing avenging swarms, traversed the disintegrating enemy cities, while more and more hatred belched upwards in screaming steel and rending explosive. Unlike the early prisoners, they were not lost souls, unbefriended and unaided. They arrived in camp knowing what to expect and what was expected of them. After the first terrible depression, they had hope to buoy them up. They knew they had friends, both in England and in the prison camps, who would help them to escape if possible. Moreover, the camps were well provided with the practical means to assist them.

The scene was darkening over Colditz. Men gradually realised that the difficulties were multiplying and the hazards of escape more problematical and dangerous as the days dragged on their infinitely slow and tedious procession. Around the cobbled courtyard of the inner *Schloss* the clack-clack-clack of wooden clogs wearing themselves out on the stones was interminable in the daylight hours; it bore into the head like the drops of water in a Chinese torture. It was a motif ever recurring in the symphony being played within the fortress.

There was only one silver lining for the escaper. German Army morale was on the decline and it was becoming noticeable among the camp guards.

It was possible, by slow degrees, to set up a black-market, in fact many black-markets. Racketeering in the produce of this illicit trade gradually became rife, until it was eventually scandalous and the German profiteers were seen to be gaining.

The matter was taken in hand so that an orderly influx of escape paraphernalia took precedence over private cupidity, and escapers, harassed by the infinite difficulties of escaping from the Castle, had the comfort, at least, of knowing that, once out they could hardly be better equipped for the journey across enemy territory.

The overture continues. The cymbals and the kettle-drums have had their turn. What of the undertones, the huge background in front of which the violins will play? What say the trombones, the bass drums and the deep-throated cellos?

November 1942 opened with the final phases of the Battle of Alamein which Winston Churchill describes as 'the turning of the hinge of Fate', adding, "It may almost be said, 'Before Alamein we never had a victory. After Alamein we never had a defeat.'"

Guns boomed from the Atlantic on the North African shore. The American amphibious invasion began at Casablanca on November 8th, and in the Mediterranean, around Oran and Algiers, on the same day. Stalingrad was relieved at the end of January 1943, with the capture of Field-Marshal Paulus and the survivors of twenty-one German divisions. Churchill was anxious to open the Second Front in Europe in 1943, and Stalin was likewise pressing for it. The British were losing an enormous tonnage of shipping every week in the Atlantic. The drain of this life-blood still had to be stopped. It was one of Hitler's few remaining trump cards. The war leaders argued the pros and cons; Churchill met the Turks at Adana. The latter would not be hurried into the war on the Allied side. Hitler put all his efforts into a Tunisian campaign. The requirements for the successful completion of the Allied North African operation 'Torch' sealed the doom of another operation called 'Round-up'.

The prayers and hopes of thousands of Allied prisoners all over Europe were centred on an Allied landing on the Continent—the opening of the Second Front—in 1943.

Although they did not know it by that name, 'Round-up' was what they prayed for.

The Colditz inmates were by this stage of the war well equipped for the wireless reception of news from the Western Allies. They had at the same time, by the continuous application of carefully aimed shafts of ridicule, silenced the German loudspeakers in the camp. The Germans no longer tried to switch on their news bulletins. Instead they set about dismantling the loudspeakers in the various quarters. Alas! they were too late. When the electricians took down the instruments all they retrieved were hollow shells. The works had been removed in good time, and were already in the service of the Crown instead of the Corporal.

The great march of events in the latter half of the war was not lost to the prisoners. Indeed, the majority lived for the news. It was a soul-assuaging consolation to the many who knew, in their hearts, that they would never make home-runs. Let the violins speak.

A seeding of players in the escape tournament began to take place. It was a voluntary affair, and brave men stepped out of the queue of their own accord. They did not speak of it.

There was no dramatic renunciation of rights; there were no recriminations. They dropped from the life-line around the overcrowded escaping life-boat and, with resignation, allowed the great ocean of world events to swallow them. They drowned their personal ambitions and drifted, each one alone

27

with his own soul awaiting the end. The end lay over the horizon and the sky was lowering.

To these men, suspended in the boundless sea of time, the broadcast news bulletins were essential for mental well-being and sanity. News was like oil poured on the waves; a protecting calm amidst the storm that threatened the balance of their minds, that was never far away, that could descend with the elemental force of a whirlwind. Sometimes, indeed, the news appeared as a mirage, deceiving them horribly, but, at least, the omissions and the veils drawn over adverse situations coming from the Western transmitters were as nothing compared with the great hoax that was played upon the German people by their wireless broadcasters. If the Allies did not tell all the truth, at least they avoided lying. So, for our men, there was always hope as opposed to the revengeful bitterness that grows from deliberate deception.

CHAPTER II

ESCAPE FEVER

NEWS of the success of the escape of Ronnie Littledale, Billie Stephens, Hank Wardle and the author, and of their safe arrival in Switzerland, soon filtered through the censor's net. Four gone-aways and four home-runs—it was great news, putting the British contingent well ahead of the other nationalities in the friendly rivalry for the lead in home-runs. Many men, whose hopes of an ultimately successful escape had almost vanished, imbibed new strength and determination. A wave of enthusiasm like a gust of fresh air swept through the Castle.

Dick Howe, of the Royal Tank Regiment and officer in charge of escape, was overwhelmed with new schemes and the resurrection of old ones. Activity became feverish, and it was clear that the Jerries were in for a difficult time. The latter soon scented trouble ahead and the German security team hardly slept at night. Hauptmann Priem and Oberleutnant Püpcke, Hauptmann Eggers and the deadbeat Hauptmann Lange, Oberstabsfeldwebel (Sergeant-major) Gephard and his Gefreiter (corporal), known as the *fouine* or ferret or Dixon Hawke, took turns at making the rounds. P.O.W. 'stooging' systems had to be double shifted to cope with the new circumstances. Hardly an officer was free from some duty or other.

For some unaccountable reason the word stooge, in prison jargon, had two totally different meanings, depending entirely on the context in which the term was used. 'Stooging' in the above case implied the P.O.W. 'look-out' organisation instituted to warn prisoners of Germans approaching on the prowl, 'snooping' as it was called. On the other hand, a stooge could be a person planted by the Germans in the camp to report on the prisoners' nefarious activities.

As the German security net became more closely drawn and the sentry layout more dense, it was brought home to the prisoners that escapes of almost any kind would have to rely on split-second timing. The old leisurely days were disappearing. This change implied long hours of stooging by an escape team, and the plotting of enemy movements for weeks on end in order to discover the loop-holes in their defence system.

Dick, thirty-two years old, had won his M.C. at Calais in 1940. He was standing the strain of the difficult job of Escape Officer remarkably well. To any outsider, he looked sallow, hollow cheeked and terribly thin, but that was normality in Colditz and passed without comment. His good humour remained his greatest friend. Demands on his time were heavy. What kept him always on top of a situation was an obstinate refusal to be flustered either by contrary events or by contrary people.

Rupert Barry and Mike Sinclair teamed up. They were a formidable pair and would take a lot of stopping. They were given what was known as the theatre-shaft job.

Rupert, of the Ox and Bucks Light Infantry, tall, dark and handsome with his big brown moustache and smouldering eyes, had been one of the first escapers in Germany. He, Peter Allan and the author, out of a tunnel at Oflag VIIC, near Salzburg, were half-way to Yugoslavia when recaught in September 1940. At Colditz, Rupert's luck had not been good. Two tunnels on which he worked did not succeed in putting him outside the wire, although the first was completed without discovery.

Mike, of the 60th Rifles, had been free in Poland for a long time, and then in a Gestapo prison for a while before he reached Colditz. He had escaped once from the Castle, only to be recaptured in Cologne. He was, by now, a fluent speaker of German. He was a few years younger than Rupert—about twenty-six. His red hair and his audacity had earned him the title among the Germans of *Der Rote Fuchs*—the Red Fox. Of medium build, tough, with a resolute freckled countenance, his life was devoted to escaping, and his determination was as valuable as a hundred-ton battering-ram matched against the walls of Colditz.

Mike and Rupert reorganised an old twenty-four-hour watching roster, which had been started many months before, on what was known as the air-shaft or light-well situated in the middle of the theatre block, where also the senior officers were housed.

The theatre itself was on the third or top floor of this block, and the square light-well was surrounded by a corridor on three sides which separated it from the theatre. A locked door gave onto the corridor, which was lighted from barred windows overlooking the well. The door was the only normal means of entry. There was no staircase. The twenty-four-hour watch was maintained in this corridor.

At the bottom of the well, fifty feet below, were doors leading into various German kitchen and canteen quarters. Thick walls, on the other hand, separated it from the prisoners' quarters at ground level. Needless to say, a sentry stood at the bottom of the well throughout the twenty-four hours.

After a fortnight's watching it was possible to confine stooging activity to some twelve hours, not consecutive, during the day; the other twelve hours being ruled out as impossible for escape purposes.

One early winter evening, as the light was beginning to fade, rehearsals of a forthcoming show were in full swing, bringing many officers of all nationalities into the theatre. It was a time of activity. An orchestra was practising; the scene painters were at work; stage managers, producers, actors and staff milled around, all providing admirable camouflage for the movement of shifts of stooges through the locked door into the corridor beside the well.

The old piano clanged out its tinny tunes. Sounds of hammering and scene-shifting mingled with the hubbub of voices rising and falling. Dick Howe busied himself around the stage followed by his Dutch stage-lighting assistant, Lieutenant

Beetes. The dreadful piano worried Dick. He mused over that dream piano—the new Bechstein Concert Grand—that had arrived one day, months ago now, in the courtyard. Workmen had toiled for hours hoisting it up the narrow staircase and had demolished a wall in the theatre in order to install it. Then the workmen's civilian coats, thrown off in the heat of the moment, had vanished. The contents of pockets re-appeared mysteriously, but the coats were never found. An ultimatum from the Commandant; stubborn silence from the prisoners; and the Bechstein Grand retraced its journey down the stairs and disappeared again outside the prison gateway.

There were no less than four orchestras now; all of them suffering from the curious version of the chromatic scale reproduced by this rickety, upright cupboard full of tangled wires.

There was the Symphony Orchestra conducted by a Dutch-man, First Lieutenant Bajetto; the Theatre Orchestra with Jimmy Yule as composer, orchestrator and pianist; the Dance Band with John Wilkins as band leader; and finally the Hawaiian Orchestra composed principally of Dutch colonial officers.

"What a difference it would make!" Dick sighed to himself. Then a flicker of a smile appeared at the corners of his mouth, and, as he stood in the middle of the stage by the footlights, surveying a scene, just completed, his thoughts were not on the set he was supposed to be examining. He was wondering if he could not, after all, spirit the Bechstein Concert Grand back into the theatre.

His mind was far away when a tug at his sleeve from the auditorium pulled him back to earth. He turned to see Vandy, the irrepressible Dutchman, plotter of a hundred escapes, smiling broadly as usual, looking up at him.

"I haf made a fine hole," said Vandy in a suppressed voice, "come qvick and see, my two escapers are preparing now to go."

"Fast work, Vandy," said Dick, jumping down over the

footlights. "I know this theatre pretty intimately and haven't noticed any rat-holes recently."

"Ach no! Dick—you vould not see. I haf been vorking for a veek and you know my plaster camouflage!"

Vandy led him to the dressing-room at the right of the stage. There in the corner was a gaping hole with all the paraphernalia of camouflage strewn around.

"Why!" exclaimed Dick, "you're using Neave's old route."

"Qvite right, it is the same. This hole—qvick! bend down and look along it—you see—it is in the roof of the causevay over the main gate. My men can now reach the guardhouse. They are putting on the German uniforms at this moment in my qvarters. They vill be here very soon. It is a blitz."

"But," said Dick incredulously, "the Jerries blocked up that route some time ago."

"Yes," replied Vandy unshaken, "but my men haf seen Germans recently through the windows of the causevay. Where there is an entrance there must be an outrance."

"H'm!" said Dick. "I'd better get our stooges out from the corridor pretty quick. Thanks for telling me, Vandy, but give me a little more notice next time."

Vandy was full of glee. There was nothing he liked more than surprising people. He was revelling in the joke he was about to play on the Jerries and missed the note of anxiety in Dick's voice. They retraced their steps into the theatre as Vandy studied his watch and signalled to a Dutch stooge at the door leading to the stairs.

At the same moment, Rupert Barry appeared from the direction of the light-well. Dick beckoned him over.

"You're in the nick of time, Rupert. Vandy has a blitz on."

They were near the orchestra, which had started running over the opening bars of Chopin's Polonaise and the piano was making a noise like a broken-down zither in Dick's ear.

"What did you say?" shouted Rupert. "The band has a blitz on?"

Dick took Rupert's arm and they moved away among the chairs of the auditorium. "I said Vandy has a blitz on. He's got two Dutchmen coming up here any moment." Dick pointed to Vandy and his theatre stooge in close conversation some yards from the theatre door.

"They're going over into the guardhouse. They're dressing as Jerries. There may be trouble. You'd better get our stooge out from the corridor. Who's in there now?"

"Peter Storie Pugh," said Rupert.

They were both looking towards the door as he spoke. Hardly were the words out of his mouth when the balloon went up.

The unmistakable figure of Priem appeared framed in the doorway, a dark outline in the gathering dusk. Vandy's stooge had been caught off his guard.

Priem took a few steps into the room. From behind him stepped Gephard who made for the electric switches, and the next moment the theatre was flooded in light. A posse of Goons followed closely at Gephard's heels. The music of the orchestra tailed off to nothing as Priem grated out his orders. Hammering continued in the wings of the stage. The scene builders went on with their work—oblivious of the unrehearsed drama taking place in front. Goons were suddenly everywhere. Vandy made for the door of the staircase, but a sentry barred the way with his rifle across the jambs.

Dick noticed that Rupert had glided away in the direction of the door to the corridor. The situation was tricky. He vaulted on to the stage and collided with Scarlet O'Hara who had just emerged from the wings. Scarlet had heard the familiar guttural shouts as he was in the midst of mixing up some scenery paint for his own use. Dick whispered to him.

"Quick! Scarlet, go and help Rupert. He needs some diversion. He's got his stooge in the corridor and must get him out."

Scarlet, the Canadian tank lieutenant, whose complexion had earned him his name, saw the situation immediately and muttering to himself, "These b—— Huns again, never let you alone for a minute, the blasted Kartoffels." He faded into the milling crowd of actors, scene-shifters, instrumentalists and German soldiery.

The Jerries knew what they were going for. Vandy's hole must have been discovered from the German side. They made for the dressing-room and herded everybody off the stage into the auditorium as Priem and Gephard held a conference. They were discussing what action to take. Vandy's blitz had shaken them.

"Will they hold everyone in the theatre and search them all?" Dick wondered to himself. It was a normal procedure. The room would be cleared, one by one the officers would be searched, and finally the Jerries would search the premises and the corridor. He stood leaning against the rickety piano, and could see Rupert and Scarlet in deep conversation in the far corner. Lulu Lawton, the black-haired Yorkshireman from the Duke of Wellington's Regiment, Dick's second in command, was weaving his way through the crowd towards him. In the distance Dick also spied Harry Elliott, a captain of the Irish Guards, who waged a private war against the Germans.

As Lulu approached, Dick said casually, "I wonder what brought Harry into the theatre. He never comes up here if he can help it. And to choose to-day! It'll be worth listening to what he has to say about the Jerries upsetting his routine. Look, he's arguing with the Jerry on the door now, swearing at him like a trooper."

"He came up to get some more yellow paint for his jaundice set-up," explained Lulu. "He's going before the medical board any day now."

Priem had apparently made up his mind what to do. He mounted the stage and addressed the assembled mixed bag of officers of all nationalities:

"*Meine Herren*," and he continued in German with sarcasm, "I am confident that not all the officers here present intended to escape through the hole I have just found. I shall not inflict unnecessary punishment on you by insisting that you remove all your clothes for searching. You will leave the theatre one by one. My under-officers will feel through your uniforms and in your pockets. I must find the instruments with which the hole has been made, and the culprit. The theatre will probably be closed, but I shall report first to the Commandant. Will you begin to leave the theatre at once and one at a time."

Dick looked anxiously towards the corridor. He could not see Rupert or Scarlet; only a huddle of French and English officers around the locked door. Obviously a scrum was being organised—but the top of the door was clear of their heads and if it was opened it would be plainly visible. Dick thought hard. A long queue had already formed by the theatre exit where several soldiers now stood while Gephard and two Gefreite—the *fouine* and another—quickly ran their hands over officers' clothing, occasionally feeling inside a pocket. The search was cursory. One by one the queue was diminishing. He noted through the open door of the dressing-room that a sentry had been posted in front of the hole. The soldiery was all occupied. Priem was the danger.

Dick deliberately avoided the queue and approached Priem, who was standing at the top of the stage steps surveying the scene before him. Dick suddenly had the inspiration he was waiting for. Looking up at Priem from the bottom of the steps he said in German:

"Herr Hauptmann, I wish to ask you a question about the theatre's requirements."

"*Na*, what is it, Herr Hauptmann Ho-ve?" said Priem descending to his level and losing his commanding view of the corridor entrance. He always pronounced Howe as two syllables, 'Ho-ve'.

Dick drew him over to the piano and, winking at Lulu who was leaning on it, he began:

"The British, Herr Hauptmann, have collected a big reserve of *Lagermarken* (prison money), which, together with subscriptions promised from other nationalities, we have calculated is large enough to buy a cinema organ for the theatre. You see, our theatre committee does not want a piano any more. This one here"—and Dick struck a few discordant notes on the keyboard of the upright—"is *kaputt*, as you know well."

"You cannot afford an organ, Herr Hauptmann!" said Priem, raising his eyebrows and smirking incredulously.

"Oh yes, we can! If you will come with me to our Senior Officer's room downstairs I can ask him to show you the figures."

"But, Herr Hauptmann Ho–ve, you do not require an organ —you need a piano." There was horror in his voice. The shaft had struck home.

"*Nein, nein*, Herr Hauptmann Priem," interrupted Dick, "we are not interested in pianos any more, everybody wants to have a fine Würlitzer organ. The Protecting Power will support our demand for one because this piano here is finished. We can say you refused to give us a new piano months ago when we asked for it."

Looking past Priem, Dick caught a glimpse of Rupert and Scarlet, and then to his relief, as the screening crowd dispersed to take up their positions in the fast dwindling queue at the exit, he noticed the figure of Peter Storie Pugh.

Priem began to walk towards the exit as well, and Dick and Lulu followed. Dick said:

"Herr Hauptmann Priem, would you like to see the accounts showing our reserve of *Lagermarken*?"

"*Nein*," replied Priem, "I believe you." He turned away to speak to his Oberstabsfeldwebel, Gephard, and Dick turned to Lulu.

"If that doesn't bring the Bechstein Concert Grand back, I reckon we'd better start saving for the Würlitzer! I have a hunch, though, that the old Commandant won't want to have a grand piano left on his hands."

The theatre emptied. Vandy had long since disappeared. Dick, Lulu and Rupert were the last to be 'frisked'. As they departed, the spare Goons were already dispersing throughout the theatre, rummaging in the corners, and Gephard approached the corridor door with the key in his hand. . . .

In the courtyard below, Vandy was waiting for Dick.

"All is not finished, Dick, I haf a plan. You must distract the sentry who stands at the hole, please."

Dick looked at him and burst out laughing, then beside Vandy he saw two bulky-looking Dutch officers. He knew them well and knew too that their bulk was not natural. There was no stopping Vandy. Weakly he said:

"Hold your horses, Vandy. Priem's still up there with his posse of Goons. Do you want to distract them all?"

"No, Dick, vait till they haf gone. Here they come—look! Ve must count them," and facing the theatre block doorway he counted, "vone, two, tree, vor, vive . . ." and then finally, "Fouine, Gephard, Priem. That is all except vone," and, as the procession of Jerries filed out of the gate, Vandy sent one of his men to check if they had locked the theatre door. They had not.

"Ve are in luck, Dick! You see, you are not suspect in the theatre; you haf much vork there, you can distract the stupid German. Then I vill send my two men through the hole."

Almost wearily, Dick turned back, asking Lulu to help him do the distraction. It was dark by now outside. They climbed the stairs again and entered the lighted theatre. They pretended to go about their work, talking and laughing. Vandy quietly hid his two escapers in the wings beside the stage door leading down to the dressing-room, and then joined Dick and Lulu.

"Ve vill go to the dressing-room by the other door and attract the sentry to us," he whispered.

After playing a few bars on the piano and banging some chairs about, the three of them filed into the dressing-room from the auditorium, apparently discussing heatedly the seating accommodation, the price of tickets, the timing of the various sets and finally in surprise . . .

"Why the hell is the sentry here?"

Dick asked him what he was supposed to be doing and offered him a cigarette. The sentry took it with a *"Danke"* and hid it in his tunic pocket, pointing out the large hole behind him which they all pretended to see for the first time.

Vandy chipped in with his good German and soon a political discussion was under way. The two of them eased around the sentry and Lulu started to look fixedly out of a window near the door by which they had entered. The floodlights came on with a searing flash. Suddenly he pointed and said, "Look! look!" excitedly. Dick rushed to the window and Vandy almost lifted the sentry forward. Nothing doing! The sentry stood rock-like.

The political conversation continued, with Vandy on one side of him, Dick on the other and both edging gradually towards the door in close animated discussion. Lulu, still by the window, interposed some comments at long range in halting German. Vandy and Dick feigned misunderstanding; they shuffled towards him; they inveigled the German to ask him questions. Lulu's German became more halting and less audible. Vandy became the interpreter and courier between them; standing half-way, he tried to draw them together. The sentry would not budge. Vandy was impatient at the best of times. He was working himself up and was on the point of giving the sentry a direct order to stand aside. He left the dressing-room with a growl and a wink, scowling at the sentry behind his back.

Dick and Lulu continued valiantly. More cigarettes passed hands and were lit. The sentry would not smoke. Lulu, who was nearest the door, sniffed.

"What've you got in your lighter, Dick?" he said suddenly and sniffed again.

"German lighter fuel," said Dick. "Why? Does it smell like eau-de-Cologne?" Then he, in turn, sniffed. There was no mistaking that smell for German lighter fuel and it was getting stronger. "Why!" Dick exclaimed, "it's brown paper—no, it's scenery paint—no! it's both."

Then he smelt wood burning and rushed from the room, followed closely by Lulu. As they turned the corner they saw Vandy circling round a blaze in the middle of the floor of the auditorium, which he was fanning violently with a large sheet of cardboard. He turned to shout "*Feuer!*" and, at the same time, piled more wood shavings, brown paper and bits of canvas, which he had collected, on to the flames. A thick blue cloud billowed upwards as Dick and Lulu took up the cry, *"Feuer! Feuer!"*

Vandy rushed back to the dressing-room shouting to the sentry: *"Achtung! Feuer! Feuer! Schnell! 'raus, schnell! Sie werden verbrennen, wenn Sie hier bleiben.* You will be burnt alive!"

The theatre filled with smoke as more paper was applied. Again Vandy dashed to the dressing-room door, gesticulating violently, and shouted to the sentry to follow him.

The sentry would not budge.

Defeated at last, Vandy threw up his hands, "It is no use, the stupid fellow vould rather burn to death."

With that the three of them set about putting the fire out. Then, joined by the two Dutchmen from the wings, they all fled from the theatre, leaving a smouldering heap on the floor. As they descended the stairs, smoke was billowing from the high windows, showing up ominously in the searchlight beams, and Germans could be heard shouting *"Feuer! Feuer!"* from the guardhouse outside.

Extraordinary to relate, the theatre was not closed and, the next day, the prison gates opened wide to allow the passage of a heavy lorry carrying the Bechstein Concert Grand piano. Amid a greater ovation than any pianist who ever pressed its keys could hope to hear, the piano was manhandled off the lorry and began its second panting, puffing journey up the narrow staircase to the theatre.

CHAPTER III

THE LIGHT-WELL

THE stooging in the theatre light-well was progressing satisfactorily and without too much disturbance. But the results coming from the graphs plotted did not give cause for optimism. After a month of watching over the most favourable sections of the twenty-four hours, a two-minute blind spot stood out as a regular feature of the graph shortly after 2 p.m. every day. It coincided with a change of guard. The bottom of the light-well remained void of German humanity for these two minutes. They did not necessarily occur at exactly the same time every day. One day the two-minute gap might be at 2.10 p.m., another day at 2.12 p.m., and even sometimes as late as 2.15 p.m. On an average, 2.10 p.m. was the psychological moment.

The escape was decided upon, and the German uniforms were put in hand for Rupert and Mike. These consisted of fatigue overalls which were the standard dress of Germans working in the kitchens and, when off duty, eating or drinking in their canteens. At the bottom of the well, doors led off in various directions into a maze of German kitchens, sculleries, store-rooms, bakeries and canteens. A corridor eventually led to a staircase, down one flight of stairs and out into the German Kommandantur courtyard.

Our two escapers were to descend by rope from one of the theatre corridor windows, a distance of fifty feet to the bottom of the well, and find their way out to the German courtyard. Once there, they had a choice of two routes, depending on the positions of the various gateway guards which were not accurately predictable. The better route, probably, would be that usually taken by the prisoners when marched under guard for their daily recreation of one hour in the park. Once in the park, the escapers could make for a secluded spot near the football enclosure, climb the barbed-wire fence abutting the twelve-foot wall surrounding the park, using it as a ladder to help them to the top.

There would be little activity in the German barracks about fifty yards away at this time of day, and they could hope to scale the wall unseen. In addition, although the trees in the park were leafless, the branches provided a good screen at fifty yards, especially as the football enclosure was at a level lower than the barracks.

Preparations for the escape were nearing completion. The German overalls were ready; the civilian clothing to be worn underneath had been fitted and checked. Identity papers were in order; maps, compasses and money provided. Bos'n Crisp, R.N., who, with a few assistants, manufactured all the ropes required for escapes, had made a stout sixty-foot length, fully tested for strength.

The time had come for Dick to start work on the bars of the light-well window. The escape would be carried out within a few days.

With Lulu Lawton to assist him and a team of stooges in action led by Grismond Davies-Scourfield, a lieutenant of the King's Royal Rifles, Dick repaired to the theatre. They entered the forbidden corridor by a small lattice window in the theatre wall instead of by the usual door. This window was conveniently placed for the escape, being situated in an angle of wall not directly facing the theatre exit. Although officially sealed, opening and closing it presented little difficulty, and it faced the barred corridor window from which the descent was to be made.

Crawling through the lattice window, Dick and Lulu surprised two young Frenchmen who were peering downwards into the light-well from one of the corridor windows.

"Hello! Hello!" Dick greeted them with mock gaiety. "Can I help you?"

"*Non, merci,*" replied the Frenchmen.

Dick continued sarcastically, "You're in a forbidden zone here. I shall report this to the Germans," and then taking them to task, "What if I'd been a German—where are your stooges?"

"We have no stooges," was the answer.

"How often have you been here?"

"A few times. We intend to escape from here to-morrow. We have been observing. We think we can descend easily into the well with a rope after cutting the bars."

At this news both Dick and Lulu nearly exploded. The Frenchmen's approach, however, was so naïve that Dick recovered himself in time to burst out laughing instead.

"You b—— fools," he said, "how long have you been in Colditz?"

"Oh! a long time now."

"In that case you ought to know better than to carry on the damn silly way you're doing. Does Colonel le Brigant know what you're up to?"

"No!"

"Then why the hell not?" said Dick. "It's about damn well time some of you gay young dogs realised that there is a Senior French Officer in the camp, and that when he orders you to keep him informed of your escaping activities he means it. Get out of here quick." Turning to Lulu he added, "We'd better all get out quick and seal up. What a b—— awful mess!"

Outside in the theatre, Dick and Lulu explained to the Frenchmen that they had very nearly ruined an escape which had been in preparation for months. The Frenchmen, unfortunately, did not take kindly to the explanation. The more they realised how inept they had been, the more their pride was wounded. They insisted on their right to escape by the light-well if and when they wanted to. The matter ended with both sides saying they would refer it to their respective Commanding Officers.

"For crying out loud!" said Lulu, as they wended their way back to the British quarters, joined by Grismond on the stairway. "Months of hard work and a first-class scheme, and

43

those two nitwits come along to break it up. I've always liked the French, but, my godfathers! the crass, stupid way they sometimes behave makes me wonder if they've any brains in their heads at all. Discipline! Great Cæsar's ghost—and they all did two years military service before the war! They're crazy!"

Lulu, the staid Yorkshireman, could not contain himself. Grismond could make no sense of it all, and Dick walked back to the quarters in glum silence. At the bottom of the stairs he said to Grismond:

"Go and fetch Rupert and Mike—tell 'em there's a hitch and will they come straightway to the C.O.'s room. You come along too. Lulu! let's go, we've got to have a showdown and the sooner the better."

There was a showdown, and when the sheafs of graph paper were produced showing the months of patient stooging that had been done in order to establish a two minutes' safe period in the light-well, the Frenchmen at last climbed down.

The curious attitude of the French towards their C.O.—towards any C.O.—was always a matter of mystery to the British. Their Commanding Officer in Colditz was one of the finest Frenchmen imaginable. Yet a large number of French officers felt no compunction in carrying on their own escape schemes without telling a soul, although it was a recognised rule of the camp that the respective Senior Officers should be informed so that they could compare notes, avoid messing up each other's plans and prevent chaos.

Frankly, some of the French were insubordinate. Presumably, they thought that so long as they told nobody at least their security was good. On the other hand, the senior officers of the army of a defeated nation did not feel in a position to enforce strict military discipline under prison conditions.

This state of affairs, fortunately, seldom displayed itself openly and, apart from one or two high spots such as the light-well debacle, the French chain of command in the camp was respected.

The French had to give way, but their stupidity in the

execution of the project was made up for by their astuteness in seizing an opportunity.

"If two can escape by the well, surely four can, without much more difficulty?" they queried, adding, "and if four can get out, there is more hope of at least one or two making home."

Dick and the C.O., and Rupert and Mike, chewed over this proposition for a while. Finally, it was agreed:

"Yes, all right. Four will go. An Englishman with a Frenchman—in two pairs." With that the pact was concluded and the escape was on. The British were not satisfied, but, at least, they were magnanimous. Extra risk was involved inside the camp; once outside, four heads were always better than two and, after all, the *Entente Cordiale* was being toasted daily in the camp!

German overalls were provided for the Frenchmen. Civilian clothes, papers and other paraphernalia they supplied from their own sources.

Dick and Lulu found themselves once more, some days later, mounting the stairs to the theatre on their way to cut and prepare the window bars ready for the descent.

Grismond's stooging was excellent. Nowadays, in the Castle it could not afford to be anything less. The Germans were jittery and their movements had to be watched with extreme caution.

The bar cutting was not so difficult, but it took time. The window being high above ground and overlooking a well about thirty feet square, Jerries at the bottom could not see anything going on inside the window-sill. Kitchen noises and the continual hubbub of movement served to drown the tell-tale sound of sawing. Dick and Lulu cut the bars successfully, replacing the loose pieces with patent sleeves manufactured by Scarlet O'Hara. These provided a perfect camouflage against observation. The bars could even stand gentle shaking, but would not survive the violent tug of a brawny Goon. If the bars were tapped, of course, they would not ring true.

Zero hour for the descent was ten minutes past two in the

afternoon of November 20th, 1942. This is where the next snag arose. An *Appell* was, more usually than not, held at two o'clock!

Appells, when properly organised, and provided there were no unforeseen hitches, could be called to attention as the German officers appeared, and dismissed again within eight minutes. Such an *Appell* was indeed a rare occurrence. The German officer had to appear dead on time, and each contingent had to be warned to behave in exemplary manner. The French were the largest group, but as two of their own number were escaping, order and co-operation could be expected from them.

There was always the haunting fear of an unknown spy inside the camp. Sometimes, as in this case, the best that could be done to combat the possibility of such treachery was not to give the traitor enough time to 'put his spanner in the works'. Only at the last minute were officers, gathering for the *Appell*, warned to behave amenably and cut the *Appell* time to a minimum.

The afternoon arrived. Everything was prepared. The rope was concealed under the bed of Duggie Bader, the Air Force ace. His room was one of the nearest to the theatre. A vaulting-horse, normally housed in the theatre, was close to the lattice window and would take the strain on the rope. Rupert, Mike and the two Frenchmen were dressed for the occasion: first, civilian clothes, then over them the German fatigue overalls, and on top of everything, army overcoats and trousers.

Rupert and Mike were both seasoned escapers. For that reason, their feelings as the crucial moment arrived were more like those of an experienced bomb-disposal officer about to begin an operation than anything else. Panic at the thought of the approaching danger, at the prospect of possibly being 'written off', was gone. With it went the worst system of physical nausea which, in earlier days, brought on vomiting. There was an outward coolness, which was deceptive. The fear, which came from knowledge of the odds, lay less heavily

46

upon the stomach. The anguish was in the conscious mind instead of in the subconscious—the entrails. There was little nervous reaction, no visible shaking.

The suffering of the conscious mind is a stage ahead. It is fearful of over-confidence. It must remember the lessons of experience. It must not forget. The beginner has no experience to forget. His fear is of the unknown. Curiously enough, escaping is one of those adventures in which experience counts a great deal. Only the seasoned escaper knows it.

Compare a tame animal with a wild animal. They are as chalk and cheese. An experienced escaper is a tame animal that has learnt something of the wiles of a wild one.

The experienced escaper feels a heavy responsibility lying at his own door. He knows how to succeed, and if he fails it is probably his fault. The odds are his own making. He knows he cannot blame 'bad luck' any more. The beginner does not know the odds, they are not of his own making. He is lucky or unlucky, and until he has passed the stage of blaming failure on bad luck he is not a seasoned escaper. The experienced bomb-disposal officer knows this, too. If he is blown sky high it is because he made a blunder, though in conditions fraught with terrifying danger for the uninitiated.

The *Appell* sounded at 1.55 p.m. and the prisoners gathered in the courtyard. Obedient to whispered commands, ranks were formed in an orderly manner and in record time. As 2 p.m. struck Oberleutnant Püpcke, tall, in his well-fitting grey artillery uniform and highly polished jack-boots, walked quickly through the gate.

"True to form," thought Dick, and he winked at Mike and Rupert forming up not far away.

The *Appell* went off without a hitch except for the ominous arrival of the *Abwehr* (security) officer, Hauptmann Eggers, in the middle of the proceedings. As the prisoners had nowadays come to expect, the Jerries were not far behind them. Eggers knew that something was in the wind, but evidently had few clues.

The parade was dismissed. Dick and Lulu made for the

entrance to the theatre block as nonchalantly yet as quickly as possible.

Eggers deliberately headed for them and buttonholed Dick.

With a slow, calculated pronunciation he rasped out in English:

"Well, Captain Howe, and where are you going?" There was suspicion in his manner and sarcasm in his voice.

"I'm going with Captain Lawton to do some boxing in the theatre. Why do you ask?"

Eggers ignored Dick's question and said slowly, looking Dick straight in the eye, "I thought Captain Lawton was a great friend of yours. Why do you want to box him?"

"This is terrible," thought Dick, holding his gaze. The precious seconds were ticking away. He replied:

"We can have a good fight and still remain friends."

"Very remarkable! very remarkable!" commented Eggers dryly, nodding his head. He moved out of earshot, and Lulu said, as they both marched into the theatre block:

"Let's call it off for to-day. He's up to something."

"No, we go on," said Dick. "He'll have to be damn quick now to catch us, and I'd much rather see him in our courtyard than waiting on the German side for our chaps to come out."

They hurried up the stairs and into the theatre to find the four escapers ready and the stooging in action. Davis-Scourfield was in charge, already giving the running commentary of Goon movements reported by signals from his staff.

"Eggers in courtyard—Dixon Hawke in sick-bay—two snoops at entrance to French quarters . . ." he reported, slowly translating the signs given to him, like a bookie's mate taking his cues from the semaphore men on a race-course.

Lulu secured the rope to the leg of the vaulting-horse and passed it through the lattice window. Dick and Lulu then scrambled through into the corridor. The four escapers were already waiting.

"We're running late," said Dick, looking at his watch, "it's ten past."

He opened the air-shaft window and listened. The next moment he was removing the sleeves and the bars. One look down the well was enough. Out went the rope, and Mike Sinclair started to descend. He seemed to be ages going down. Grismond's voice came from the theatre.

"Eggers has entered theatre block . . . he's coming up the stairs to the first floor. . . ."

Without further ado Dick and Lulu picked up the first Frenchman and threw him out of the window shouting, "*Allez, vite!*"

There was a violent jerk on the rope as the Frenchman's slack was taken up. Grismond's voice could be heard:

"Eggers on way up to second floor."

"Get the rope away, Lulu," Dick shouted, and to Rupert and the waiting Frenchman, "run for it, vamoose *vite!*" He was already sealing up the window bars and applying the camouflage.

"Eggers coming up the last flight to theatre," came through steady as a rock from Grismond.

"You must come out," said Lulu hoarsely, as Dick applied the finishing touches to the bars. Dick made a running dive through the lattice window and as Lulu locked it quietly, Dick picked himself up and gave him a clout in the solar plexus.

Eggers walked into the theatre.

What he saw was a first-class rough-house. On the floor of the theatre auditorium with chairs flying in all directions, an irate Yorkshireman made it plain to the world that the Christian beatitude of turning the other cheek did not apply where he came from.

This might have been enough for Eggers, but, to his perplexity was added bewilderment, as the French chapel choir, which had foregathered for a practice at the other end of the theatre, intoned the opening lines of a dignified *Kyrie Eleison*.

Eggers pulled himself together. He was accompanied by two snoops before whom he had to keep up appearances. His sly eyes roved the theatre quickly, then, with a sudden movement, he unlocked the door into the forbidden corridor.

Dick and Lulu stopped fighting and innocently pressed forward towards the door to see what Eggers was up to. One of the snoops tried some of the window bars, but missed the ones that had been out. The procession retraced its steps. Eggers relocked the door and turned to continue his tour of inspection.

Spying the two Englishmen, he grinned at them, then shaking his head as he departed, he quoted, "Mad dogs and Englishmen . . ."

The stooges reported that Mike and the Frenchman had walked casually out of the German courtyard by the deep archway leading to the park. Turning to the right, they had walked downhill, then through a wooden gateway on the left-hand side, down the steep winding path to the bridge over a stream which bounded one side of the park and they were lost to view.

Half an hour passed without any alarms. It could be safely concluded that the two had succeeded in leaving the camp.

Dick had little time to congratulate himself on this achievement. The next problem loomed up like a black cloud. Rupert and the second Frenchman had not been able to go. Dick was determined that Rupert should not be disappointed. He felt his reputation was involved. If he could 'fix' three *Appells*, and provided neither of the first two escapers were recaught, it should be possible to repeat the escape. It would have to be done the next day at the same time or never.

He decided to try a method of fixing the *Appell* which had not, to his knowledge, been used at Colditz before. It was known as the 'rabbit' method. He had heard of its use elsewhere, but in Colditz it was thought generally that there were too many sentries present to allow of its success. He conferred with the French adjutant and called Lieutenant Gigue of the French Foreign Legion to his rescue. It was agreed that both contingents would adopt the same system and conceal one absence each at the next three *Appells*.

Bruce, 'the medium-sized man', the indefatigable and ever-willing young R.A.F. officer, who stood about five feet one inch in his socks, would be Dick's 'rabbit'. The operation required the co-operation of a large number of officers.

With the help of Rupert and Lulu, Dick rounded up thirty of the tallest British available, and in a secluded corner of a dormitory, his audience lolling on the beds and seated on the floor, Dick called for attention and began:

"We managed to get Mike away this afternoon with a Frenchman, but it was a near thing. Eggers was hot on the trail—so hot in fact that Rupert who was the next to go couldn't make it. If we can fox the next three *Appells*, one to-night and two to-morrow, we should be able to send Rupert out immediately after the 2 p.m. roll-call. This is why I want you fellows to help. I'll have to grade you for height first. So will you please all stand up in line facing me as if on *Appell*."

With some jostling and banter a line was formed, then re-shuffled, so that the tallest was at one end and the smallest at the other.

"Now," said Dick, "I think the quickest way to get what I want is for you to number off. Squad," he shouted with mock seriousness, "from the left, number!" This was followed by "even numbers, two paces backward, march!"

Having obtained two similar rows of fifteen men each, he explained:

"We've now got to reshuffle each line so that it looks fairly natural, but I'd like the tallest in the middle of each line."

This was done and Dick continued:

"Will each of you please note your positions carefully, that is, the man on each side of you. Got it? Good, now let's break up and try a rehearsal."

The team broke up and when Dick said, "Form up!" the two lines reformed without a hitch.

"That's fine. Now, for heaven's sake, remember your positions carefully. A lot depends on it. The next step is this: your two lines are to form the middle portion of the second and third ranks of the parade turn-out. There will be half a dozen officers on your right flank in each row; there will be a complete rank of chaps in front of you. Those left over will tag themselves on to the left flank. Now, this is where Bruce comes in." He shepherded Bruce to the right of the front rank."

"As soon as the Jerries have counted Bruce's file of three, and have passed on towards your left, Bruce will duck and run between your two ranks to the left-hand end of your front rank. Let's try it, Bruce."

Bruce ducked down between the two rows and reappeared in a few seconds at the far end.

"O.K.," said Dick.

Rupert, who was watching carefully, butted in, "Dick, both ranks had better form up pretty close. I could see Bruce easily between their legs."

Dick agreed. "You'd better all wear overcoats on the *Appell*, it's cold enough, and form up close," he said, and to Bruce, "Carry an R.A.F. cap with you on *Appell*. Don't wear it to begin with, but when you reappear, have it on your head with the peak well down. Last man on the left of the front rank: remember, on the actual *Appell*, to keep a gap on your left just sufficient for Bruce to fill in."

The parade reformed from scratch with Bruce in position, hat in hand.

"Now I'm the Jerry officer and there's a complete rank in front of you. Rupert, see how it goes as I do the counting."

Dick started to count the files in the German fashion, and as he passed three files from Bruce, the latter glided out of sight and was in his new position, with his hat pulled well down over his eyes long before Dick reached him.

"That'll do," said Rupert.

Dick then gave some final cautions and the party broke up.

The rabbit method was more foolproof the bigger the number on parade. The French were a hundred and eighty strong by now compared with the British eighty, and little difficulty was expected with their contingent. This was the kind of game which appealed strongly to the French mentality.

The evening *Appell* and the next morning *Appell* went off serenely. The French, noticing what was happening, thought it a great joke. For Dick, there was the satisfying feeling of an operation going according to schedule, but behind it was always a haunting misgiving—the stool-pigeon; the unknown traitor who might be in their midst, who had his own secret method of transmitting information to the Germans within the prison, and who could ruin the best of schemes.

The midday *Appell* assembled as usual. Dick, Rupert and Lulu formed up at the end of the rear rank. From here they could witness the rabbit performing. To their right they could see the French forming up. Nothing looked unusual. The parade came to attention and Oberleutnant Püpcke entered the courtyard on time. He was always punctual. The counting began. As it passed Bruce, he could be seen stiffening for the 'off'. He bent his head down, looking at his feet, and as the counting reached the fourth file beyond him he seemed to slip to the earth and in a second was diving along the closely formed corridor between the two rear ranks. He reappeared, if anything rather suddenly, in his new position.

As Püpcke reached the end of the counting, a sentry near the canteen door came smartly to attention and left his post at the double. He halted in front of the German sergeant-major, and spoke hurriedly to him. The sergeant-major saluted Püpcke, and spoke to him. Together they accosted the sentry and a consultation took place. This was the signal for the prisoners to start barracking and shuffling their feet to register impatience. The sentry had obviously seen something. He was the one nearest to the point where Bruce reappeared. Püpcke, however, did not appear convinced. Turning away from him, he ordered the parade to dismiss.

Dick and Rupert had little time to congratulate themselves on their good fortune. In less than a minute they were in the theatre where the drill was laid on as before. Rupert, calm and collected, not showing a trace of the excitement seething within him, took up his position in the corridor and his French colleague soon stood beside him. He, too, was behaving himself well. He could hardly be excited with the coolness all around him.

The operation worked like clockwork. Dick gave no orders. The men who were on this job were old hands.

The rope went over the sill; the bars came away and Rupert was outside. As he dropped down Dick whispered hoarsely after him, "Good luck, Rupert! Remember they can't shoot a British officer."

Grismond Davies-Scourfield's voice could be heard as yesterday, but to-day there was a ring of optimism in his reports:

"Püpcke walking out of courtyard through main gate . . . Gephard talking to Dixon Hawke in centre . . . two snoops at sick-bay entrance . . . all clear in theatre block. . . ."

The Frenchman followed Rupert and as the rope slackened it was whipped up and removed immediately to its permanent hiding-place. The camouflage replaced and the windows closed, the whole team quickly dispersed. Dick and Lulu transferred their activities to genuine theatrical preparations on the stage and awaited the reports of the stooges watching the progress of the escapers.

Ten minutes later, small, ginger-headed Peter Storie Pugh bounced into the theatre. "They've been caught, Dick," he said, "at the gateway down to the park."

"What the hell!" exclaimed Dick. "How were they caught there? There's no sentry."

"Quite, but there was when Rupert and his Frog got there. He appeared from nowhere and stopped them."

"What happened?"

"I couldn't see much for the trees, but there was quite a lot of talking before he made them put their hands up. Then they were marched back to the Kommandantur."

"Somebody's been quick off the mark this time, if you ask me. That's Eggers' work all right—but what gets me is that he should know when our men were going and the direction they'd take."

"I'm afraid it's the old story, Dick—a traitor in the camp," said Peter. "This always happens when too many people get to know an escape's coming off. The whole camp knew about the escape to-day."

"You're probably right, Peter, but we'll never know for certain. A stool-pigeon would certainly account for Eggers' behaviour yesterday. But we were one step ahead luckily. Eggers wouldn't have known any more than his informer, who could only tell him an escape was likely in the afternoon and that we should be watched closely."

"But to-day," Peter interrupted, "he'd know a lot more. You can't stop people talking. He'd know about everything—except probably the actual light-well."

"A damn shame!" said Dick. He was boiling with suppressed anger. He was sure in his own mind that an informer was at work, and he was impotent to trace him. The whole camp would have to be treated as suspect.

A Polish informer had been found—it was old history now—but he had been found by the Poles themselves. Dick might be able to set some sleuths at work among the British, but nothing could ever be done about the French—that was the trouble—it was his Achilles heel.

Scarlet O'Hara walked into the theatre. He had been watching the German courtyard.

"They're caught," he said, grinning broadly.

"Thanks for the news," said Dick. "I can't see anything funny in it. What's the joke?"

"They were marched into the Kommandantur about ten minutes ago, from the park. I stayed put to see what happened. They've just been marched out again, and they're off down to the town jail, dressed in their underpants, with their hands up and four Goons trailing 'em."

"I bet Rupert's cold, his pants always remind me of a piece of wire-netting," said Dick. He was thinking, "Thank God, two are out, anyway—not as depressing as it could be."

Lulu had joined the group. Peter and Scarlet were recounting their stories again. Dick changed the subject.

"I don't think the rabbit will work again in a hurry. We'd better lay up a couple of ghosts while we have the chance. That means three absent from the British ranks next *Appell*. The Jerries may call one any time now."

Lulu said, "I think Monty Bissell's our man for that. He's got the best hide-out in the camp."

"Let's get cracking," said Dick with sudden energy in his voice. He disappeared through the theatre door, and down the stairs two at a time, followed by the others.

They found Monty in the prisoners' mess-room and a hurried consultation took place. Monty had recently embarked on a tunnel scheme in the chapel, under the pulpit. The entrance was cleverly concealed by a slab of marble forming one of the steps up to it. There was already ample space in the tunnel for the concealment of a couple of bodies which, it was now agreed, should be permanently housed there. Volunteers were quickly called for from among Monty's tunnelling team, and two were elected for the job. They went straight to the chapel and were walled in.

The *Appell* siren began to moan.

On a previous escape attempt Dick had put away no less than six ghosts. It had been too much for the Jerries to swallow. Besides, the ghosts were not superlatively well hidden, and were all, eventually, discovered. On this occasion Dick decided to compromise with two ghosts.

What was the purpose of a ghost? It was this: after a gone-away escape the chances of success of the escaper increased tremendously the farther he was from the camp. The area of search to be covered by the Germans increased, mathematically, by the square of the increased distance away.

Thus it was of the utmost importance to give an escaper the longest start possible by concealing his absence on *Appells* as long as possible; for this purpose ghosts were created.

In this particular instance, as the two gone-aways—Mike Sinclair and his French colleague—had a good twenty-four hours' start, Dick considered it unnecessary to conceal their absence any longer. On the contrary, it was now more important to think of the future. The two ghosts in the chapel would 'fill in' on *Appells* after the next escape, whenever that might be.

German sentries entered the courtyard and took up their positions for the roll-call. Their officers appeared. The parade came to attention. The count was taken. Four officers were missing. Messengers were dispatched to the Kommandantur. After a long delay they returned. The parade was dismissed.

Dick now had two cards up his sleeve.

*   *   *   *   *

Optimism ran high after Mike's escape. He was known to be heading for Switzerland, towards the hitherto almost foolproof secret Colditz frontier-crossing route.

Then after five days came the news of his recapture. The Germans were never slow to announce the recapture of an escaper: in fact, it was by the absence of such announcements that the successes were counted. An almost audible groan went up from the whole camp. He carried the hopes of so many and bore personal messages with him to so many loved ones waiting patiently at home in England for their husbands and their sons.

Within ten days Mike was back in the Castle, in a solitary confinement cell. His story came through.

When he and his French companion had walked through the German kitchens from the theatre light-well, they found their way down the stairs and into the German courtyard without mishap. One quick glance had been enough for Mike to assure him of the direction to take. The gateway to the park lay open. There did not appear to be anyone on duty there. Without a word the two men, in their German overalls, passed the court-yard sentry, heading for the gate. Through this they walked and on down the hill, turning through the next gate to the left of the roadway and then down farther along the steep, wide path into the park, over the bridge.

Within ten minutes they had climbed the park wall and were free. Mike parted company from his companion *en route* and in two days he was in Singen. The Frenchman made for the city of Leipzig, where there were many French workmen and where, also, a convoy of lorries started for France, at regular intervals, with supplies for the occupation troops. Mike was re-caught near Singen. His was the story becoming menacingly common these days; an air-raid had started a round-up for parachuted airmen. Thousand of civilians were out on the man-hunt. He was picked up by a patrol within half a mile of freedom and three days out from Colditz. The Frenchman was already in the cells on his return; his contacts in Leipzig had failed him.

Mike was not allowed to communicate with anyone during his stay in the 'cooler', which lasted six weeks. He was left alone with his thoughts, disconsolate and dejected, to brood upon his failure, 'so near and yet so far . . .' Mike would take himself to task seriously. He had a strongly developed conscience and an unswerving devotion to duty. A feeling that he had let down his fellow prisoners would not leave him in peace. At twenty-six he could stand a fair amount of loneliness and introspection without ill effect, but—six weeks was a long spell and, besides, Mike had taken more than his share of punishment with the Gestapo in Poland.

Resolution was the healing salve that would conquer the putrefying poison of morbidity. He would try again. He would not give up; that was certain.

PART II: 1943

CHAPTER IV

RADIO NEWS

DURING the autumn of 1942, Dick Howe had entered into private negotiations with a French clique which possessed one of the two wireless-sets in Colditz. A second group of French headed by Lieutenant Gigue owned the other. The first set had been smuggled into the prison with the arrival of a batch of Frenchmen from a camp where they had had considerable contact with the outer world, mainly through orderlies and French workmen in the town and countryside. Gigue's set had been smuggled into the camp in parts hidden in thirty-five parcels, received over a period of months, from France.

The British had no set of their own and a purchase was arranged. Dick had been Escape Officer for some months by then. From the many contacts he had and the many rather morbid impressions he picked up, he saw, only too clearly, the value of possessing such a link with the outside world. He was preparing the hide for it when a hitch occurred. The proposed purchase became widely known among the French contingent; their senior officers were told of the transaction and were prevailed upon to stop it. Feeling among the French ran on the lines that as they were likely to be moved at any time—which was true—they would probably be separated into groups for different destinations and would need both sets. After all, they argued, Frenchmen had gone to much trouble to obtain them, so why should they dispose of one? They even argued that as British morale was higher than theirs, they had more need of the boost given by Allied news broadcasts. Of course, as long as they remained in Colditz the British would continue to use translations of their bulletins. Dick retired from the scene.

Lieutenant Gigue came from the South of France and had spent most of his life in Marseilles. He had the typical French accent of the region, which differs from normal French, enunciated between the lips and teeth. The tongue plays a great part in producing the Marseilles accent by giving the impression of always sticking to the palate a split second too long.

Gigue carried a huge scar across his cheek and neck. His hair and eyebrows were jet black and his skin a deep sun-tanned brown. A pair of mischievously flashing dark eyes and a ready grin completed an appearance of good-humoured energy. His movements were unbelievably quick, and he had the knack of changing his position without being thought to have moved at all. It was a most curious and even eerie propensity. If it had not struck so many different officers at different times, the likelihood is that each one would have thought he had had an hallucination or was just suffering from prison slow-wittedness. But after about a year or so, when men repeatedly found themselves talking to thin air where they had thought they saw Gigue a moment before, the matter became one of public interest. It was even advanced that possibly Gigue was endowed with occult powers. Certainly it was most disconcerting for Englishmen to be found talking out loud to themselves in French in the middle of the courtyard; Gigue understood no English. He moved without a sound wherever he went.

Marseilles is not so far from Corsica. It is said that Napoleon had the cat-like propensity of walking, not on his toes and heels, but somewhere in between. Nor was Gigue unlike a Corsican bandit in that he had a faithful company of followers who, in all escaping ventures, appeared to understand his every mood and interpreted his unspoken wishes with unfailing accuracy. Gigue's heart was made of gold, and the English had no better friend among the French contingent. Long before the French left Colditz, Dick Howe and Gigue had become close collaborators, and the friendship between them paid dividends.

One spring-like day in February 1943 Dick careered down the spiral staircase from the French quarters out into the courtyard and nearly bumped into Colonel Guy German who was taking his morning constitutional.

The sun just climbed high enough at midday to peep over the steep roofs of Colditz and send a few shimmering sunbeams to scatter the shadows that ruled unchallenged in the yard during the long and dreary winter months.

There was a glow in Dick's heart and triumph in his voice as he spoke to his senior officer.

"Good morning, Colonel."

"Good morning, Dick."

"I've got good news for you, sir."

"What is it? You sound excited. Coming from you that means it must be very good."

"The French are going, as you know."

"Yes, they're going very soon, I think. Colonel le Brigant has told me. He has it on good authority from his own stooges. Incidentally, he's also told me the move is to make room for British. You remember the rumours we heard of the big breakout from Warburg? Well, the British are reported to be coming from Warburg—at least some of them. So the rumour may have been true."

"Well, sir, my bit of news concerns a wireless-set."

"Ah ha! are the French coming round, then? We don't want a repetition of the last effort. There was some bad feeling over that—you remember?"

"Yes, I remember well. But this time they want to present it to us."

"In that case it must be given through the Senior French Officer so that we know where we stand. I'm afraid I'll have to insist on that point."

"I think that's all laid on. Gigue tells me that he has the agreement of Colonel le Brigant to leave one of his sets behind. You see, Gigue has two now. He's damn decent about the whole business. He can claim that the sets have been obtained entirely through his efforts, and he is pressing his claim and the right to dispose of the set as he likes. He says there'll be practically no opposition from the French quarters. They've two other sets now which will travel with them."

"Of course, Dick, there's our own set on the way. . . ."

"Yes, but . . . it's not here yet and may never reach us. Gigue knows about it, too, and says his C.O. knows it."

"Very well! It looks as if we can accept with a clear conscience."

"Colonel le Brigant will be speaking to you about it soon."

Dick was about to turn away when his senior recalled him.

"One moment, Dick, that's not the end of the matter. What about the use of the set? Have you thought about that? First of all there's the maintenance, then there's the stooging and the recording, and we'll have to decide on reception times and the best wave-lengths and produce the best news bulletins possible."

"Yes, I've thought about it," said Dick, and the slightest trace of weariness crept into his voice. He knew what was coming. The Colonel was thinking. He had, when in thought, the unusual habit of raising his eyebrows and wrinkling his forehead. They walked together round the yard—now in shadow, now in sunlight. The Colonel always walked briskly. He had a robust physique and was still tough in spite of the years of weakening. His was a forceful character that stood no nonsense from Germans or anybody else. He could be frighteningly abrupt. To those in whom he placed his confidence he was a towering pillar of strength. He could scent out weakness like a bloodhound after his quarry, and he wasted no time. He was the ideal Commanding Officer in a difficult situation.

It was his regular exercise hour and the circle he walked never varied, though the direction in which he walked it changed unpredictably. Dick walked beside him as they speeded round in clockwise direction. The Colonel, as if to jolt his thoughts, stopped suddenly and reversed direction. Dick was well trained in his habits, and had caught him up again in a yard.

The Colonel had been ruminating and now he spoke as if unwillingly:

"I see no way out of it. You are our best wireless engineer. I daren't put the machine in anyone else's hands. It's much too valuable—our only link with reality, in fact. If it broke down it would be like cutting an artery. Yes, Dick, I'm afraid it means more work for you."

"I know that."

"What you must do, at least, is to try to relieve yourself of all the news routine, and arrange the security so that you're free of that responsibility. Pass it over to someone else."

"Lulu Lawton?" queried Dick, who had already given thought to the problem of stooging.

"Yes, by all means."

"Gigue has shown me the works," Dick continued, "and they're first class. We have absolutely nothing to teach that crew. I must hand it to Gigue. I can understand why the Jerries have never found it."

"Well, it's up to you, Dick, or rather to the man you appoint for stooging and camouflage to see that the Jerries continue not to find it. If they do—it'll look bad and we'll have only ourselves to blame."

Early in 1943 Gigue had received a second brand-new receiving set in another round of thirty-five parcels from France. They were smuggled, as usual, out of the German parcels office before the Germans ever set about examining the day's parcel delivery. The French were consequently happy to leave the British one of their three sets before they departed from Colditz.

There was no need even for the British to construct their own wireless hide. They took over the French set in its stronghold, lock, stock and barrel. It says much for the ingenuity of Gigue and his French colleagues that, although towards the end of the war the Germans knew the British had a set in action they never found it. They searched until they were blue in the face without success. Eventually our prisoners made no concealment of the news bulletins which were read publicly at the evening meal. The war situation was discussed openly with the Germans; their arguments controverted and their alleged facts and figures contradicted.

As to the situation of the receiver, it was concealed in the eave of the steep sloping roof above the French quarters—which became British on the departure of the French.

When a roof is forty feet high from gutter to ridge, it can be appreciated that at least two floors may be built inside it having dormer windows and comparatively high ceilings. The floor area of rooms within the roof becomes reduced at each level upwards, not only because the two sides of the roof are approaching each other, but usually because a vertical wall is built around the sides of the rooms so that the inmates do not have the impression they are living in a tent. This vertical wall, in the case of rooms at Colditz, was about five feet high and concealed behind it a small triangular space bounded by the three sides; slanting roof, vertical wall and horizontal ceiling of the room below. Actually the architectural features were slightly more complicated than this description implies. The triangular space had to be enlarged out of the seven-foot-thick walls. Within it the wireless installation was set up, complete with electric light, switch-gear for the receiver, earphones, a table and two chairs for the operator and the shorthand writer acting as news-recording telegraphist. Beside it, a second cavity was enlarged to provide a hide for contraband.

Entry to these secret apartments was made from the attic which formed the apex of the roof itself.

*   *   *   *   *

Jim Rogers, the mining engineer from South Africa, could not have lived long without the news. The progress of the war could be foretold by the tilt of his broad moustache. This had grown from nothing at the time of his capture. Jim had once been a burly, tough six-footer, but the lengthening war was telling on him. He seemed to grow smaller. As his stature shrank and his body grew thin, his moustache alone waxed in splendour. His strength, like that of Samson, was going into his hair.

64

Where Samson had wielded the jawbone of an ass, Jim wielded his guitar.

Before ever the B.B.C. news bulletins became an organised part of the daily schedule, Jim had developed his own system of news summaries, which he recited daily, with infinite relish, to the whole British contingent assembled for their meagre evening repast. What Jim really needed was a huge beefsteak in front of him, but alas! as that dream dish never materialised, the best that he could do was to whet his appetite with words. He revelled in his phrases and smacked his lips over his metaphors. His war appreciations were full of meat, peppered with doubtful facts, heavily salted with assumptions and blanketed with the opaque rosy-coloured sauce of optimism. His prognostications were sweet fruit to the easily gullible, enriched as they were with the cream of the latest rumours. The 'Old Horse' as he was affectionately called, really had very little information to go on. His principal source was the meagre French bulletins which were often garbled with news coming from Vichy. In addition, he had the German Press and the hearsay of the latest prisoner arrival from another camp.

As a writer may use a true story for the basis of his novel, so Jim used the news. He would come rushing into the common room just before the midday meal, eyes glistening, a lock of straight hair falling over his forehead, and his moustache quivering with excitement.

"Great news to-day, boys! Great news! I've just got it all straight from the horse's mouth—a chap just in from Marlag Nord—he's in the delousing shed. He was on that Dieppe raid some time ago—won't say any more now—keep it all for to-night—managed to get the whole story at last—it's terrific. It'll shake you."

"Aw, you don't say!" would come from Don Donaldson, the Canadian, often called 'the Weasel', who had once climbed into the cockpit of a German Messerschmitt, but could not find the starter.

"Come on, Horse! Don't hold back."

Jim would then become as close as an oyster, "Awfully sorry, old chap, but simply mustn't jump the gun—besides I might give the wrong impression—got to draw the right conclusions, you know—that means some thinking—there's big strategy behind this."

It was a cat-and-mouse game. Don and Jim's other messmates would feign indifference. At lunch-time, over the table, surrounded by eight glum officers, silence would reign. After ten minutes, with the meal practically finished and not a word spoken, Jim would realise an opportunity was slipping from him. Bursting to tell his story and thoroughly put out at the lethargy of his companions, he could not hold out any longer. In an offended tone he would blurt out:

"My God! I think you fellows are a lot of bums! Nothing to talk about—no interest in the war—I can't understand chaps not taking an interest in world events . . . terrific things going on."

There would be a pause as Don would drag out the comedy. It was like teasing a big Newfoundland dog which was your greatest friend. Jim knew he was being teased. But his nature could not be suppressed. When Don judged he had wrung the last ounce of patience out of him, he would say again:

"Aw now, Jim, you're playing with us! We just can't wait to hear about Dieppe straight from the Old Horse's mouth. Just give us a hint."

So Jim would unbend, and gathering the 'chaps' around him, with their heads all bent close together over the table, he would tell them in a hoarse whisper:

"The Allies have the whole invasion buttoned up. It's coming any day now. Dieppe was terrific strategy—I've worked it out. It was all a hoax to make the Jerries think that we'd think that invasion was hopeless and so ease up on coastal defence. No more now, chaps, but I'll give you the whole works to-night. Keep it dark—I want to shake everyone. Damn good for morale."

And indeed it was. Jim was our camp Goebbels—but he did a much better job than that despicable propagandist, probably because he just could not have told a lie if he had tried. He was, by nature, a good story-teller. He was a spider who could weave a tantalising web to enveigle even the most suspicious fly. Once in his net, his listeners were wrapped up in a pleasantly soft cotton-wool of optimism and hope which curiously, through all the years of despair, became a wonderful protection against the lengthening shadows; the misery of the polar extremes of the unknown and of reality. He was a magician who, by pretending not to be able to deceive his audience, by even encouraging their laughter and their ridicule at his naïveté in the lesser tricks of his trade, cast over them the greater spell at which he aimed; succeeding with genius, so that they were completely unaware of what he had done to them. There is no doubt he kept hope high and courage strong even in the darkest days. He was the Knight of the Silver Lining.

As with Dieppe, so it had been with the loss of the two great battleships, with Singapore and the retreats in the Libyan desert.

When Singapore fell, the French were terribly upset. The Poles were full of sympathy, and the Dutch were calm but silent. The British treated it as if one of their favourite football teams had been beaten, and as if the coming defeat had been known beforehand because the star forward line had been changed.

The fact was that the British contingent had been cushioned for the coming fall for some time by the Old Horse and a confederate, Colonel Kimber. The French came to our quarters with long, glum faces, wringing their hands as soon as the news was confirmed. The war in the East was over for them. They could see the Japanese hordes in the Mediterranean. They did not come to condole, but rather to join the British in a common act of despair. Singapore appeared to them to be for the British what Dunkerque had been for themselves. They found their allies in good spirits and were dumbfounded.

Colonel Kimber had worked on the defences of Singapore before the war. He had, even in those days, fumed at the pig-headedness of men who installed enormous guns with a traverse that covered attack from the sea, but gave no protection whatever in the direction of the Causeway.

By the time Singapore fell it was old news to the British, and Jim passed over it lightly:

"Singapore has gone, but I told you all about that three weeks ago, so there's no need to bother about it now. It merely serves to bear out the accuracy of my forecasts."

Loud cheers interrupted him, and French guests, who were present, sat with mouths agape at the spectacle of British officers cheering the news of the fall of Singapore. It is not without reason that Europeans speak seriously of 'mad Englishmen'.

When the cheering, catcalls and whistling died down Jim continued his summary of the news of the day.

When he had finished and the clatter of plates and hum of voices had resumed its normal cacophony, as if to emphasise the complete indifference of the British to a huge catastrophe, Don Donaldson's Canadian drawl would intervene:

"Come on, Old Horse! Tell us a good story."

Jim had quite a fund of them, and they grew longer and more elaborate with every telling.

"Well, chaps! when I was mining in Yugoslavia some queer things happened to me—you just wouldn't believe them. D'you know there was a princess out there and guess what she did?"

"No! What?"

"Well, you just wouldn't believe it."

"Aw, you don't say! Come on, Old Horse, tell us all about it."

And Jim would tell the story how, once, when prospecting in the mountains of Yugoslavia, his camp had been visited by a royal party. They were entertained lavishly by Jim's mining team and the *Slebovitza* flowed freely. A beautiful princess became quite incapable of retracing her steps, after the party, down the rocky gorges to the mountain road, where the cars and retinue attended. Jim and a mate formed a comfortable chair for her with their four hands interlaced, and seated upon them she slept peacefully as they carried her down the stony path.

"What happened then, Jim?"

"Her little head was against my shoulder." He paused.

"Go on, Horse!"

"I slipped on a rock. It gave the princess an awful jolt and she promptly pee'd into my hand."

CHAPTER V

THE FRENCH TUNNEL

THE French had been digging a tunnel for eight months. It looked as if there might be a race between the tunnellers and the Germans; the former to finish the tunnel and escape before the latter moved them all from the camp. A small party of French had already left for Oflag IVD.

The French architects of the tunnel consisted originally of a team of nine officers who constituted themselves the 'Société Anonyme du Tunnel de Colditz'. To make sure that it was *anonyme* the tunnellers had no chief. *Liberté, Egalité, Fraternité* was the motto they lived up to. They were: Jean Brejoux, a professor of German; Edgar Barras, the strong man and the champion French 'stool-ball' [1] player; Bernard Cazaumayou, the weight-lifter; Roger Madin, an engineer who was the tunnel electrician; Paillé, French Sappers and Miners; Jean Chaudrut, the chief stooge; Georges Diedler, from the Vosges; Jean Gambero, the astute Parisian; and Léonce Godfrin, from the Ardennes.

The conception of the tunnel was curious yet typical. The French are a logical race. They had read in the German Press that the Leipzig Fair was to be held in spite of the war. Leipzig was only twenty-two miles away. It would provide wonderful cover for the escape of a large body of prisoners. Leipzig would be full to overflowing with visitors, coming from all parts and speaking many languages. The only way, it seemed, to dispatch a large body of prisoners to Leipzig was by tunnel—but not the whole way by tunnel; that opened the discussion of the next problem. Again, the French decided where they would like their tunnel to debouch so as to provide a safe get-away. From

[1] Described in *The Colditz Story*.

there they worked backwards into the Castle to see where the entrance should be. Alas! none of the French quarters touched ground level; underneath them on the ground-floor were rooms occupied by Germans during the daylight hours; the sick ward, the parcels office and Gephard's office. Once more, logic saved the day. "If we can't start at the bottom," they said, "let's start at the top." And that was what they did.

The clock tower provided them with a means of access to the cellar. The clock had not worked for years and the weights, with their long chains, had also been removed, leaving empty cylindrical sleeves which extended from the clock down to the ground-floor. There were small cubby holes, presumably inspection chambers, giving access to the sleeves at each floor level. The cubby holes had long ago been bricked up by the Jerries.

A heavily barred steel door on the top landing of the French quarters, at fourth-floor level, was the first object of attack. It led to the clock-room. With men like Gigue and Roger Madin in the camp, the padlocks, mortice locks and cruciform locks securing the door were soon provided with keys. Once in the clock-room, a camouflaged opening was constructed in the floor and in the ceiling below, which let the Frenchmen down into the cubby hole on the third floor. They could have descended through the sleeves, but these were a tight squeeze for any adult, being only sixteen inches in diameter, and coming up again would have been difficult. They constructed ladders instead, piercing holes in each cubby-hole floor down to ground level. Here the first serious tunnelling began. It consisted of a vertical shaft through the stones and mortar of the arched roof of the Castle cellar.

Once in the cellar, which, of course, was subject to examination by German patrols, the Frenchmen had the choice of digging in any direction they wished. Having already chosen their direction—they started breaking out a hole, four feet from the ground, in the wall facing the chapel.

The cellar contained a stock of old Hungarian wine reposing in bottles under a layer of dust—a serious temptation to the

French. They only weakened once, according to their own admission. That was the night when they examined the cellar from end to end in search of a secret passage or other ready-made exit from the camp. They were unsuccessful. Momentarily depressed at the prospect of months of tunnelling, they 'won' four bottles of wine.

Having made an entrance door on pivots like a safe door out of the original stones from the wall, they continued, digging a horizontal tunnel behind it, through the heavy foundation which supported the dividing wall between the chapel and the spiral staircase to the French quarters. This continued for a distance of fifteen feet.

Once under the chapel, they dug a vertical shaft upwards for a distance of nine feet until they met the beams of the chapel floor. Progressing under the floor, they searched for the entrance to a crypt, but found none.

The team realised, at last, that there was no short-cut and that they would have to continue the tunnel until they were outside the wire. They decided to increase the number of shareholders in the tunnelling company. They had been working by day and night for two months and were ready to welcome new blood.

The S.A.T.C. obtained its recruits without difficulty. Many eyes had watched with envy the guarded movements and mysterious disappearances of the founder members, and had noted the surreptitious washing of the dirty sweat-stained underclothing of the Société Anonyme. The company increased from nine in number to thirty. Tunnelling continued in three shifts throughout the twenty-four hours. The spirits of the French rose as yard after yard of tunnel opened in front of them.

When the tunnel was nearing completion in the early days of 1943, Gigue, who was by then a long-standing member of the company, and Madin, who had been one of the original members, offered to take Dick on a conducted tour of the premises. It was January, and they were hoping to break soon. When that took place the British would never have an opportunity of seeing the work they had carried out, and they were genuinely proud of their tunnel.

"You know," said Dick, gladly accepting their invitation, "we've heard you digging away for months, and of course your own people have, too. Haven't you been running a tremendous risk all this time? The Germans must know well enough that a tunnel's in progress."

It was a fact that at all hours of the day, but more especially at night when the Castle was wrapped in the silence of sleep, tunnelling could be heard. The sound was definable as high up as the third floor of the Castle above the chapel, where some of the British lived, and it even kept light sleepers awake. It could be compared to the regular, consecutive landing of high-explosive shells over the hills some miles away. There was a gentle concussion which appeared to come from various directions, carried by the air, the walls, the floor and even the ceiling. The dull, heavy thuds struck the ear from all sides. Eventually, it was possible, by continued careful listening, to eliminate echoes and secondary sound waves, and to establish with some certainty where the sounds emanated from. Indeed, the Germans must have done this by now.

"The Jerries may know it well enough," said Gigue in French, "but as long as they can find no entrance we are safe."

"But the Germans will persevere. . . ."

"Come with us this evening and you shall see why they will not find the entrance," replied Gigue. "We are on the night shift and you will spend it with us."

They met again after the last *Appell* of the day. Dick had finished his supper and was prepared for a night's vigil. Lulu would make up a dummy in his bed. He had been warned to put on plenty of warm clothing.

The Castle was in darkness, except where the reflection from the searchlights glowed. Dick mounted the French staircase with his two friends. They reached the attics at the fourth floor. From the landing to the left was the Ghetto where the French Jewish officers lived; to the right were attics, locked and uninhabited.

Gigue looked at his watch. It was 9.30 p.m. If all went well there would be no further *Appells* until 7 a.m. the next morning.

They waited for the remainder of the shift workers to appear. It was to be a 'removal' shift. Tons of debris from a week of tunnelling had to be cleared away that night. While they were waiting Gigue explained to Dick:

"We have been lucky to find a good place for the debris of the tunnel. When we go through the steel door over there," he said pointing, "you will see a ladder leading to a skylight in the roof. Outside on the roof within a distance of two metres there is a window in the gable of the attic above your English bedroom, the one over the chapel. It has bars which we can remove and replace. In this attic we have found plenty of space for hundreds of tons of rubble between the slanting roof and the partition walls." Gigue flashed a sly grin at Dick as he caught his puzzled expression. Dick asked:

"But how do you pass the rubble from the skylight into the attic?"

"*Eh bien!* A man sits on the roof outside the skylight. He passes the sacks from one man on the ladder to another inside the attic."

"So that is why you do this at night?"

"Yes, indeed. If it was done in the day our man could be seen from the town and the countryside. At night he is in a dark shadow cast beyond the searchlight beams."

"He must get damned cold up there," said Dick. "Why, it's freezing hard."

"He freezes to begin with. But when he has lifted sacks weighing twenty-five kilos for half an hour, he is not cold any more."

The *équipe*, as the French always called their team, had by now all arrived. There were twenty energetic Frenchmen milling around them on the small landing. Dick was aghast at the crowd. Gigue and Madin, receiving the 'all clear' signal from their stooges, began work on the locks. Within a matter of minutes the steel door opened and the whole *équipe* was soon

74

safely inside the clock tower. The door was locked behind them. Everybody seemed to know what to do. At signals from Gigue, who stood near the door keeping contact with a stooge outside, the team set to work. The secret trap-door in the floor was disclosed, and bodies disappeared downwards through the hole. A ladder was hoisted from below and propped against a skylight window which Dick saw for the first time. Around it gathered half a dozen Frenchmen ready to go out on the roof. If there was an alarm this section of the team would have to leave the clock tower. Jerries might enter and search the room. Those who descended would have the trap-door sealed above them, and would remain hidden unless they had to come out because of an *Appell*.

Gigue handed over his post to a colleague and invited Dick to descend the ladder. Madin had already disappeared below. Gigue followed and the trap-door was closed above them. In the small chambers, at successive levels, men were changing into their tunnelling kit. Dick noted a gaudy variety of designs and colours in woollen vests, pants and stockings which the Frenchmen donned, layer upon layer. It was evidently going to be cold. Some of them wore tin helmets, and, as if answering his unspoken question, Gigue said to Dick: "Put on this English Tommy's helmet. It's the only English one we have and it's right that you should wear it. When my friends start shifting the rocks you may need it."

They were soon ready to descend to the lower regions. They stood for a moment surveying each other laughingly.

"You look like an old Roman warrior," said Dick, "with that helmet on."

Gigue indeed looked like something out of a nightmare classic. He wore gaily coloured stockings and knee-pads, a pair of dirty dark blue shorts over several pairs of pants and a bright red thick woollen sweater drawn in at the waist by a broad leather belt with a brass buckle.

Dick looked no less peculiar. From the plimsolls on his feet two pairs of long woollen pants stretched up to his waist, while, over them, a pair of white rugger shorts covered his buttocks.

Three short-sleeved vests clothed his chest and the tin hat crowned his head. He looked like Tommy Atkins after a bomb had blown off his uniform. Gigue said:

"You need not laugh at me. Laugh at yourself. You remind me of an English general going to have his bath in the trenches."

They climbed down the next ladder, one after the other, and carried on downwards, passing, at each floor level, through a small room packed to the ceiling with loose stones and rubble until there was scarcely sufficient room to manœuvre.

"You are now at ground level," said Gigue. "The team is about to start work—we shall watch it from here for a moment." As he spoke a blue and white checked sack the size of a laundry bag rose through a hole in the floor. Dick recognised the pattern of the standard German palliasse cover used throughout the camp.

The sack was seized by a Frenchman, standing over the hole, who checked and tightened the cord which closed it at the top, and then lifted it into a cradle made of rope with a heavy steel hook attached. Dick lifted the sack himself, out of interest, and estimated that it weighed half a hundredweight. The cradle, with the sack in it, was hooked to a loop on an endless rope that disappeared upwards through the two round sleeves which had housed the clock chains and weights. The Frenchman pressed an electric button beside him. The cradle started to move upwards and was greedily swallowed by the mouth of the sleeve above Dick's head.

"An endless rope lift?" queried Dick.

"Yes," said Gigue, "we use the original pulleys and a reduction gear from the clock at the top. It makes the work much easier for our men."

Another sack rose through the hole in the floor, was hooked to the lift and began its ascent to the attic.

"How much debris do you move in a night?" asked Dick.

"We can move nearly one ton per hour," replied Gigue. "We shall work to-night for seven hours. If you stop for long you catch cold. So we carry on continuously."

Dick said he could well understand it. He was already feeling the chill of a strong draught coming up through the hole in the floor. The clock tower was acting like a chimney.

"Let us go down further while the way is clear," said Gigue. They dropped through the hole, feeling for the ladder beneath them. Dick went carefully downwards in a narrow shaft for a few feet, then found himself again in the open. Descending further he landed on the floor of the Castle cellar. A closely shaded electric light was focused on the ladder to direct the worker mounting it with a heavy sack on his shoulder. Beyond the light was impenetrable darkness. Dick looked around him wonderingly.

"Where do we go from here?" he asked Gigue quietly.

"Wait, a sack is coming," Gigue whispered as if that explained everything.

Dick heard a rumble that seemed to come towards him out of nowhere. Gradually his eyes became more accustomed to the dark and he could see a rectangular glow of light, bright at the edges, which appeared to shine out of a wall at eye level some yards away. Then the rumbling stopped, shadows moved across the glow and suddenly a bright square patch of light showed in the wall. A Frenchman passed him and began to climb the ladder with a sack on his shoulders.

"This is the entrance to the tunnel," said Gigue in an undertone. "The noise you heard was a sack moving along on the sled. We can now go forward." He beckoned Dick to follow.

They approached the hole in the wall. Dick looked along the tunnel. It was a little higher than it was broad; about two feet four inches by two feet in section. It had been hacked through stones and mortar and he began to understand the sounds he had heard for so many months. "There's certainly no need for any shoring or timbering here," he mused.

An electric bulb burned brightly at the far end which was five yards away. The walls of the tunnel gleamed white with light reflected from stone surfaces polished by the frequent rubbing of passing bodies.

Dick stepped on to a large block of wood placed on the floor under the entrance. Then he noticed the heavy door which shut the tunnel. It was a complete section of wall, a foot thick, which had been built inside a wooden casing. A long piece of steel, three quarters of an inch in diameter, acting as a pivot, ran vertically through one end of it. The lower end of the pivot rested on a steel plate hollowed out to receive it. The plate was concreted into the floor of the tunnel. The upper end of the pivot passed through a hole in another steel plate concreted into the roof of the tunnel.

Dick recognised something familiar about the design and asked Gigue:

"Who made the door?"

"I did," was the reply. "I saw Van den Heuvel's door after the Jerries had found his secret room—you remember?—and I copied it."

Dick remembered. It had been impossible to find Van den Heuvel's door, sealed. The irregular edges of the present door were obviously carefully set to fit into crevices in the wall as a pattern fits into a mould. Putty, cobwebs and dust completed the camouflage which would defy minute investigation.

Dick was lost in admiration at the work when he heard Gigue calling from the far end of the tunnel.

"*Dépêche-toi*, Dick. Another sack is coming."

Dick hoisted himself into the hole and crawled to the far end. A rope, made of bedsheets resembling those produced by Bos'n Crisp, ran the length of the tunnel between well-polished tracks of wood at each side. These, Dick realised, carried the sled with the sacks of rubble.

"Here," said Gigue, "we have buried the largest stone of all. We have had them of many sizes, but the one upon which you are kneeling weighs about one hundred and fifty kilos."

"Did it bother you?" said Dick mockingly.

"Yes, it was at the top of the shaft which you see over you."

Dick looked upwards. Above him in the glare of another electric bulb was a vertical shaft, some nine feet in height. Their breath, forming clouds of vapour, rose upwards into it. Dick asked:

"How did you get rid of the stone?"

"Flynn's bar was the answer," said Gigue. "You know that he is the only Englishman with a place promised on this tunnel. Well, if he had not stolen the bar from a lorry in the courtyard, I don't think we would ever have passed that rock. I will show you the bar later. We use it all the time. Barras and Cazaumayou worked upon the stone. It could easily have killed them, for it was as big as the shaft. They made a hole here to receive it. Then they worked underneath it for days, loosening it. It was touch and go. Finally they needed a long bar so that they could free it and escape from underneath it as it fell. At that point Flynn produced his bar. The stone fell one night while they worked, here, where you are. It shook the building. They escaped in time. Afterwards our work was simplified. You know, we had reached the floor of the chapel. Now follow me up the shaft."

Dick climbed upwards after Gigue on a skeleton timber scaffolding that had been erected inside the shaft. Below stood a helmeted Frenchman whom he left with a grin saying, "*Excusez-moi si je tombe sur votre tête.*"

At the top Gigue disappeared again. Dick thought of Alice in Wonderland. Then he reached the top, looked over and reflected that he was not so far wrong. Gigue was lying in front of him completely blocking the view. Not a ray of light penetrated past him. He was struggling and panting as he moved forward. Dick waited patiently at the top of the shaft thinking, "They won't shift a ton this hour. We've put paid to that."

All transport of sacks had ceased. Beside him was a rope suspended from a wooden pulley above his head. The tackle carried the sacks down the shaft.

The puffing and blowing continued, growing more distant. Then Dick heard a "Pssht!" and looked forward. Gigue's head appeared round a corner a long way off.

"Come quickly, Dick, you are occupying the place of one of our men who must handle the sacks."

Dick had already realised this.

Now it was his turn to push and squeeze, to twist and turn,

to sweat and rest, wondering if he would ever see again the light of day. He squirmed himself forward eight yards under what was the floor of the chapel between heavy oak timbers which had been sawn through. At last he found himself in a large space, deeper than before, about two feet, but almost a living-room in other respects—about six feet square, in fact. Here Dick collapsed to recover his breath while a gentle rumble told him that the sacks had started moving again along the tunnel corridors.

"How did you get past those timbers?" asked Dick.

"They nearly finished us," said Gigue. "They are of oak, only six hundred years old, and forty centimetres square. We had to cut through seven of them, each twice, and our saws were made of German table knives!"

Dick felt the sweat clammy around his waist. He suddenly thought of something and asked Gigue:

"Did your fellows cut those seven beams in this freezing cold without getting pneumonia?"

"It was worse than that, Dick. It was very cold lying on those blocks of granite out there, you know, but they were not even allowed to catch a cold! We are under the chapel floor and a German in the church would think it funny if he suddenly heard a cough coming from the dead underneath his feet. We have had stooges always in the chapel when we worked underneath. They warned us if a Jerry came in."

"Pious chaps, I suppose," said Dick.

"Oh yes! they were very pious. They held a retreat which lasted for months. One after the other, for two hours each, they came to the chapel and prayed for our success. If a German came—well, you know, as we say, it is not prayer alone but good deeds also that count, so our friends did the good deed. They banged on the floor as they knelt, with their toes. There was not even a sneeze from the dead below after that."

"I suppose we are near your heading now?" Dick asked.

"No, we are not half-way," replied Gigue. "We are underneath the sacristy. You see the switchboard in the corner. That is where the electricity is branched off from the main chapel supply. Ah! here is Roger. He will explain all to you."

Madin's head appeared through a large hole in the floor of the tunnel some yards away. His pink face, appearing out of the ground, reminded Dick of a ferret. He had a long nose that looked as if it could smell out anything. His angular forehead was surmounted by a wispy crop of fair hair and he wore thick-lensed glasses. His teeth were conspicuously undershot so that his huge triangular-shaped chin protruded outwards giving the impression of complete separation from the remainder of his physiognomy. He smiled on the least provocation, and when he did so the sparkle in his eyes, enlarged by the spectacles, emanated humour and good temper as a fire radiates warmth.

"Hello, Dick!" he said, pulling himself up higher out of the hole. "How do you like our tunnel? Not so bad, eh? Do you approve of it? I have just been checking the electric wiring."

Gigue said to Madin:

"Roger, will you tell Dick all about the electrical installation. I shall leave you—I must go forward to the digging face. Come along later, when you are ready. *Au revoir.*"

He disappeared into the hole, leaving Madin in charge.

"I must tell you how we obtained electricity for the tunnel," said Madin, grinning above his large chin. "We should never have had it without the aid of our curé Jeanjean. You know that the chapel was closed for a while after the morning service. Jeanjean protested he could not continue the spiritual instruction of his converts unless he was allowed to teach in the sacristy. He obtained permission for two hours a day. I was his principal convert! I worked on the wiring, and whenever a German came near the sacristy I was on my knees beside the curé praying hard or listening to his exhortations."

Roger was lying on his stomach, with his head resting in his cupped hands, chuckling away as he told his story: "Gephard came once and even tried to enter the room when wires and floor-boards were lying loose all over the place. Neither the curé nor I have ever prayed so loudly, either before or since, in our whole lives. The curé gave Gephard such terrible looks that he had not the courage to enter and he left us in peace."

"Now, you see the power comes down from the sacristy to this switchboard," Madin continued, pointing to a wooden frame adorned with switches, fuses and lamps.

"The whole tunnel has electric lighting which serves at the same time for signalling. At the entrance there is a switch, and our stooges up above pass messages to the man at the entrance who passes them to everybody in the tunnel by means of this switch."

"When do you think the tunnel will be ready?" Dick questioned.

"We are working very hard to finish before the Germans remove us. You will take over, of course, if it is not finished in time. But we are near the end. We have only about fifteen metres to dig now in loose subsoil. You know how long the tunnel is?"

"No," said Dick.

"It is over forty metres long, including the vertical shafts. The latter total up to eleven metres. The one in the corner over there which you will go down in a moment is the deepest, it is six and a half metres. We had to go underneath the main foundations of the Castle."

Dick was shivering again. The cold was intense. Movement was the only means of keeping warm.

"Take me down the mine, Roger," he said, "before I freeze to death here. You've been working, but I haven't."

"Come along, then," said Madin, leading the way. "After the next sack we will go."

A rope-and-pulley tackle was suspended over the hole and every few minutes a sack, appearing as if from nowhere, was unhooked by a worker who transferred it to the waiting sled. Empty sacks were also making their appearance from the other direction, heading towards the working face.

"Be careful to place your feet firmly in the prepared footholds," said Madin as he disappeared. Dick followed. The shaft was well lit and was about three feet square. It was lined with a timber framework, and a rope, attached at intervals to the frames, served to steady the climber. Dick descended warily, using the easily recognised, well-worn footholds on the frames where the rock had been hollowed out so that the toes could take a good bite. A fall here would be dangerous. When he reached the bottom, Dick looked up. The top seemed to be miles above him. A sack full of stones was swinging in mid-air half-way up the shaft. Dick turned to Madin:

"I see now why you all wear tin hats. I wouldn't like to get a rock on my head from twenty feet, not to mention a half-hundredweight sack."

The Frenchman who was hauling on the tackle grinned. He understood enough English to know what Dick was talking about. He remarked in French:

"*Je ne permets à personne d'enlever les sacs sauf celui qui est là haut. J'ai plein confiance en lui!*"

Dick nodded expressively, looking upwards. He was wondering what it would feel like to walk in the open air again. Here in the bowels of the earth, surrounded by tons upon tons of rock, a sudden fear gripped him. He wanted to breathe freely and expand his chest, but was cramped and confined by the forbidding walls closing in upon him from every side.

"Good God!" he thought. "I'm getting claustrophobia."

In spite of himself the thoughts recurred, "One fall of rock would be enough; we could never get out. The air in here would only last half an hour with all these bodies around. A self-made tomb in just the right place," he muttered, "underneath the chapel."

He followed the tunnel forward. Madin had vanished. He soon saw why. There was a staircase ahead of him. He had to squirm himself round so that he lay on his stomach with his feet facing downhill. He descended steps, cut out of the layers of stratified rock, until he reached a new level five feet lower. Here he turned himself round again and crawled forward on his hands and knees. The tunnel was now of more spacious dimensions and he could kneel almost upright on the floor. Tunnellers could pass one another, and half a dozen men were hard at work

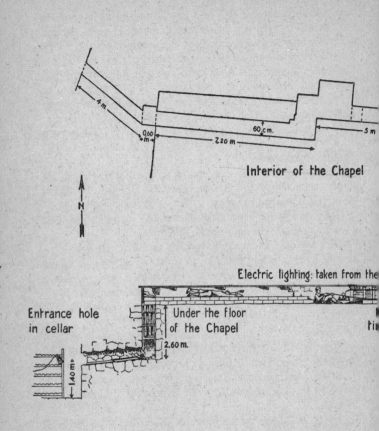

4 m

0.60 m

60 c.m.

2.20 m

5 m

Interior of the Chapel

N

Electric lighting: taken from the

Entrance hole
in cellar

Under the floor
of the Chapel

2.60 m.

1.40 m

THE FRENCH TUNNEL

This drawing has been traced from the original plans made by the Germans after the discovery of the tunnel. The plans were kept in the Escape Museum in the German Kommandantur. When Colditz was relieved, the Museum was found by a P.O.W. and Rupert Barry procured the originals.

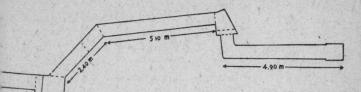

Total length: about 44 metres
(48 yards)

Final depth below Castle Courtyard
8·60 metres (9·4 yards)

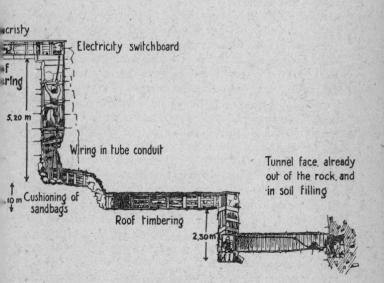

cristy

Electricity switchboard

f
ring

5.20 m

Wiring in tube conduit

Tunnel face, already
out of the rock, and
in soil filling

10 m   Cushioning of
sandbags

Roof timbering

2,30 m

filling sacks with rubble which was piled to the roof at one side as far as Dick could see. Madin was a long way ahead, beckoning to him. Then he disappeared again.

Dick followed as quickly as he could, greeting the Frenchmen one after the other. They were working at top pressure filling the blue and white check sacks as fast as they could, then tying them with cords already sewn into the tops and stacking them ready for departure. They were dripping with perspiration and Dick asked one of them:

"Why don't you take off your shirts?"

"*C'est dangereux*," came the reply, "*aussitôt qu'on arrète, même pour un instant, on attraperait froid si on n'est pas bien habillé.*"

Dick arrived at the end and found himself looking down another shaft. He counted. "That's the third shaft in this tunnel," he thought, "not counting the clock tower. The place is just a rabbit warren."

A large square wooden tub rose up towards him from the depths, hoisted by another pulley tackle. As it came to the surface the Frenchman next to him unhitched it, emptied it to the side of the tunnel, hooked it on again, and the tub descended. Not a word was spoken. Unseen hands worked the lift from below. The operation had become mechanical.

Dick followed the tub, descending carefully one foot at a time. This shaft was not so deep, about eight feet, Dick estimated. He could see that he was nearing the working face. Rubble, earth and large rocks were cluttering up the passage, making progress difficult. Three men were at work filling wooden boxes as fast as they could, while a fourth carried them and emptied them into the tub on the lift. Dick passed them, caught up with Madin, and looked beyond him.

There was Gigue hard at work on the tunnel face in front. He was digging in comparatively loose earth and rock with a short-handled spade. It was coming away easily, and he was working so fast that there were not enough wooden boxes to keep him supplied and he was piling earth up behind him, leaving it to his mates to clear away.

86

Gigue turned a sweating countenance towards them and flashed a broad smile at Dick. He wiped his face with a piece of towelling. "What do you think now, Dick? If we can get enough timber for the roof we shall finish in a week. The digging is easy, but it is dangerous, too, without supports. It could easily fall in."

"I'm lost in admiration," Dick replied facetiously, "but not only in admiration. I've been up and down, backwards and forwards so often I'm lost in any other way you like to think."

"You see the tunnel just behind you? It's completely timbered—floor, walls and roof—you notice? Well, we had to do that. It is the most dangerous section of all. It is under very old foundations which are loose. There are some big stones above and there is not much holding them."

"Thanks for telling me. I shall move faster next time," said Dick feelingly. "Where exactly are we?"

"We are outside the wire and approaching the side of the valley which drops down to the stream in the wood. We should surface in about twelve metres."

"You deserve to have a break after all this," said Dick. "I've never seen a tunnel like it."

Gigue was patting affectionately a steel bar an inch and a half thick and four feet long. "Flynn's bar," he said. "The most useful tool we have."

At that moment the lights went out.

"Great Cæsar's ghost," said Dick, "what happens now?"

The lights flashed on again. Then off and on a second time.

"That means there is a German patrol in the courtyard," explained Madin. As he said the words, the lights blinked three times in quick succession, then went out completely.

"Danger! Stop work! Remain quiet!" whispered Madin. "The Jerries must be heading either for the chapel or for the cellar, probably the chapel. They suspect the chapel very much. They have heard our digging but cannot trace it. All they know is that it is in this region. I suppose their instruments cannot get close enough. We are very deep here."

87

They sat huddled in total darkness at the end of the tunnel for ten minutes waiting for the 'all clear'. Dick was catching cold rapidly. Madin, beside him, was shivering. The lights suddenly went on again. Everybody breathed a sigh of relief but remained motionless. The lights might signal again. They remained steady and bright. After a further minute, the tunnellers started moving, stretching cramped limbs, blowing on their hands, massaging and rubbing.

Work was resumed at full pressure. Dick looked at his watch and gasped as he realised how quickly time had passed. It was 3 a.m.

Madin now took over from Gigue at the working face, and Gigue said to Dick:

"Come back with me to the sacristy junction. There is more room there. We are in the way here, if we are not working. We can eat something up there and relax for a moment."

They both set off, Gigue going first. Dick followed closely, looking upwards now and then through the cracks between the boards—bed-boards, of course, he noted, almost subconsciously —to see whether any large rock was about to tear through the timber, crushing him to pulp in its fall. They passed the danger zone and retraced their steps to the 'junction' as they had come.

Dick breathed a sigh of relief as they reached it. He was warm again from climbing and crawling, and he was feeling hungry. He had come provided for this. Seated with his back against one of the heavy chapel timbers, he removed a bright yellow handkerchief, that had once been khaki, from the pocket of his rugger shorts, and, unfolding it gently, revealed a thick sandwich composed of two slices of German bread enclosing a slab of Canadian cheese.

Gigue was not slow to follow him. His equally cumbersome sandwich, however, did not contain cheese but a thick, strongly smelling paste. They munched in silence for a while. Then Dick's curiosity made him ask, "What's that high-smelling paste you've got, Gigue?"

"It's home-made *foie gras*," said Gigue. "I make it out of everything that's left. It smells good, doesn't it?"

"I'm not so sure," Dick replied. "If it tastes as it smells, I think it should make excellent manure."

"You don't know what's good," said Gigue.

Together they sat for a while, each wrapped in his own thoughts. Dick was reflecting upon the extraordinary twist of fate that could bring about the present situation; a Londoner and a Frenchman from Marseilles a thousand miles away, sitting side by side eating sandwiches in a burrow underneath the floor of a fifteenth-century chapel in a medieval castle in the middle of Germany. How would it end, this great upheaval of mankind all over the world? Would he ever come out of it alive? Dick questioned and, as always, reached the usual conclusion: "Probably not. The Nazis will see to it—the lousy bunch of gangsters."

In spite of the cold, he began to feel drowsy. The rumble of the sleds and the pulleys was monotonous and the sacks passed interminably before his eyes. Gigue was already asleep. Dick dozed fitfully, shifting uncomfortably now and then, growing steadily stiffer with cold and cramp. At one point he awoke and noticed Gigue had gone. Then dozed again, as he thought, for five minutes. . . .

Madin was shaking him.

"Wake up, Dick, it's time to go," he said. "Follow me."

The shift had ended, and the tunnellers were filing past, one after the other, on their hands and knees. Madin and Dick joined the queue.

At 6.30 a.m. Dick found himself once more out on the landing at the top of the French staircase. It was all so strange. He felt as if he had been living for months in the tunnel, and he had to pull himself together to realise where he was. In Gigue's dormitory he was given a mug of hot coffee. He drank it quickly, lay back on an empty bed and fell fast asleep.

Three days later the fate of the tunnel hung in the balance. According to the French, one of their own men, who had gone to Oflag IVD, had talked too loudly or too openly about a French tunnel at Colditz which started on the top floor. The

Germans were after it in earnest. Search followed upon search. Work on the tunnel had to cease completely with only five more yards to dig to finish it. The situation was ominous.

Then there was peace for three days. Work started again— cautiously. But the Germans had not finished. Gephard made a surprise attack. He probed the long weight sleeves in the clock tower, he could see nothing as he flashed his torch down into the darkness, but there were men below. He sent a messenger out to the Kommandantur by the hand of the sentry who was with him. Had he heard a movement? A cough maybe?

Within ten minutes several Goons appeared with a small boy amongst them. A coil of rope was produced. The boy, a fair-haired young Teuton, pale and trembling with fright, suffered the rope to be tied around his waist. He was led to one of the sleeves. With promises and blandishments, he was encouraged to descend. He was lowered slowly through the sleeve into the blackness below. In his hand he carried a torch which he aimed at the floor beneath him. As he landed he flashed the torch around him and screamed in terror.

"Hilfe! Hilfe! Hier sind Leute!"

There were three Frenchmen in the chamber. Gephard was occupying the only exit. The Frenchmen knew of a last desperate way out. At one corner of the chamber, a comparatively thin wall, nine inches thick, separated them from a bathroom used by patients from the sick ward.

As the terrified youth, sobbing with fright and shouting *"Hilfe"*, was hauled up again through the sleeve, the Frenchmen attacked the dividing wall with crowbars like demons, and in five minutes had battered a hole through it. The noise they made was deafening, yet the Germans above them were so occupied with the youth that, when they awoke to reality and sent search parties in frantic haste to locate the new hole being pierced with all the publicity of a battery of pneumatic drills, they were too late. The birds had flown.

A Belgian Army Major, Baron Lindkerke, was peacefully reading a book, lying in his bath, when the earthquake started.

The wall beside him began to pulsate and heave. Long cracks appeared, accompanied by earsplitting crashes from the other side. A brick shot out of the wall into the bath, landing on his stomach. It was time, he thought, to evacuate. Something was under pressure at the other side and an explosion would occur at any moment.

He rose from the bath and reached for his towel. Plaster was flying in all directions, and brickbats were leaping outwards, splashing into the bath around him. A jagged hole suddenly appeared. Iron bars flayed the opening, enlarging it. As he stepped from the bath, a head and shoulders came through the opening. Then a half-naked body scrambled over the bath on to the floor, bespattered, sweat-stained and dirty. Another body followed and then a third, more bulky than the others. It had difficulty in squeezing through and fell into the bath.

Major Lindkerke picked up his belongings and rushed from the room shouting: *"Mon Dieu! Mon Dieu! c'est le comble!"* Which translated means, "My God! My God! this is the end!"

Soon the whole Kommandantur was alerted. Squads of workmen appeared with crowbars, pick-axes and sledge-hammers. The chambers at each successive floor were broken into and the finger of fate pointed ever downwards to the cellar.

For a time the French hoped that the Germans would not find the tunnel entrance in the cellar; but alas! the scent was now too strong. The Germans were hot on the trail. The cellar was combed from end to end. Every inch of wall was sounded. No camouflage could stand up to German thoroughness indefinitely.

The next day the news came through: "They've found it!" That was all that was said. With those few words disappeared the hopes of more than a hundred Frenchmen. So many dreams smashed, so much yearning for the sunny lands of France; so many wives who would never hear the sound of a familiar voice on the threshold; so many hours, days and months of dangerous toil for nothing.

And through it all came the voice of the French conscience: "Was it our own fault? Was our stooging at fault? Were we too confident?" Like the masters of the *Titanic*, they had thought their ship could not founder.

CHAPTER VI

THE PARCELS OFFICE

THE French were still leaving. Throughout the spring of 1943 the rumour persisted. They were repeatedly warned they were going. One day it was, "*Nous partons demain*"—the next day it was, "*Non! pas aujourd'hui, mais dans une semaine—certes —l'information est toujours juste par nos tuyaux.*"

They packed and unpacked many times; their *couvertures*, and rucksacks, their valises and portmanteaux, their *poussettes* —push-chairs and prams. Some were glad to go, looking forward to the move as a relief from the overpowering walls of Colditz. Many of the French Jews saw the writing on the wall and were, quite legitimately, not so keen. Men like Gigue and Madin would leave with mixed feelings. They would have more opportunities in another camp—but not the same atmosphere. . . .

A dead Goon was found in the parcels office one morning. There was a bullet wound in his chest and his revolver lay beside him. The Germans said he had committed suicide. The question they never answered was: "What was he doing in there, locked up for the night amongst the parcels belonging to the prisoners?"

The dead German was removed from the parcels office without ceremony and hurried out of the courtyard. Few prisoners were about at the time. The Germans chose their moment. The mystery was never solved and the reader, with this outline before him, knows as much as at least ninety-nine out of each hundred prisoners at Colditz. The odd ones are not talking. . . . The author is not one of them.

The office was naturally a focus of interest among the prisoners and many would have liked to have access to it. The entrance, however, gave straight on to the courtyard and on to the beats of two sentries placed there day and night.

During 1942, the British had been greatly troubled by the installation of an X-ray machine in the parcels office. Most valuable contraband material was lost, which, incidentally, never came in Red Cross parcels at any time throughout the whole war. The contents of other parcels, if in the least suspected, were passed across the X-ray screen, which showed up secret cavities or metallic objects. The British quarters were a long way from the parcels office, and nothing much could be done about it. A burglar alarm in the guardhouse, wired from each of the two locks on the entrance door, warned the Germans of any tampering. They installed it so secretly that the fact was not known for a long time. The Germans were obviously taking no risks.

Parcels were normally opened on a long counter behind a grille; suspected items were submitted to X-ray and then the contents passed to the recipient through the grille, which was opened for the operation and shut again immediately afterwards. The opening and shutting of the grille for every parcel was an unmitigated nuisance. The German N.C.O.s on parcels duty agreed with the prisoners on this point and occasionally became lax.

Some days after the dead Goon had been removed, the British were drawing parcels. Lulu was Parcels Officer at the time. He had been planted there because contraband was expected. Bill Fowler, who had escaped from Colditz in September 1942, was by this time in France. Lulu's official duty as Parcels Officer was to be present at the opening of all parcels— a witness for the defence. The job was intriguing for the first twenty parcels or so, and thereafter became steadily more boring until, at the end of a fortnight, "one grew a beard" as the French would say.

John Hyde-Thomson stood in the parcels queue on this particular day because the parcel list, posted on the notice-board outside the office, had his name upon it. He arrived in front of the open grille. An N.C.O., known as 'Nichtwahr' because of

94

his irritating habit of ending every sentence with this ejaculation, and who had the local reputation of being a Gestapo man, searched among the stack for John's parcel. It was unearthed and opened on the counter in front of him. Lulu stood beside him. His thoughts at that moment were in the Yorkshire Dales.

As the seals were broken and the maltreated cardboard cover burst asunder, there was a clatter of steel on the counter which brought Lulu's reverie to an end as conclusively as might a clap of thunder. John Hyde-Thomson was expecting warm woolly underwear and some good books. Lulu was not expecting the consignment which was on the counter at that particular moment. Wires had crossed somewhere.

He was not going to be outdone, however. Before the grille could be slapped down, he enfolded the parcel in his arms and was careering out of the office door as an astonished Goon held aloft a brand-new pair of wire-cutters, screaming, "*Halt! Halt!*" and struggling with the pistol in his holster.

Lulu was too quick for them all. He tore across the courtyard, as German banknotes fell like autumn leaves in his wake. Not a shot was fired. Up the spiral stairs he ran and collapsed at the top of seventy steps, shouting for help. Willing hands took over, and the contents were distributed and hidden within a few minutes—long before the pursuing riot squad was able to mount the stairs and seal the doorways into the various quarters.

The spectacle in the courtyard after the meteoric passage of Lulu was out of the dream world of a prisoner in a high fever. The two sentries in the yard stood transfixed. They had never, in their whole careers as soldiers and P.O.W. guards, been given instructions as to what to do when German banknotes rain like confetti around prisoners of war, whose principal aim in life is to have enough money to travel as fast as possible out of Germany.

The notes were like manna from heaven. Prisoners who had, one second before, been ambling aimlessly around the yard in their clogs and khaki overcoats did not take long to realise, unlike the sentry, that they had witnessed a miracle and had suddenly become the chosen people. As Lulu disappeared through the staircase doorway there was a rush, and before the sentries could gather their wits together there was not a note to be seen.

A search followed, but nothing was found. The Germans were disillusioned. So many searches had yielded so little that searching had become a disheartening pastime. Since Priem's nocturnal visit in 1941 when his hatchet, tearing some floor-boards asunder, had impaled a trilby hat concealed underneath, the Germans had had no luck. But the initial search after this episode would not be the end of the matter. A report would go eventually to the Gestapo. The Castle was heading for another ransacking, of this there was no doubt.

Lulu Lawton was removed from his post and sentenced to a month's solitary confinement. The contraband parcel contained everything that an escaper dreamt of, from wire-cutters, files and dyes to cameras and photographic materials.

This kind of bull-in-the-china-shop operation, however, frankly disgusted Gigue. He had an advantage, of course, in that he lived in the French quarters over the parcels office, but, to be perfectly honest, he returned the compliment the British had paid his countrymen in connection with the theatre light-well escape—with interest. As a parting gift before he left, in addition to the secret wireless-set, he bequeathed to Dick his method of entering the parcels office.

Gigue had spirited seventy parcels out of the parcels office for his two wireless-sets alone. He had caused no rumpus, no publicity and had lost nothing.

First of all, he manufactured his own cruciform keys for the two parcels-office locks. The cruciform lock is roughly equivalent to four different Yale locks rolled into one. While the office was open and in use, he had searched for, and discovered, the carefully concealed wiring of the burglar-alarm system. This travelled, at one stage, along the ceiling under an electric-light tube conduit. Gigue made a careful survey. Any civil engineer would have been proud of his work. Under the floor-boards of his own quarters, he pierced a minute hole through the plaster of the ceiling below, immediately over the alarm wires. He then tapped the wires and, manufacturing his own switch, he placed it in the circuit. He could thus control the burglar-alarm system at will.

The method of operating his switch was equally ingenious. The switch was fixed under the floor-boards which were replaced permanently and made to look as if they had not been touched for fifty years. A hole, about one-eighth of an inch in diameter, was pierced through the board directly over the switch, which was then operated through the board by employing a long, thin electrician's screwdriver. When camouflaged, it was impossible for anyone to find this hole unless he possessed the secret of the measurements from two recognisable points in the floor.

Gigue's method of entering the canteen was simple enough when carried out with a first-class team. It consisted of providing distraction for the two courtyard sentries while Gigue manipulated the keys with the help of two assistants at the parcels-office door.

Dick initiated a team of his own into the secrets of the parcels office, and when the French left in the summer of 1943 this team carried on successfully until the end of the war. The British had no further trouble in removing such parcels as they required at will.

Dick's key assistant, in both senses of the word, was Vincent or "Bush" Parker, an Australian and a Flight-Lieutenant in the R.A.F. He might equally well have been called "Fingers" Parker, for his wits and his hands were as quick as lightning. He learnt to handle locks with consummate skill. Bush was a colourful character, which makes it worth digressing to shine the spotlight upon him. Colditz would not have been quite what it was if Bush had not been there, and his activities throw a revealing sidelight upon the life of the prison.

Bush was well knit and strong, a good athlete and an outstanding stool-ball player. Though not more than five feet seven inches tall, he was handsome, with the features of a young Adonis and a winning smile which showed off his fine teeth. Black wavy hair crowned his classic-shaped head. He had a charming manner which must have made him the complete lady-killer in those happy far-off days when Bush was a Battle of Britain Spitfire pilot.

All that he could exert his charm on now was the sour, sensible Oberstabsfeldwebel Gephard, from whom he could wheedle more of the rationed coal than anyone else in the camp. Gephard thought the world of him and the coal came in handy. Bush was one of the three directors of the British Distillery Monopoly, which developed by the natural process of free enterprise, unhindered by anti-cartel laws and appreciated by the drinking public because of the excellent service rendered.

Bush was definitely talented. He was an amateur card sharper of the highest professional standing!

One evening Dick sat in, as sixth player, in a regular poker school of five. The other players were "Rex" Harrison of the Green Howards, head escape tailor, an indefatigable worker for the escapes of others and unfailingly good humoured; "Bag" Dickenson, a bomber pilot in the R.A.F., second director of the British Distillery Monopoly; Bush Parker; Teddy Barton, the camp theatrical producer; with Scarlet O'Hara making up the sixth.

After a quarter of an hour's desultory play, Bush whispered to Dick, "Watch this one carefully," as he started to deal.

Dick found himself, after the deal, with the ace, king, queen of hearts and two nondescript cards. The pool was opened with four players, Bush and Teddy Barton throwing in their hands.

Dick was watching Bush. He asked for two cards. Picking them up he found he had the knave and ten of hearts. A royal straight flush—unbeatable!

Bag Dickenson drew two cards, Rex drew two and Scarlet three. The bidding started with Rex making the running. Dick tagged along and Scarlet soon fell out. When the 'raises' reached a hundred *Marken* (about £7) a time, Bag looked worried and said to Rex, "I warn you, I've got a power-house."

Neither of them seemed interested in Dick, who stayed in,

and the bidding continued. Finally, coming to the fore, Dick raised another hundred, whereupon Bag said, "I'll see you."

But Rex was not satisfied. He began another raising spree—two hundred *Marken* this time—putting three hundred into the pool.

A few onlookers had gathered round the table. There were nearly two thousand *Lagermarken* in the pool. This was worth £140, which in Colditz was no mean kitty on a single hand.

Dick and Bag called a truce and 'saw' Rex, who laid down on the table three aces and two kings.

"You're daft," said Bag, "raising like that on a full house. I've got fours," and he put down four nines. He had drawn a nine and another to fill three nines.

Bag could see the *Lagermarken* already in his wallet—and began to pick them up when Rex asked casually:

"What did you have, Dick?"

Dick replied by firmly removing Bag's hand from the pile of notes saying, "Just hold everything, chaps, for one moment. I think you'd like to see this," and he laid down his 'royal'!

All the prisoners in the room gathered round the table to see the hands as the immediate onlookers announced jubilantly to the world, "Boys, come and look! Dick's drawn a royal straight flush!"

Bush and Dick roared with laughter as they saw the look of utter disappointment on Bag's face, and Rex sat back, stunned.

Bush spent much of his time teasing Bag and this occasion was a high-light. When he had pulled his leg enough about his four nines power-house, Bush and Dick revealed the conspiracy and all the cash was refunded.

Not for one moment throughout the dealing and playing of the hand had the players suspected anything, and Dick, who tried hard to see how Bush manipulated the cards, was none the wiser.

Dick could rest with an easy mind, assured that the parcels-office keys were in good hands.

The others of the parcels-office team were "Mike" Harvey,

a lieutenant of the Royal Navy, Lulu Lawton, "Checko", the black marketeer, two stooges and Dick. They started the habit of sitting on the office steps to read and chat, so that, eventually, when the French left, sentries would be accustomed to seeing Englishmen seated where, formerly, Frenchmen had had the priority. The team-work was interchangeable among the four assistants who distracted the two courtyard sentries, warned against patrols and passed the 'all clear' to Bush and Dick at the door. Bush performed the opening and closing ceremony. Dick slipped inside to seek out the parcel to be smuggled. The relocking of the door was carried out in the same manner as the opening, and the complete operation usually required not less than an hour, giving Dick twenty minutes inside the office.

CHAPTER VII

ATMOSPHERE

AN atmosphere can cling to a building just as cobwebs to its walls. It is intangible, but it is there. In the years to come, man will, doubtless, invent instruments of such finesse that they will be able to pick up sound waves emitted in a room centuries before. The voices of great men of the past will be recaptured by detectors of microscopic accuracy, magnified and broadcast.

If man can measure the amount of heat radiated by a candle at a distance of a mile, if he can prise open the oyster of the atom, it is only a matter of time before he will hear the voices of the past talking in the present.

Dogs have been known to return home hundreds of miles across country; pigeons fly homeward across the seas. Animals can smell what man cannot smell and hear sounds that man cannot hear.

The human brain is found to emit wireless waves; if it can emit, surely it can receive.

The scientific explanation of the working of the refined senses, of instincts and of the brain, is writ large inside a deep scientific tome of which this generation is now opening the introductory pages.

Certain of man's senses have been dulled. One of them is the ability to appreciate consciously the proximity of fellow beings in the present, not to mention out of the past, without the aid of the simpler senses which remain man's standby—sight and hearing and the nervous system.

Yet, dulled as the senses have been, something remains; an inchoate attribute by which man can sense vaguely what he commonly calls 'atmosphere'. Undoubtedly, much that provides the reaction in human beings which is often loosely termed the sixth sense, comes into the brain subconsciously through the other senses. The eyes particularly will take in much more than is consciously registered by the brain and will perform unconscious permutations and combinations with memories much like a calculating machine. The answer is then handed over to the conscious mind which registers 'an atmosphere'. At the same time, almost certainly, this other indefinable attribute reacts within the brain.

Colditz had an atmosphere. Naturally a castle that had stood for centuries would. But it was not the atmosphere of antiquity, of the passage of history within its walls, that struck every new arrival upon entering the courtyard.

Colditz had more recently been a lunatic asylum. There was a weird, bleak and depressing air about the place which struck the newcomer so forcibly that he knew, without being told, that the Castle must have been filled at one time by a great sadness.

It was not the place to encourage a sane outlook upon life. The high, dun-coloured walls surrounding the tiny cobbled yard; the barred windows—even those opening on to the yard were barred; the steep roofs which hung precipitously overhead; the endless clack-clack of wooden sabots; the cacophony of voices in different languages and musical instruments in different keys were not calculated to breed contentment or resignation. As a lunatic asylum it had never been a sanatorium where insanity might hope to be cured. It could only have been a home for incurables and a dungeon for the violent.

Into this prison the Germans threw the men who, of all the prisoners of war in Germany, were the most likely to chafe and strain and pine under the stifling confinement of its oppressive walls. Those who had found resignation were not for Colditz. Those who had broken their chains and would continue to do so filtered into the Castle.

Colditz was a fruitful breeding-ground for frustration and might easily become a prison full of mentally unbalanced men.

How easily it might happen is illustrated by the proportionately large number of officers who actually became unbalanced. The development of the malady could be seen and the symptoms usually followed a regular course. The process was known as 'going round the bend'. It started, commonly, with a passion for classical music, often followed by a demoniacal lust for physical training, after which the particular form of 'unbalance' of the individual developed—plain for all to see.

In one, it would be sheer violence, and the officer became a danger to his fellows but even more so to the Germans. A sentry was the red rag to a bull, and the demented prisoner would have to be held down by friends to stop him from hurling crockery, bottles, anything that came to hand, at the victim of his 'hate' complex. In another it would take a suicidal turn. These two forms were the most trying for the community. The Germans were appallingly slow in taking action to remove the sufferers to a proper house of treatment, and in the intervening months a constant guard had to be maintained by the prisoners themselves, which wore down resistance to a malady that almost became infectious.

Other forms of unbalance were as innocent as they were amusing, but their general effect was not to fortify the sanity of the other prisoners.

One would become eternally sullen and develop a baleful glare. It was disconcerting to a man, sometimes consciously aware of his own liability to 'go round the bend', to be fixed by this stony and hypnotic gaze. Thoughts of the fabled 'Old Man of the Sea' mingled with an uncontrollable desire to run. The glassy eyes could change their expression from mild to murderous without a flicker.

One officer of this type retained a devilish sense of humour, concentrating on the German sentries in the courtyard. He would approach one of them stealthily and fix him with his stare. The sentry was not aware of the attack until he turned and faced him. For a full minute their eyes met as the satanic hypnotist scowled at him. Then, with no warning, the insane one suddenly leapt high into the air and the unnerved Jerry jumped equally high in sheer terror. The lunatic then walked off, quite unconcerned. Eventually, the sentries grew accustomed to this treatment. When they did, our man ceased to plague them.

Another 'leg-puller' type made a habit of puffing smoke from a filthy home-made cheroot in the faces of the same unfortunate sentries. Having done so, he flicked the ash off his cigar on to the cobbles in front of the sentry, then produced a dustpan and brush from behind his back, swept up the offending ash and marched off to the dustbins.

A soulful, melancholy type used to play the guitar for hours in the bathroom, seated on a stool with his head inside an empty suitcase. This officer was once removed to a hospital where he displayed remarkably good sense by denuding the hospital garden, in one night, of a good crop of ripening tomatoes.

Yet another type gave up washing and became so filthy that he was not allowed to eat at table. He sat cross-legged all day long on the top of a seven-foot cupboard, occasionally eating from a bowl a nauseating mixture of his own concoction consisting of egg-powder and an inedible semi-dried vegetable, a German issue, called 'rabbi' which the prisoners normally used for stuffing pillows and mattresses.

The Germans did nothing about the 'whackies' unless they were violent, and then only after several years. Others they picked out, like the guitarist, as if they were picking an apple out of a basketful. There was no logic in their methods. One officer, who was not mad, pretended to be so, following medical advice as to symptoms and behaviour. The 'fake' lunatic, after nearly a year, became discouraged and returned to normal. The attempt was known only to Dick Howe and a doctor. The community, as a whole, considered him a genuine 'round the bend' and were encouraged at the sight of a recovery.

Then there was the religious maniac of the proselytising variety who unlocked the staircase door in the dead of night and sallied forth into the lamplit courtyard where only the sentries monotonously paced their beat. Dressed in a flowing sackcloth robe and holding aloft a large wooden cross of his own manufacture, he recalled the world to prayer in loud, ringing tones, chastising the stolid sentries with his tongue, accusing them of dreadful sins and demanding their immediate submission and repentance.

* * * * *

Each prisoner had his own personal struggle and suffered his own fears. In the silence of the night, in fitful sleep, they rose uncontrolled to take on grotesque proportions. Waking from dreams of long unending tunnels, of the search for an opening that never appeared, tearing at stones with bare hands, lying prone in the clammy earth amidst worms and maggots, queer thoughts came uninvited. Waking from a nightmare race, thrashing the blankets, cursing, sweating and gasping for breath, fleeing for life, always uphill, with the Jerries close behind; hearing their shouts merge into the crescendos of the proselytising preacher in the echoing courtyard, then melt away into silence; no! not peaceful silence, but another sound, travelling upwards through the windows, along the searchlight beams, the pad—pad—pad of the enemy—a sentry on his beat; at such a time men wondered if they were sane. The preacher in the yard might be funny no longer, the joke had lost its savour. Lying awake on his straw palliasse in the eerie half-light, a prisoner could see himself swaying on the tight-rope of sanity, could visualise himself bearing down on the sentries with a cross or sitting like a Buddha on the top of a cupboard.

Such moments were the testing time, and much depended on the prisoner's reaction. A sense of humour was a healing balm of incalculable worth. If a man could laugh at the vision of himself seated cross-legged on top of a cupboard, it was as if he tore himself clear of the encircling tentacles of a strangling octopus. He promptly slept and woke up refreshed in the morning. If he did not laugh, a red light glowed threateningly before him. Soon he would not dream his nightmares. They would begin to occupy the stage of his conscious, wakeful mind. He would rise in the morning nervous, irritable and depressed. That way lay danger.

Of all the qualities that make for sanity in such surroundings a sense of humour stands paramount. Thank God there was no lack of it at Colditz! It was small wonder that men returned in spirit to their boyhood days and took refuge in the antics of a schoolboy. What can be saner than a schoolboy!

The masters had guns instead of canes and might use them; the antics had a steely edge to their humorous side, but that way, nevertheless, lay sanity. The majority of the prisoners of Colditz instinctively found comfort and solace in the carefree, day-to-day psychological outlook of the schoolboy. It was another of the many secrets that the Castle held; a secret that the prisoners did not whisper about, for the simple reason that they were unaware of it.

CHAPTER VIII

THE COCOA 'V'

In spite of a few deceptive spring-like days in February, winter took a firm grip upon the Castle in the early months of 1943; it was proving to be worse than the last. It was the winter of Fate for the Germans in Russia: the siege of Stalingrad.

There was less coal for the prisoners; fewer bed-boards that could be removed with safety from beds for fire-wood. Relief from perpetual shivering was only obtained by retiring under the blankets. Rations deteriorated further. The most plentiful food consisted of sugar-beet residue, dyed red and brought into the camp in barrels labelled, '*Nur für Kriegsgefangene*'—only for P.O.W.s. It was issued as a jam ration and was uneatable.

In these conditions of cold and hunger the German Commandant decided to alleviate the lot of the P.O.W.s by purchasing a luxuriously complete and up-to-date equipment for the barber's shop. The finance was provided by what was known as 'The Commandant's Fund', which depended for its revenue on canteen profits.

One frosty morning, a decorator's van arrived, accompanied by a representative of the contractors, a civilian plumber, a fitter and four sentries. Such an exciting intrusion was a gala occasion for the prisoners. To look upon civilians, to see a civilian lorry, why! if a prisoner were to put his fingers in his ears so that he did not hear the clack-clack of wooden clogs nor the guttural sound of German voices; if he half closed his eyes so that he saw nothing beyond the lorry—neither the field grey nor the khaki around him; and if only he could stop shivering, why! he could imagine himself standing on the pavement in Regent Street beside a lorry drawn up at the kerb; a real live motor vehicle—a delivery van. Such a phenomenon was only seen in Colditz once a year, if that.

Enough of day-dreaming. There was work to do. The four sentries would require a considerable amount of skilful distraction. That merely meant a little more exercise for the talents of men like Scarlet O'Hara, Rex Harrison, Bush Parker, Peter Storie Pugh and Scorgie Price.

While the contractor and his men disappeared for a moment into the barber's shop, Rex and Peter, looking like Mutt and Jeff—Peter was not much taller than 'the medium-sized man' —on their way to commit a burglary, set about deflating one of the back tyres. They did not succeed because they were not meant to. Instead they started a loud argument in bad German with the two near-side guards protesting that they were only interested in the type of tyre and the shape of the wheel, which, they maintained with significant gestures, was not round. This brought the other two sentries over to the near-side of the car which was the signal for redoubled angry protestations while, on the off-side Scarlet removed the road maps from under the driver's seat and Bush Parker disappeared with the tools. It was on an occasion similar to this, a year before, that "Errol" Flynn, a Flying Officer in the R.A.F., had 'won' the four-foot-long crowbar which earned him a place on the fated French tunnel.

The contractor's men reappeared as Peter and Rex concluded their harangue and walked away exuding an aura of righteous indignation.

The workmen opened the van and began to off-load a highly polished adjustable barber's chair. Scarlet, returning to the scene, noted a hydraulic jack reposing on the floor of the van not far from the doors. The two sentries on normal duty in the yard, stationed on the near-side of the lorry, could see the open van doors. Rex and Peter were sent off to distract them, while Bush Parker and Scorgie Price took over the two sentries at the rear of the van.

The secret of the operation is synchronisation. It is impossible to distract a person and to keep an eye on three or four other people as well. It is difficult enough to look at one person out of the corner of an eye while concentrating upon a second, the sentry. Scarlet only has to watch one of the four, namely Bush Parker nearby. Bush cannot see Scorgie at the far side of the van but only has to watch Rex, Rex watches Scorgie, Scorgie watches Peter, and Peter watches Scarlet. The circle is complete.

Peter, farthest away from the scene, starts the action upon a signal from Scarlet, who then turns his gaze on Bush. Peter, facing so that he can see Scarlet, stops in front of his sentry who is momentarily standing at ease and begins talking to him mockingly about Stalingrad. The sentry is not supposed to talk, is confused and turns to march away, which is what is required. Peter follows him, still talking. Scorgie has now started work upon his sentry. He has a book in his hand. He is looking at a funny picture and roaring with laughter. His sentry can only half see the picture and is tortured with curiosity. Rex has seen the effect of Scorgie's effort and busies himself beside his sentry whittling a curiously shaped piece of wood. The sentry is intrigued. Bush then comes into action by showing his sentry a card trick. Scarlet vaults quickly into the van, seizes the jack, jumps off and walks casually away with it under his coat. This action is completed in five seconds. Peter has seen Scarlet walk off and retires. The others follow.

Later, when the balloon goes up, the sentries will all swear they never took their eyes off the van.

Having removed the jack, handle and all, Scarlet now contemplates 'winning' a wheel. He needed a heavy flywheel for a lathe he was manufacturing. The rubber tyre and tube would always come in useful. The wheel brace was among the tools already taken. An off-side back wheel would give his stooges an opportunity of practising their art upon the two sentries on the off-side of the van.

The wheel nuts are loosened first. They are very resistant. A new distraction has to be brought into action at five-minute intervals for each nut. The whole operation will take well over half an hour. . . .

The German contractor's representative, in a 'natty' suit, long, green, heavy tweed overcoat with a strap at the back and a dark green Homburg hat, was busy supervising the unloading and transporting of his equipment into the room which was to be transformed into the palatial barber's shop. He did not become aware of the gradual disintegration of his lorry for some time. Then suddenly he missed the jack which he had seen not half an hour before. He gave tongue in no ordinary manner. He screamed with anger, and his invective was aimed, mostly and quite rightly, at the German guards. He demanded that the security officer be fetched at once. Scarlet had to give up his task of wheel removing—with the job only half done. Four of the five nuts holding one rear wheel had been removed. Nobody noticed it. Scarlet thought it might be tactless to point out the fact.

"It would be more reasonable," he said, "if the Goonery let me finish the job. Then they would notice the wheel missing and put on the spare which is chained inside the van. It would save the back axle anyway," he continued. "I hate to think what's going to happen after a few hundred yards' running."

Sadly Scarlet returned to the British quarters, carrying under his coat three bricks on to which he was going to lower the brake drum. He had no intention of leaving the jack.

Hauptmann Eggers was apparently not available. Instead, Hauptmann (Rittmeister) Lange, another security officer, arrived on the scene with another sentry. He and the irate civilian retired to the *Evidenz Zimmer*—the interview room—which had just been swept out for the day. The civilian, taking off his green Homburg, put it on a table near the half-open window. He did not remove his coat as it was too cold. The sentry stood at the door. A heated discussion took place. Rex Harrison took the opportunity to remove the hat with the aid of a long piece of wire passed through the bars of the window.

The civilian was gradually mollified by promises from Hauptmann Lange that a search would be conducted and restitution made. He turned to pick up his hat and leave the room. He stood with mouth agape for several seconds, then raised his clenched fists above his head and turned his goggling eyes heavenwards.

"*Was ist?*" asked Lange innocently.

"*Mein Hut! Mein Hut!*" screamed the German, stamping his foot in a fury. "*Er war bestimmt hier—Donnerwetter—eine neue Schweinerei! Mein Hut ist verschwunden. Ich bin in eine Verücktenanstalt gekommen.*" He stormed out of the *Evidenz Zimmer*, shouting for his driver to come immediately and take him out of the madhouse while the lorry still had four wheels and an engine. The dramatic irony of his own remark was lost upon him.

By implication the solitary nut and bolt must have held the rear wheel for at least two days, because the workmen returned, albeit on foot, in the afternoon and all the next day to complete the installation. If the wheel had come off—the prisoners argued with reason—they would not have returned at all.

*   *   *   *   *

The big search was well overdue and everybody looked to his hide carefully and with some anxiety. It came one morning as the first snow of the year began to fall. The Germans made the fatal mistake of 'letting slip' to the British, before the first *Appell*, that they were to leave the camp for a day's outing. That was enough, and every possible precaution was taken. The whole contingent, now nearly one hundred strong, marched off after 7 a.m. *Appell*, across the causeway of the Castle and down into the town. They were accompanied by a guard of one hundred Goons and half a dozen Alsatian dogs.

The walk was greatly appreciated by the contingent although it lasted only ten minutes, hardly enough to warm up the body, ending on arrival at a building called the *Schützenhaus*. Upon entering the building after a roll-call in the yard outside, the prisoners were delighted to see signs of a festive occasion. There, at one end of the *Schützenhaus* hall, stood a large canopied platform. It was already adorned with decorations and a long rosary of coloured electric bulbs. Outside the snow continued to fall gently.

Although some officers had set out with the intention of making a break, the weather was not propitious. The overpowering company of guards, who took up their positions around the building, did not serve to dispel that impression. Still, there was one vague possibility which was hawked around the hall by Dick Howe. The British were settling down for the day. Groups gathered around the few tables, and, on the floor in the corners, blankets were spread. Cards were produced, chess was soon in progress, Red Cross food appeared and the air grew heavy with tobacco smoke. Someone obtained permission to boil water in an adjoining scullery and tea was served. With all this luxury in new surroundings Dick found only one officer sufficiently enthusiastic to attempt an escape which had the remotest chance of success. Captain Geoffrey Munro Pemberton How, R.A.S.C.—alias "Pembum"—was prepared to have a go in spite of the fact that he had just received a new pipe from England; a treasure which would have kept him happy, even in Colditz, for many a long day. Pembum was renowned, among other things, for his voice, which resembled that of a corncrake. Added to this, he spoke in staccato monosyllables. He had a ruddy face with a ruddier nose and, being somewhat older than the average at Colditz, he was looked upon kindly, as might be an uncle. Pembum wore, over his uniform, a British Warm which was a colour that could pass as civilian attire; like his pipe, it was brand new.

In the late afternoon, the order to return to the Castle was given. The British paraded in front of the *Schützenhaus* over a predetermined spot, a manhole cover in the yard. The snow had almost ceased and was melting into a slush on the ground.

It says something for Pembum that even when the manhole cover was opened and a revolting slime revealed, his courage did not desert him. Down he went in a second, and the cover was closed on top of him.

The parade count was fixed. All went well and the company marched out of the yard, turning left along the road. Dick looked back as the column wheeled and was shocked to see a conspicuous cloud of smoke rising around the manhole cover. "The blighter's smoking his damned pipe," he thought.

There were so many Goons in the yard that it was impossible the cloud would remain unnoticed for long. Within a few seconds and with the yard still in sight, the company was halted. An *Unteroffizier* returned, at the double, to the yard as one of the sentries at the rear, shouting a warning, called for assistance. The *Unteroffizier* lifted the manhole cover, saw Pembum, dropped it again and then jumped up and down on the cover several times whooping like a Red Indian war-dancer.

Only the rear of the column saw Pembum removed and led off ignominiously, his brand-new overcoat dripping with the grey brown filth from the walls of the manhole and his head bespattered with droppings from the underside of the manhole lid, the result of the poundings of the *Unteroffizier*.

Dick accused Pembum, on his return from a month in the cooler, of succumbing to temptation by smoking his pipe in the manhole. Pembum denied it and explained that the smoke was condensation in the cold atmosphere of the manhole rising with the air heated by his body. His explanation was correct, but in spite of protestations of innocence he took a long time to live down the jibe that he had sold an escape for a pipe of baccy.

The procession returned to the camp, but not empty-handed. The *Schützenhaus* platform had lost its rosary of coloured lamps and the *Schützenhaus* itself was the poorer by a dozen electric-light bulbs, several electric fittings and switches, some yards of cable, a useful length of lead pipe from the lavatories and some linoleum from the floor, window curtains of a good neutral tint, half a dozen chairs which had been converted into small firewood and, finally, the four legs sawn off a table and made into presentable logs, while the table top remained, leaning neatly against a wall.

The Germans discovered all these later in the evening, but they were by then disheartened. An exhaustive search of the

British premises had been carried out over a period of eight hours that day, and the Germans had only some useless contraband—chicken feed—to show for their hard work. The quarters looked as if a bomb had burst in them, furniture and belongings lay in shambles all over the floors. The Dutch reported that immediately after the British contingent had left the camp with their escort, another company of a hundred Goons had marched into the courtyard headed by four bloated-looking Gestapo officers. They had filed up the stairs into the British rooms where heavy thuds and rumbles continued all day which Vandy described as 'like the noise of many vindmills all turning round at vonce'.

To consider a further search at that moment for electric-light fittings and other paraphernalia, though admittedly enough to stock a reasonably sized jumble sale, was out of the question.

Where was the contraband hidden? The type and dimensions of hiding-places varied enormously. The beams across the ceiling of one of the larger rooms were supported by simply designed cornices protruding from the vertical wall face. These plinths were of stone and mortar covered with plaster. The architect had omitted one, perhaps with his thoughts on the evil eye. Lulu Lawton, who was officer in charge of 'Hides', made good the architect's omission and the evil eye winked. The false cornice, with its trap-door always repainted with plaster of Paris and sprinkled with cobweb mixture after use, survived the war without a tremor. Other places, of course, had to be found for articles such as the hydraulic jack. Take a good look at a lavatory-pan!

The French must have had the impression that the Germans were weary that night and would not be on the alert. Their notion was a good one. Two of their number, Edouard Desbat and Jean Caillaud, decided to attempt an escape over the roofs of Colditz, which they had been planning for some time. Snow lay on the ground, though it was melting on the roofs. It would make the climb more difficult, but there were signs of a mist coming up, which was exactly what they wanted.

After the last *Appell* at 9 p.m., the British retired to their bunks and most of them were soon asleep.

Shots rang out in the stillness. Men stirred and turned over; some sat up. Scarlet O'Hara was heard to remark, "Coo! Did you hear that? Three *grosse coups de fusil!*"

More shots followed.

Blackout blinds were raised.[1] Lights went on in courtyard windows like patches in the quilt of night. Windows opened. There were shouts, orders, jeers, counter-orders and laughter. Windows shut again, blinds were lowered, and the lights went out one by one.

Only two Frenchmen, one clinging by means of a lightning conductor to the vertical face of a chimney-breast eighty feet from the ground, the other perched on a roof ledge close at hand, knew what the shouting was about.

Desbat, hanging perilously from the conductor, knew it because he was being shot at, and Caillaud was taking the strain on the safety cord linking the two of them, ready to save his friend if he fell, wounded by the German attack.

Their objective was the outer end of a roof ridge, from which they could descend two hundred feet in comparative darkness, clear of the encircling wire and the ring of guards. The mist had failed them. They still might have succeeded, relying on the supposition that sentries seldom look skywards, and upon the fact that the chimney-breast was in half-light, reflected from floodlight striking an adjacent building.

A loose piece of mortar was Desbat's downfall. His foot dislodged it, and it fell with a crash to the ground near a sentry in the outer courtyard. The sentry looked upwards. Desbat saw him out of the corner of an eye. He did not move. The German, accustomed to the glare of the lights, could see nothing at first. He called another sentry. Together they peered, shading their eyes, trying to pierce the gloom. They saw Desbat.

[1] Although the outside of the Castle was floodlit, prison orders were to the effect that blinds must be drawn. It was a precautionary measure in the event of air-raids, when the floodlights were always extinguished. The order was, needless to say, flagrantly disobeyed.

Shouts of "Halt!" were followed by three shots which loosened bricks around Desbat's head, sending dust and splinters flying into his face. He yelled, *"Schiessen Sie nicht, ich ergebe mich"* ("Don't shoot, I give myself up") several times.

The guard was turned out. In spite of his yells which could be heard clearly below, fifteen more shots were fired at him. They may well have been warning shots, but the nearest hit the brickwork only three inches from his head and the volley was unnerving to say the least of it.

The alarm having been given, the sentries inside the prisoners' courtyard caught sight of Caillaud on his ledge and covered him, ordering him to descend.

The Jerries might have been tired early in the evening. They might justifiably have been in high spirits later in the evening at the recapture of two escapers; but they were ill at ease, jittery, uncertain of themselves and trigger-happy by midnight.

There was an atmosphere of *Macbeth* abroad. Men slept restlessly. Dogs barked in the distance and would not settle down. The familiar tread of the sentries in the courtyard was not audible. They moved like ghosts in the snow, silent and unearthly. It was a night for witchcraft. Indeed, Priem was plotting. With a mug of Schnapps beside him, he sat brooding in his office in the Kommandantur. He would have a revenge on the British after his own style.

At 2 a.m. he ordered an *Appell* for the British P.O.W.s. His heavy-booted Huns came striding through the dormitories, switching on the lights and shouting, *"Aufstehen—Appell! Sofort! Schnell!"*, hardly giving the officers time to don overcoats over their pyjamas and stuff cigarettes and food into their pockets, before being herded without ceremony into the courtyard, now thickly carpeted with snow. They were met by a posse of Goons with their guns in the rabbiting position. This meant the Jerries were ready for trouble.

Priem himself appeared while the rooms were being cleared by his men. The floors were still littered with the debris from the search of the day before. Officers in pyjamas and Goons, tripping over their guns, were milling around the beds and tables in a glorious congestion of confused humanity. The Goons were shouting and the prisoners were all talking at once.

Harry Elliott, still lying in his bunk, yelled across the gangway to Dick, "What the hell's happening?"

Dick, struggling with one leg in his trousers, replied above the din, "Priem's on the warpath again."

Harry said, "Ask him what the devil he thinks he's doing."

"Ask him yourself," shouted Dick.

Harry jumped out of bed and strode off, in his pyjamas, in search of Priem. He found him on the staircase and said:

"Captain Priem, what the hell do you think you're doing? Go away and leave us alone."

Priem, saluting with mocking humour, replied, "Hauptmann Elliott, please go down to the courtyard."

"You go to hell!" said Harry, "I'm going to do a pee," and with that he marched back into the quarters and headed for the *Abort*. Harry relieved himself and returned to bed.

In the meantime, one of the German rifles had been stolen. The tempo of movement and the clamour redoubled. Guards charged around the rooms searching in the beds and under them for the missing weapon. Priem was sent for. He arrived as the scene reached a climax of pantomime chaos. He could not make himself heard. The more rebellious prisoners, who had not yet descended to the yard, were chanting all the songs they could think of at the top of their voices. Strains of the *Siegfried Line* mingled with "B—— and the same to you." Suddenly, Priem spotted the rifle inside an officer's pyjama leg. There was a mad rush of Goonery. The officer was completely smothered and then almost carried bodily out of the room under 'Strengen Arrest'. Jeers, whistles and catcalls rose to a deafening *crescendo*. The Germans were losing control and began to manhandle the prisoners towards the staircase with the usual, "*Los! Los! Schnell! Los!*"

Priem now took it into his head to visit the Dutch, living on the floor above. He mounted the stairs, followed by a squad of

Goons, and also a party of British in pyjamas and overcoats led by Rupert Barry, determined not to miss the fun. Sleepy Dutchmen rose on their elbows and blinked with astonishment at the incredible procession as it burst into their quarters. Priem was greeted with roars of laughter on all sides. Beside himself, he ordered the Dutchmen out of their beds, then turned to his soldiery and saw the cause of the laughter: a pyjama column of twenty Englishmen in attendance on the Germans, chatting innocently, grinning, waving to friends and generally awaiting developments. He emitted a bellow and went for Rupert, thumping him on the chest with his fists and screaming between the punctuating blows, *"Gottsverdammter englischer Schweinhund!"*

His squad were meanwhile pulling the blankets off the Dutchmen and turning them out of bed. Priem could not hold all the English. He was gripping Rupert with his two fists clenched over handfuls of pyjama and overcoat. The others mingled with the Dutch and the hubbub increased.

Within seconds the scene in the Dutch quarters became a repetition of the act in progress on the floor below. The shouting and singing, wafted up the stair-well, was soon drowned by a chorus upstairs.

Priem countermanded his order, screaming at the top of his voice that the Dutch should return to bed. But by now they were all awake, enjoying the fun and had no intention of doing so. Priem sent in his men to force them and a steeplechase began around the clusters of bunks. The Dutch and British were indistinguishable in their night attire, and the hide-and-seek continued fruitlessly until Priem, in despair, called his men off and left the prisoners to sort themselves out.

Down in the courtyard everybody was singing. Blackout blinds were going up again and faces looked down upon the rioters below.

The *Appell* had been extended to the senior British officers from the theatre block. They descended, sleepily, one by one. The S.B.O., Lieutenant-Colonel Stayner of the Dorsetshires, known as "Daddy" because of his grey hair and gentle, fatherly manner, walked into the yard. He looked frail and tired. He stopped for a moment under the lamp near the doorway, surveying the unruly mob before him, his tall thin frame silhouetted against the darkness beyond. Wisps of hair straying from under his fore-and-aft cap, were caught by a swirling gust of wind which sent a myriad snowflakes pirouetting. He heaved a tired sigh, shrugged his shoulders and took up his accustomed place for the *Appell*, resigned to a long session in the cold.

The French and Dutch began booing from the windows as Priem appeared on the steps outside the entrance to the British staircase. Priem held up his hand, waving at the windows and shouting orders that nobody could hear.

His N.C.O.s must have understood him. They gesticulated warningly up at the windows as the rifles of the sentries came up to the shoulder. The French and Dutch wisely retired. There was a momentary expectant lull. David Hunter, a lieutenant of the Royal Marines, could not resist the temptation. He yelled "*Feuer!*" and a salvo of shots echoed through the yard, as bullets flew into the night or embedded themselves in the walls. Slates rattled to the eaves.

Daddy Stayner remonstrated half-heartedly, "Hunter don't do that again, you're aggravating the Germans."

He knew his junior officers well enough. He had no intention of attempting seriously to call for order. In fact, he was beginning to enjoy the fun.

A sly smile played about his mouth as he watched the German N.C.O.s, led by Gephard and the Ferret, running around the yard demanding of the sentries, "Who gave the order to fire?"

Priem ordered the S.B.O. to command his men to form ranks for an *Appell*. Daddy Stayner maintained a stubborn ignorance of the German language and called for the British interpreter.

Flight-Lieutenant "Bricky" Forbes, R.A.F., the interpreter, was nowhere to be found. He had a Balaclava helmet well over his face and was determined to remain incognito. A German interpreter was sent for.

At this point a blackout curtain in the British quarters went up, and Harry Elliott poked his head out as far as he could to see the fun. Priem saw him and exploded. He bellowed orders at Gephard, who headed up the stairs at the double with two sentries. He returned in five minutes without Harry. Harry was back at the window.

From behind the blinds in the windows of the French quarters a plain-song choir could be heard chanting. The voices rose and fell in monastic rhythm.

The French were intoning their usual litany:

"*Où sont les Allemands?*"

"*Les Allemands sont dans la merde.*"

"*Qu'ils y restent.*"

"*Ils surnagent.*"

"*Enfoncez-les.*"

"*Jusqu'aux oreilles.*"

Gephard reported to Priem:

"Hauptmann Elliott says he is too ill to parade in the snow."

Harry, it may be remembered, was cultivating a chronic jaundice at this period of his captivity.

"Escort him downstairs to the doctor's dispensary," ordered Priem. "He will parade in there."

Gephard clicked his heels, saluted and disappeared upstairs again at the double.

Bedlam continued in the courtyard. The prisoners were still singing and shuffling around in a turmoil of movement like a bubbling cauldron, with the legitimate excuse that they were trying to keep warm.

The monotonous chant of the French inside their building provided a background of continuous sound like seas breaking on a distant shore.

A German security officer appeared, accompanied by an elderly, wizened little German corporal who was to act as interpreter. The latter had obviously just been dragged out of his bed and was half asleep. What he saw on entering the yard made him blink, wondering if he was still dreaming.

Priem was at his wits' end. If he threatened again with the rifles of his men a Machiavellian voice would shout *"Feuer!"* and he would be ultimately responsible if men were killed or wounded. He had lost the substance of power for a failing shadow—his voice.

Harry descended the stairs under escort and was greeted with vociferous cheering. He was led to the dispensary and locked in.

The Germans conferred with Colonel Stayner, then turned and faced the mob. The S.B.O. raised his hand, motioning for attention. Almost miraculously a lull descended on the unruly mob.

The intoning of the French could now be clearly heard and the quavering sound of Harry's voice—he did not see the S.B.O. from the dispensary—wafted into the yard rendering, to the tune of *Mademoiselle from Armentières*, an extempore composition:

> The Huns were hanged, one by one, parley-vouz,
> The Huns were hanged, one by one,
> Every b—— mother's son,
> Inky, stinky Hitler too.

The S.B.O. continued to demand silence as a wave of laughter threatened to bring new disorders in its wake. For a moment there was silence.

The German interpreter uttered in ringing tones his first words:

"All British are warned to mutiny."

They were his last.

A roar of applause greeted the pronouncement. Priem threw up his arms in despair, giving up the unequal fight. He turned to the S.B.O. and spoke to him.

Colonel Stayner turned towards the prisoners, "Parade dismiss!" he shouted as loudly as he could. The order was greeted with wild cheers and the British broke up in high spirits. They had won a signal victory.

Gradually they filed back to their quarters under the sullen gaze of the bewildered sentries.

The courtyard emptied and the sound of voices dropped to a distant murmur issuing from the turret staircase door. The guards faced each other across the yard waiting for the order to 'fall in'. On the snow in front of them, where the British had stood a few moments before, was an enormous dark brown 'V'. An enterprising spirit had thought it worth the expenditure of iron rations—a tin of Bournville cocoa!

CHAPTER IX

FRANZ JOSEF

INTROSPECTION had little place in Colditz. On rare occasions a prisoner became interested in psychology. As a rule he went on—'round the bend'. Psychological studies, in fact, could be dubbed a third form of the initial symptoms of the disease; the other two being, as already mentioned, the inordinate passion for classical music and the untiring cult of the body—physical jerks.

The majority of the Colditz inmates seemed to prefer the more simple variety of self-examination—an occasional examination of the conscience. After all, it had the prestige of a few thousand years of beneficent usage, whereas the modern version achieved, in prison, sometimes startling, sometimes comic, but never satisfying results. The difference between modern psychological introspection and the Christian examination of conscience was described by a wag at Colditz as the difference between a Futurist nightmare and a Michelangelo masterpiece; only the canvas and paint were common to both, as the mind of man to the two forms of mental approach.

A new British escape scheme was afoot. There was little time, opportunity, or inclination for the self-indulgence of morbidity. The project was big: it would involve the breakout of a large party. As usual, it started in a small way.

One bright morning in April 1943 Dick Howe was looking vacantly down from a window in the British dayroom at the sentries below. He was joined by "Monty" Bissell, a six-foot Irishman who was a curious mixture of two temperaments. He had the temperament and the physique of a prize-fighter and his bones must have been made of case-hardened steel. He had no fat on him whatever. Yet, although he was as thin as a rake, his weight remained well over fourteen stone. He charged everywhere with his head down, like a bull. He could not walk slowly, with the result that he frequently bumped into people. It was like being hit by a shunting engine. He had black hair which fell over his forehead, and a long face with a beak of a nose and hawk-like eyes. When he laughed, which he did at the most incongruous moments, accompanied by a loud snort and a satanic jerk of the head backwards, his mouth opened, revealing several yawning gaps where once had been a fine row of teeth. Boxing had done that for him.

Monty had the soul of a poet. He would quote Shakespeare and Yeats—in equal mouthfuls—lovingly, with the tenderness and complete unselfconsciousness of one to whom the music and the meaning of the words were ineffably majestic, imposing and intuitive.

Monty leaned on the window-sill beside Dick. Neither spoke for some time. Then Monty recited with his huge hand on Dick's shoulder:

I've looked too long at life through a window
And seen too often the freedom I crave.
Yes, I've looked far too long at life through barred windows,
But I'll look much longer at death from my grave.

"Not bad, not bad, hah! What do you think, Dick? I got it from Black Campbell. Didn't know he was a poet, did you? Ha! Hm!"

A long pause intervened. Dick was in a reverie. Monty might have been on the moon, but his heavy hand came down again with a resounding thud on Dick's shoulder.

"What's all the thought about, Dick? Listen to this!" and he intoned with almost fierce intensity:

Come,
Close your eyes, see the graph of expression
Traced by the pencil of Modernity,
Watch those steep ascents and sheer declines
Marking the course of enthusiasm

Whose fire consumes itself and Phœnix-like
Creates once more the spark of quick desire.
These jagged peaks must needs record some trend.
Dizzy heights and abysmal nothingness
Can cancel out : but nothing cancels out.
In Time all that does not move is stiller
Than the still. We must progress or perish,
And being able must progress yet more,
Else perish sooner. Man as yet unborn
Has all but solved the mystery of birth.
This Science cannot aimlessly suffice,
For one must know the 'I' to know the all.
To know this 'I' each age has creased the brow,
But ours of all the ages sets small store
Against the value of this seed of hope.
Philosophies, Religions, Mysteries,
Give way to stark Reality . . .

"That's Humanity! Huh! not bad, eh? for a caged bird!
Black Campbell again."

Dick replied without looking up, "I was thinking that, if we
could change a sufficient number of the sentries on one side of
the Castle, we could let out a large number of chaps through a
prepared window and nobody would be the wiser."

"Eh? What's all that?" queried Monty, taken aback. "I was
talking about Humanity."

"Were you?" said Dick. Leaning again on the sill with his
chin cupped in his hands he continued his reverie.

Monty did not go away. Instead, he elbowed Dick over to
give him room so that he, too, could cup his chin and stare out
of the window—out and then down. Thus they both remained,
silent and absorbed in their own thoughts for a long time.
Then Dick drifted away and Monty was left alone.

That was how the escape attempt started.

*   *   *   *   *

At the end of April, Monty Bissell and Mike Sinclair could
be seen frequently walking together around the cobbled yard

in deep conversation. Mike was back in prison circulation again after his long spell in solitary. He was looking, it seemed, paler than before, but then he had red hair and the sunless winter was only just beginning to recede before the onslaught of spring.

Now, as they strode around the yard, Monty displayed, at times, great agitation, flinging his arms wide, slapping Mike on the back and walking at a pace that often brought his companion to a trot. Mike was of medium build, just about the same height as one of the German guard commanders, who was known in the Castle as Franz Josef.

Franz Josef was indeed the subject of their subdued discussion as they tore around the yard. It was not long before they buttonholed Dick.

One evening, after the five o'clock *Appell*, they approached him.

"Dick," said Mike, "we want to have a chat with you. Would you spare Monty and me half an hour in a quiet corner somewhere?"

"Come along to my room. We can sit on the beds. There's nobody there and we've got lots of time before supper."

They climbed the long spiral flight of steps to the room, where, in a secluded corner, well away from the door, was Dick's bunk. Nearby were the two-tier bunks occupied by Lulu Lawton, Rupert Barry and Harry Elliott. The room was long and the ceiling high, but the windows were in deep casements which kept out much of the light. They sat or lay on the beds as the shadows slowly deepened in the evening light.

Mike began:

"Monty has an idea for an escape which, at first sight, appears pretty crazy, but we've talked about it a lot and I, for one, think it can be done. Roughly—without going into details —it's this; I dress up as Franz Josef and with two others, dressed as German guards, we get out of a certain window at the psychological moment. I relieve the guard below our old quarters, the ones that are empty. There are two sentries; the chap on the cat-walk and the fellow at the barbed-wire gate.

I send the real guards back to the guardhouse and my two men take over. Then, having the keys of the gate and having possession of that side of the Castle, you can send out a batch of say twenty chaps—more if you like—through another prepared window and the whole lot of us clear out as fast as we can."

"H'm!" said Dick, lying back in his bed and appearing to examine intently the canvas palliasse and the bed-boards of the bunk above him. "I see, Monty, you haven't been idle!"

"Eh? What? No! by Gad! I've been working up this scheme ever since you mentioned the idea, weeks ago. I think it's terrific—a cinch—I can't sleep at night for thinking about it. All we need are two more German speakers—three German uniforms—Teddy Barton fixes up Mike to look like Franz Josef—we cut the bars on two windows—the guards are relieved and off we all go—first-class railway tickets to Blighty." A torrent of words flowed from Monty as he stood up excitedly and enacted the escape with his long arms.

"All right, Monty. That's all right, old boy. Sit down now and let's have a few details, quietly. First of all, this is how I see it. We'll have to do a long period of watching so that we know exactly what motions Franz Josef will go through on the particular evening—assuming it will be in the evening—of the escape. Then we must also do a lot of stooging so that we know which sentries will go on the posts we're going to relieve—we want dumb ones." He paused for a moment, thinking, then continued:

"We've not only got to make three uniforms complete, and mighty good ones—better than we've ever made before—but we shall have to make two rifles and a revolver in its holster for Franz Josef—also the two bayonet scabbards. Changing the guard means plenty of time for the Jerries to notice the uniforms and the lights may be on. Anyway, it's not at all like a couple of chaps, in uniform, marching past a sentry in a hurry. That's how I see it. The answer is stooging—hours and hours of it, and the best uniforms we've ever made. Apart from that, I'd like to see how Mike makes up as Franz Josef; and lastly, which windows do you propose to work from?"

There was a moment's silence before Mike spoke:

"We'll show you the windows now if you'll come with us. I think Teddy Barton can fix me up as Franz Josef. I've asked him about it already, and he's fairly confident about it. I'm the right height."

"You'll have to examine old Franz with a microscope for a couple of weeks at least, to pick up all his mannerisms. You've got to be word perfect," Dick interrupted.

"Yes, I know," continued Mike. "Have you any ideas for my two Goons?"

Dick thought for a second. "Where do you come in in all this, Monty? You'll never pass as a weedy little tich of a sentry."

"No! I'm going to lead the storming party out of the second window," announced Monty with gusto. "What a show it's going to be! Hah!" and he threw his head back with a devilish grin.

"I thought, maybe, John Hyde-Thomson could be one of my guards," said Mike. "He speaks German well enough. I hadn't fixed on another yet."

"All right," said Dick, rising slowly from the bed, "let's go and have a look at the windows. The idea's crazy all right, but if everything is word perfect—well—who knows! We must think about your guards and I'll talk to the C.O. about it."

They walked downstairs, across the now darkening courtyard and into the sick-bay corridor. Monty led the way into the sick ward itself, and they stood, huddled together, by a window. Monty then explained, in subdued tones, that this window was 'blind' from the sentries at night unless one of them walked the full length of his beat, and he could be expected to stand still for part of his duty period. Dick checked up and thought there was something in what Monty said. Two or three officers could be let down quickly out of this window, and, provided they were suitably dressed, they could walk away, round a corner, towards the next sentry without causing suspicion. The bars, of course, would have to be very carefully dealt with.

They continued their tour of inspection, to the window

where it was proposed to let out the main body. This was on the park side of the Castle. The window was in quarters now vacated and in darkness, in which the British had once lived. Keys were employed to make an entry, and here, beside the second window, Monty and Mike pointed out the two German sentries who would be involved in the escape.

One of the two sentries was stationed on a high cat-walk surveying a long frontage of the Castle. The second sentry was posted at the barbed-wire gate, for the keys of which he was responsible, and which opened on to the roadway leading downhill towards the park and the German barracks. The gate was also next to the deep tunnel-like archway leading into the Kommandantur courtyard; the one through which Mike and the Frenchman had sortied not many months earlier.

With the window-bars prepared, if these two sentries could be relieved by ours, the way was clear for a rope descent by a large party.

The scheme was daring, to say the least of it.

Dick put the wheels of his organisation into action. Another "Mike", namely Michael Harvey, R.N., one of the parcels-office team already mentioned, kept a regular stooging roster on call for such eventualities. Dick arranged with Mike to put his roster at the disposal of Monty whom he charged with the task of obtaining sufficient data to be able to forecast with certainty, *three days* ahead of any given date, when Franz Josef would be on duty as Commander of the Guard; to map out his complete circuit and the frequency of his rounds with the time intervals between posts; the exact hours of evening guard changes; the times required for guards to regain the guardhouse from different posts, (*a*) if walking direct and alone, and (*b*) if in a squad on the circuit. The posts taken up by respective Goons were to be noted and particular Goons seeded out, leaving only dumb-looking ones in the running, whose tours of duty on the cat-walk and the gate were to be graphed with accuracy. It was a job the team were accustomed to, but it would necessitate at least a month of concentrated effort.

Dick required the *three days'* grace to provide ample time for completing the cutting of the bars of the two windows concerned. This was an operation which called for the greatest patience and for much experience. The work demanded such delicacy of touch that only saws made of razor blades could be used. The sick-bay window would be comparatively simple, but the window opening in front of the sentry on the cat-walk was an extremely ticklish job. The escape depended on the success of both cutting operations, and the awkward point was that they would be the last part of the scheme to be completed. This work was put into the hands of Lulu Lawton and Bricky Forbes.

Two thirty-foot lengths of rope were required. They were ordered from the marine department, Bos'n Crisp in other words. So much to begin with, but it was only a beginning.

Rex Harrison, blond, six foot two in his socks, with a long, curling moustache, even-tempered and patient, would have to produce three perfect German uniforms, one for a sergeant. He no longer had Bill Fowler to help him expertly with the embroidery and cloth insignia, but there were other willing hands to fill the gap. "Andy", Major W. F. Anderson, R.E., and Scarlet O'Hara were commissioned to produce two German rifles, two bayonet scabbards and a holster complete with revolver, and Scarlet was to deal also with the foundry work for buttons, badges, medals and belt clasps.

Finally, the principal actor in the whole drama had to be coached and transformed into the mirror image of Franz Josef.

The elderly and somewhat stout N.C.O. who was to be given a twin brother was not called Franz Josef for nothing. He was a living impersonation of Franz Josef, Emperor of Austria, King of Hungary and Bohemia; ruddy complexion, puffy cheeks, grey hair, portly bearing and an enormous Franz Josef moustache which covered half of his face. Provided this could be faithfully copied, it would in itself provide a magnificent mask.

Teddy Barton was one of the theatre past-masters. Besides producing shows and acting in them, he had the professional touch when it came to 'make-up'. His 'girls' on the stage had at once been the delight and the despair of theatre audiences. His male efforts could not have been bettered by Madame Tussaud. He and his principal aide, Alan Cheetham, manufactured fourteen Franz Josef moustaches before they were satisfied with their handiwork. The face, hair and even the hands were practised upon with like thoroughness.

Teddy Barton, Mike Sinclair and Alan Cheetham studied Franz Josef's gestures, facial expressions, manner of speech, accent, and intonation for a month on end. Franz Josef was dogged every time he entered the courtyard. He was engaged in long futile conversations while, unknowingly, he was scrutinised microscopically by three pairs of eyes that took note of every muscle he moved, every cough and splutter, every smile and grimace he made. Mike rehearsed, was criticised and rehearsed again and again, until he lived in the rôle of Franz Josef.

His moment was approaching. Two sentries had been chosen to accompany him. They were John Hyde-Thomson and Lancelot Pope. Both were good German speakers. They rehearsed with Mike the German words of command, and practised all the movements of guard changing according to the German routine. It was Pope's second effort of this kind. He had once marched out of Eichstätt prison with "Tubby" Broomhall (Lieutenant-Colonel, R.E.), posing as a German general.

It was decided to prepare a first wave of twenty men to make the rope descent from the old British quarters immediately the guard had been relieved and was out of sight.

The factor, limiting the number in the wave, was the time it would take the first German sentry relieved to march back to the guardhouse and report to his N.C.O., the real Franz Josef —Franz Josef I. Then the balloon would go up. This interval of time was checked repeatedly as a minimum of three and a half minutes and an almost certain maximum of four and a half minutes. Twenty men would, in this space of time, be able to drop down the rope and be well on the road to the park. If there was no violent reaction by the time the twentieth had descended the rope, more officers were ready to follow, but responsibility rested with their leaders not to lessen, in any way, by their action the chances of the first wave. There might be German reactions other than from the guardhouse and much nearer the scene of the escape. Late departures might cause suspicion or an escaper might even be seen on the rope. This would shorten the start of the first twenty which, in all conscience, was short enough!

An escape of this calibre involved the co-operation of about fifty officers in its preparation. In addition to the month of preparation before the day of the escape, there had been the months of earlier work put in by the artists and the printers reproducing the maps, identity papers and passes carried by the officers who were to make the attempt. These personal credentials were now brought up to date and officially stamped. German money was issued. Each escaper, of course, had to produce his own civilian attire. In this task he was assisted by the expert advice and practical help of the tailors.

The team had gathered for briefing several times and at the final meeting Dick wound up with a wry smile:

"I'm sure you'll have an exciting time and plenty of fun. You can rely on it, there'll be some shooting, but keep your nerve and go on running. You know the password: 'They can't shoot a British officer!' We have the advantage of darkness. Make for the three points indicated for climbing the park wall, splitting up into your respective groups. And remember, once you're out we don't want to see your ugly faces here again."

The main body was to make straight for the park at the double, followed closely by Mike—Franz Josef II and his two sentries. If a stray Goon appeared they were to keep running. Franz Josef II would give the impression of chasing the party and would intercept any such stray Goons and order them to run in the opposite direction, towards the Castle, with instructions to raise the alarm.

The revolver and the rifles were nearing completion. Scarlet spent hours trailing the sentries in the courtyard, holding sometimes a long piece of string, sometimes a ruler in his hand. When a sentry was stationary, Scarlet approached him casually from behind then surreptitiously measured a particular section of the rifle. Andy prepared the plans. Each measurement was recorded, the ruler providing the details in fractions of an inch. Then they set to work and made the dummies. The result was perfection. The rifles could pass close inspection in daylight. Contours, colours, shape and sheen were all correct. Only the weight would have given them away. Rifle straps were made to match. The revolver and holster followed the same high standard.

D-day had to be fixed. Careful examination and discussion of the reports of Monty and Mike Harvey, resulting from their exhaustive stooging, settled the date, which was to be May 19th, and the hour was to be—immediately after the 9 p.m. *Appell*. Franz Josef I would be the guard commander on that day and a particularly dumb-looking Goon was calculated to be on duty at the gate.

Among those remaining behind was Lulu Lawton, Dick's second in command, Bricky Forbes, Bush Parker who was to release the Franz Josef II party from the sick ward, and the stooging team for the event under the command of Mike Harvey. Monty headed the main escaping party.

Signalling was to be done by flashlight. It was laid on as a two-way code between three look-out points; one, at a window on the floor above the sick ward in charge of Bush Parker, with communication to the sick ward by tapping on a water pipe; a second, with the main body in the old British quarters; and the third overlooking the German guardhouse.

The most delicate operation in the whole scheme now had to be accomplished. The bars of the two windows in the different parts of the Castle had to be cut. Complete concentration and devotion to the job in hand was essential. Months of work and the desperate hopes of many men were at stake. Failure would involve much bitterness. For this reason, Dick chose the two men in whose conscientiousness the whole British contingent had confidence. It could be said with conviction that if they failed to do the job, no other officer would have succeeded.

One window was 'comparatively' simple. The second window was in direct floodlight. 'Comparatively' is a relative term. In other circumstances the cutting might have been deemed very difficult, but as bar cutting had by now become a stock-in-trade of the Colditz convicts, only the cutting of bars in full floodlight with a sentry immediately below attracted comment and a mild compliment from those who knew what was involved; the ear of a gazelle, a hand of iron controlled by a thread of silk, a heart of ice, a brain calm as a mill-pond and as quick to react as a trout flashing in the stream. During the five years Colditz was used as a prison in World War II, the operation of cutting a bar in full floodlight was performed successfully only three times.

The bar cutting was accomplished successfully and camouflaged.

May 19th arrived. The day passed slowly. There was suppressed activity everywhere, concealed by an over-all air of casualness. The men taking part in the attempt were not beginners. What worried most of them more than anything else was the short start. If the first stage—the relieving of the guard —came off, that in itself would be tremendously exciting, but the real fun would start when twenty P.O.W.s were out, the first with perhaps a three-minute start, and the last with less than a thirty-seconds start, in front of the pursuing enemy. The hounds would be in full cry. Colditz had never known such an attempt before and the consequences were unknown.

Monty, six feet of heavyweight boxer, strode around the quarters all day like a rhino in search of a muddy pool in the Sahara.

Mike remained outwardly calm while the turmoil of nervous anticipation was inwardly tearing at his entrails and gripping his throat.

Dick spent his time checking up on everybody's instructions, amplifying them, where necessary, to cover every possible hitch or misunderstanding. The escape was the largest and most daring so far attempted from Colditz. If it succeeded, it would make history. If it failed—"Well!" thought Dick, "it'll still make a good story!" He watched the final rehearsal of the guard-changing squad and thought they were word perfect. Franz Josef II could have walked out of the Castle with ease.

The hours dragged heavily towards the 9 p.m. *Appell*. Those in the escaping team lay on their bunks, trying to sleep. They yawned and stretched themselves nervously, finding no relief for the tension around the heart or the nausea threatening the stomach, for the hot flush or the cold sweat. Then, when everybody least expected it, the siren began to wail. The show was on.

The *Appell* went off normally. Immediately afterwards, Bush Parker and the guard-relieving party—Mike, John Hyde-Thomson and Lance Pope—faded off towards the sick ward. The second stooging contingent disappeared to their respective posts on the upper floor overlooking the guardhouse. The main escaping party with its stooges, led by Dick, Bricky Forbes, Lulu and Mike Harvey and followed by the members of the second escaping wave—altogether thirty-five strong—passed silently through locked doors into the dark unoccupied rooms of the old British quarters.

Dick looked down on to the sentry path below. "The ivory-headed Goon's at his post on the gateway—so far so good," he whispered.

Sounds of life in the Castle died down. Soon a deathly stillness reigned. Thirty-five men waited for the warning signals.

The first message came through:

"Franz Josef returned to guardhouse," Mike Harvey reported in an undertone. Then came, "All quiet in German Kommandantur."

That was the signal for Bush to act and release Franz Josef II and his party through the window, down the rope, on to the sentry path.

A silence, vibrant with tension, followed. Then, suddenly, Mike Harvey spoke in hoarse excited tones:

"Our guard party on their way—past first sentry."

A moment later, Dick, Lulu, Monty and Bricky Forbes, crouching near the window, heard the crunch of marching feet on the path and a loud heel-click as a sentry, out of sight, saluted the passing patrol. Then they came into view, round the corner of the building. This was the crucial moment.

Franz Josef II, followed by his two guards, walked to the gate and spoke to the dumb sentry in German:

"Sie sind abgelöst. Sie werden Ihre Wache diesem Posten übergeben. Gehen Sie sofort in die Wachtstube! Dort sind Sie nötig, denn einige Gefangene sind geflohen."

Lance Pope took up his post beside the gate. Franz Josef II mounted the ladder to the cat-walk and repeated his orders to the second sentry who started to descend. John Hyde-Thomson took over his post.

"My God!" whispered Dick, in a dripping perspiration, "it's going to work. Get ready!"

The cat-walk sentry had reached the ground and was marching off. Then Dick noticed the gate sentry had not followed. Franz Josef II was talking to him. Dick could hear the gist of it through the open window and repeated it to the others.

"The sentry says he's under orders not to move. Mike's demanded the keys. The sentry's handed them over . . . but he won't move. What the hell! . . . Mike ought to go. He's wasting time. The three of them can make it. He's getting annoyed with the sentry . . . he's told him to get back to the guardhouse. No! . . . it's no good . . . the dumb bastard won't budge . . . why the devil won't he move? Mike's getting really angry with him . . . this is awful. He's got to go! He's got to go! Mike's shouting at him." Dick was in a frenzy. "Good God! this is the end. The time's nearly up."

Mike was having a desperate duel with the ivory-headed Goon and the precious seconds were slipping away. He was thinking of the main party—he was determined that the main party should escape at all costs. He had cast his die—it was to be all or nothing. He was sacrificing himself to win the larger prize.

As soon as he started to raise his voice, Dick's stomach began to sink. The game was a losing one. He wanted to shout at Mike to make a run for it, but dared not interfere with Mike's battle. He was impotent, helpless, swearing and almost weeping with a foreboding of terrible failure. The scheme within a hair's breadth of success, was going wrong. Mike might possibly have disarmed the offending sentry, but it was too late for violence now with less than half a minute's start. If he had been disarmed at the very beginning it might have been different, but who would have done that when persuasion was the obvious first course. Alas! persuasion meant time and the precious minutes had flown. Four minutes had gone. It was nearly hopeless now.

The two British sentries stood their ground. John Hyde-Thomson was solemnly pacing his beat up and down the cat-walk.

Mike's voice rose to a typical Franz Josef scream of rage. Even as he shouted, there were sounds of hurrying feet and discordant voices shouting in the distance. A dozen Goons came through the archway near the gate, running fast with their bayonets fixed. At their rear, panting hard and bellowing commands, ran Franz Josef I. The game was almost up, but Mike was determined to play it to the end. He would challenge his rival; let the Germans choose between them. Franz Josef II outbellowed Franz Josef I and countermanded his orders. A scene of frenzied confusion ensued, in which the Germans obeyed first one and then the other—turned down the hill and then reversed—looked towards Franz Josef I and listened to Franz Josef II, seeing yet not believing that Franz Josef had suddenly split into two violently opposed personalities.

The German sentry who had been relieved was prominent. He was yelling at his rival, pointing upwards and dancing with excitement, completely out of control. His substitute stood quietly at his post on the cat-walk looking down innocently upon the chaos below.

N.C.O.s ran backwards and forwards in a panic, waving their revolvers. They were no longer certain of the allegiance of the men they commanded. Lance Pope had mingled with the Germans and Dick could not distinguish him. In the alternate searing floodlight and darkness around the searchlights men who were dressed alike looked alike.

Mass hysteria broke out. A German voice began screaming: "Armed mutiny! Armed mutiny!" which was taken up by a chorus, waving rifles in the air.

A shot rang out.

One of the Franz Josefs swayed and sank to his knees. A confused mob of soldiers gathered round him, all talking at once.

"They've shot Mike—I think it's Mike—I can't be sure," said Dick, turning to the men around him, "I can't see what's happening."

The panic and the hubbub continued for a moment, then subsided. Lance Pope was in the middle of the mob of Germans. John Hyde-Thomson was being pushed down the ladder of the cat-walk with a revolver in his back.

Dick spotted the Franz Josef on the ground. "It's Mike all right. I'm sure of it."

Monty at the window was shaking with rage, thumping one fist into the other and shouting, "Let me get at 'em! Let me get at 'em."

"The bastards!" said Dick; then turning to the waiting men, "they'll be in our quarters in a minute. Everybody clear out! Lulu, see to the bars. Mike, signal to the others to return to quarters."

Then after a pause and another look through the window as Lulu carefully reset the bars: "They've left Mike on the ground. My God! The filthy swines aren't even attending to him!"

Dick and Lulu did not see the end. The *Appell* siren was moaning and Germans were already in the courtyard. They had to leave the premises in haste, removing traces and locking up behind them.

For nearly ten minutes, Mike was left lying on the ground, bleeding profusely from a wound in the chest. His Franz Josef moustache had been torn off his face. A squad of Goons was standing by, evidently waiting for orders.

An N.C.O. appeared and Mike was picked up. He was semi-conscious—fainting from loss of blood. They carried him away to the Kommandantur.

In the courtyard, feeling among the prisoners was running high. Many thought that Mike had been killed. There were struggles on the British staircase. David Hunter, shouting *"Deutscher Mörder"* at the top of his voice and resisting arrest, was hustled off between four Goons with rifles and fixed bayonets in the rabbiting position, and thrown into a cell in his pyjamas.

Monty Bissell spotted the Goon who, he thought, had shot Mike. Shaking his fist in his face, he confronted him with *"Kaltblütiger Mörder! Deutscher Mörder! Deutscher Schweinhund!"* He was promptly surrounded by another four Goons, who manhandled him across the courtyard and pushed him into another cell.

There were fifty Goons in the yard waiting for the *Appell*, with their bayonets fixed and rifles at the hip. Priem had evidently learnt his lesson and was taking no chances. The guards were in an ugly mood. They had tasted blood. The atmosphere glowed hot and red with sparks that might start a nasty conflagration.

Oberst Prawitt, the German Commandant of the camp, hurried into the yard. He spoke to the S.B.O., who called the prisoners to attention and announced amidst a frozen silence:

"Lieutenant Sinclair is wounded but out of danger."

Mike's time had not yet come.

CHAPTER X

UPLIFT

THE kitchen stove in the British quarters was naturally a centre of activity around which life hummed all day long and all night too. Then the distillers were at work. During the daylight hours a former Merchant Navy engineer officer, Lieutenant Ernest Champion, R.N.R., more widely known as Ernie, constituted himself like an Arabian genie, the guardian of the stove. He knew all about cooking as it should be done at Colditz because "Bertie" Boustead, an ardent amateur, asked him, one day, when he had some pale-looking potato rissoles on the fire, "How do you know when these are done?"

Ernie, who was sitting beside the stove, told him:

"When they're brown they're burning, and when they're black they're finished."

Lieutenant John R. Boustead was a thin, six-foot length of Seaforth Highlander, who had been taken prisoner in June 1940. He possessed unfailing good humour, and at the same time somewhat hazy ideas about the mundane matters of everyday living. He was, at first, welcomed with great enthusiasm into the cooks' circle. They saw in his desire to cook a descent from an Olympian detachment.

Ernie was naturally anxious to help him, so that when he saw Bertie early one morning stirring hot water in a small saucepan on the stove he asked him, "What are you stirring it for?"

To which Bertie replied with the enthusiasm of a pupil who was at last benefiting from his cooking course, "To prevent it burning, of course, you ass."

But Bertie never lived down the reputation he earned as a cook when he approached Ernie with a sizzling frying-pan in which an egg gaily cavorted from side to side. The shell was brown in patches, black in spots and cracked all over. He said:

"Ernie! I can't seem to get this egg to fry properly. Can you help me?"

The kitchen stove would have told some soul-shattering stories if it could have spoken. One scandal which leaked out, fortunately after the dish concerned had been greedily consumed and appreciatively digested, concerned a delicious curry. The chef was Derby Curtis, a captain of the Royal Marines. When his curry was only half cooked, it took fire without warning. With consummate aplomb, which was only witnessed by a few onlookers, he lifted the frying-pan quickly off the stove, put it on the floor and stamped out the flames with his heavy-booted feet. He then wiped his boots off carefully on the edge of the frying-pan and continued to cook the curry.

In the evenings, when all meals were concluded, the stove was taken over by the distillers.

The origin and early development of this industry dates from the year 1941.[1] In 1943, however, an efficiently run firm grew from small beginnings and eventually mastered all competition and became a monopoly. The head of the concern was a Dutchman, A. Van Rood, a Flight-Lieutenant in the R.A.F. who had been studying medicine in England when the war broke out. He joined the R.A.F. and, as a fighter pilot, was shot down over St. Omer in 1942. Van Rood was a good-looking blond type and was born to be more than a doctor because he was an authority on every subject known to man. His opinions were definite on them all, and he did not hesitate to expound his views at any hour of the day or night, when given a cue and an audience, in a loud voice in any one of the four languages—Dutch, English, French or German—which his audience might care to choose, because he was fluent in them all. He became a skilful brewer, and was the Chemist, as well as a Director, of the Company. Scarlet O'Hara christened him 'Good Time Charlie Goonstein' after the Damon Runyon character who ran a speak-easy off Broadway. The name stuck.

[1] See *The Colditz Story*.

His brother Directors were Bush Parker who acted as the fuel contractor for the combine, and "Bag" or "Ming" Dickenson. The latter came from Bristol, was also a Flight-Lieutenant in the R.A.F., and before the war had been an engineer working for the firm of Rotol Ltd. He was shot down on a bombing raid over Germany. He liked to escape in an impromptu manner, on the impulse and alone. His best effort from Colditz was from the solitary confinement cells in the town. Returning from exercise, he stepped behind a door—it sounds so easy—and, while the guards marched upstairs to the cells, he marched downstairs, out, into the town, dressed as he was, in mixed khaki and R.A.F. blue. Reaching Chemnitz, he thought himself conspicuous, so casually left his purloined bicycle at the kerb and entered the best hotel in the city. He walked into the lounge and over to a nice collection of coats hanging on a stand. He chose the best-fitting one and walked out. Alas! The owner was not far behind him and that was the end of Bag's outing.

He was tall and thin, with a fair complexion and his temperament was essentially placid. He could not be ruffled—hence his alternative nickname "Ming". When Bush was not hauling coal, playing cards or tasting liquor, he was teasing the old Bag, but in three years at Colditz he never succeeded in rousing him. Bag's placidity extended to his clothing. He disbelieved in the old adage, 'A stitch in time . . .' With a fatalism reminiscent of the East, when a button fell off, a shoe lace broke or a seam came apart, his shrug expressed the spirit enshrined in the words, 'Ins' Allah'—'Allah's will be done!' His equanimity reached distressing extremes when his bed caught fire as he lay on it. This happened frequently because he had a habit of dozing off in the afternoon with a lighted cigarette in his mouth. Scarlet O'Hara, who slept next to him, kept a bucket of water under his bed for the sole purpose of extinguishing Bag's fires—he may also have been tempted to use it sometimes when there was no fire. Bag would come to, soaked to the skin, while the acrid smell of burning hair mixed with smouldering straw and canvas dispersed itself through the room. Bag would stretch his long frame and rise slowly from the bed to say, between yawns, "Thanks, Scarlet, old boy, but try and keep the water off my feet. You've soaked my only good pair of socks."

Bag was the Distilling Engineer. He was ever producing bigger and better stills at the expense of the Castle plumbing system. At other times he manufactured keys and tools of all kinds, beautifully finished and correctly tempered or case-hardened, out of pieces removed from iron bedsteads in the senior officers' quarters.

The three Directors ran their business on a barter basis and always had stock in hand to satisfy demands. An official exchange value, with a margin of profit, was placed on both sugar and raisins, and a given quantity of alcohol of any desired flavour handed over the counter for a given quantity of the two raw materials.

Flavour and colouring were the fruit of careful experiments under the direction of the Chemist. Very passable imitations could be purchased of gin, rum, crème de menthe and whisky.

Apart from the concentrated spirits, Good Time Charlie Goonstein and his mates displayed ingenuity in finding a use for the barrels upon barrels of almost uneatable 'jam' supplied by the Germans which littered the canteen and the camp kitchen. This was the stuff, already mentioned, made of sugar-beet waste, dyed red, and distributed to prison camps all over Germany in barrels marked '*Nur für Kriegsgefangene*'.

The distillers transformed half a dozen casks into vats, where the 'jam' fermented, giving off a foul smell. The ferment was distilled to produce Jam-Alc. Van Rood really deserved his nickname for this 'speak-easy' alcohol. It tasted of old rubber tyres. The Company conscientiously tried to improve its quality, but experiment how they would, even after three distillations Jam-Alc still tasted of rubber.

In spite of this gastronomic disability, it had a ready sale at a low rate of exchange—for instance, three bottles of Jam-Alc for a bucket of coal—among a clientèle who seemed able to stomach it without immediate undue ill effects. One gay party, however, which began on Boxing Day, 1943, as a fancy-dress party, continued until February 29th, 1944. Undoubtedly Jam-Alc played a part in the celebration of such a happy and glorious anniversary as the fourth New Year spent in a Nazi prison.

Coming round from it, after a debauch, was unpleasant. So much so that the sufferer was tempted to return to the comatose condition rather than face the horrors of the no man's land which lay between him and sobriety. Jam-Alc then became known as 'the needle', after the hypodermic variety. One reveller spent New Year's Day sprawled on the floor with his head in a lavatory-pan. The cisterns had been arranged to flush automatically as soon as they filled. Every time a cold douche of water poured over his head, he raised himself a few inches on one elbow to splutter, "Thanks ver' much, old boy—ver' kind of you," then dropped his head again, ready for the next two gallons.

* * * * *

As 1943 dragged out its endless repetition of daylight and darkness, and as the significance of the capitulation of Stalingrad slowly sank into the reactionary recesses of the Teutonic mind, German morale became noticeably poorer. Like the weeds which show themselves when a soil is badly cared for, so the German temperament sprouted corruptive practices when the selective weed-killer of propaganda lost its force and hold upon the people.

Nineteen-forty-three saw the birth and growth of the corruption of the Colditz guards. In 1944 it grew to such proportions and involved such a large quantity of the consumable Red Cross foodstuffs, cigarettes and tobacco that even a casual observer could deduce that the prisoners were not obtaining value for money. There was undercutting, throat cutting, Dutch auctioning and blackmail. There were rings, cabals, cartels, subsidiaries, commodity monopolies, short- and long-term contracts and financing houses.

In the midst of this tumultuous sea rode "Checko" in an unsinkable boat. Flight-Lieutenant Cenek Chalupka, R.A.F., was, metaphorically, made of cork. In the hey-day of Neville Chamberlain he flew for his country—Czechoslovakia. After Munich he flew for Poland; after Warsaw he made his way to France; and after Paris he flew for England. He was decorated by every nation for which he fought.

He was tall, dark and handsome and full of vitality. He spoke English with a catching accent in a manner that would rival Maurice Chevalier. How the women must have fallen for him!

He was the only prisoner in Colditz who could claim to have kissed a girl while imprisoned there. It happened in 1944. "Checko" was escorted to the dentist in the town for treatment. One look passed between him and the pretty German receptionist. It was enough. The next day she contrived to deliver to the camp a muffler Checko had 'inadvertently' left behind! She persuaded the guard commander to send for Checko to come to the prison gates. There, through a tiny grille in the massive oak, no bigger than the palm of a man's hand, the muffler and Cupid's dart passed simultaneously, and a pair of rosy lips presented themselves for their reward.

Checko was an adopted godson of Eric Linklater. Indeed, his was a character that would fit admirably into this famous author's portrait gallery: puckish, virile, humorous, dynamic, unroarious and explosive. Checko, in the course of 1943, flooded the Colditz market with maps, files and hack-saw blades; dyestuffs, photographic materials and coloured inks; stamps, identity papers and time-tables; tools of every description, paints, plaster, cement and chemicals. He had rivals and he had difficulties. Racketeering among the French—until they left—was reaching alarming dimensions, and whereas he concentrated as far as he could on the accessories of escape, he was up against firms that worked only for the bodily comforts of prisoners. Extra food and fresh food, eggs, butter, cheese, vegetables and fruit commanded high prices and threatened, at times, to run him out of business. For a while he sailed with the wind, keeping his head and gathered allies to his cause until public opinion in the camp was eventually roused and came to the rescue of those seeking escape, as opposed to luxury.

All this, however, did not happen in a day. Not until December 1944 did order develop out of chaos. David Stirling, the tall Scotsman whose exploits as the Commander of 'L' Detachment, S.A.S. Regiment [1] are written in war history, was detailed by the S.B.O. to co-ordinate and to regulate the black-market activities of Colditz. Prices came down with a crash, distribution became orderly and goods remained plentiful. In addition, by way of bonus with every exchange, 'pieces' of military intelligence were collected When these were all put together they solved the jig-saw puzzle of the local German Command; the division of responsibility between *Wehrmacht,* Gestapo and *Landwacht,* the pressure groups and personalities, the weight of weapons and military supplies and the local forces that could be deployed. But this is jumping ahead in time and sequence. . . .

Returning to the spring and early summer of 1943, when racketeering was still in its infancy and the Goons were not demoralised, one of the principal aims of the Colditz convicts was, naturally, to try to demoralise them by every means pos-sible. Goon-baiting is a self-explanatory term. It meant simply baiting the Goons. This activity, like distilling, gained impetus and attained dizzy heights in 1943.

There were few officers at Colditz who had not, at one time or another, faced court-martial charges. There was, generally speaking throughout the war, at least one officer languishing in a solitary confinement cell under sentence of death.

Appeals took a long time and the first appeal was not usually successful.

No death sentence was, in fact, carried out from Colditz, but this did not lessen the heavy toll of suffering inflicted on the unfortunate ones imprisoned for years, alone with their thoughts and with the shadow of the shroud spreading over

[1] 'L' Detachment eventually became the 2nd S.A.S. Regiment. The S.A.S. should not be confused with the Long-range Desert Group, which was under the command of (then) Lieutenant-Colonel R. A. Bagnold until August 1941, when it was taken over by Brigadier G. L. Prendergast. Later, in 1944 in Italy, it was commanded by Lieutenant-Colonel David Lloyd Owen.

them. To die or not to die—that was their question. It was worse than knowing the final outcome because, during the eternity of months, there was hope manacled to frustration and utter impotence on the part of the prisoner to help himself. It is one thing, for instance, to struggle madly against death in the depths of the sea, but it must be a far worse agony to lie, pinioned and helpless, in the depths in a submarine, dependent on the help of others that may never come or which may, when it comes, be ineffectual.

The situation in which some of the prisoners thus found themselves became almost intolerable. They were spirited men of fine character, expiating no crime, and the strain told heavily on their nerves. Some indeed were insane before they were finally reprieved. As far as is known, they have recovered.

Goon-baiting was not therefore a pastime to be undertaken lightly. A little surreptitious baiting here and there was always good fun and the risks attached to it added to the excitement. But there were some who attached a more serious view to this side of prison life. Goon-baiting was a weapon—of some potentiality in the prison 'cold war'. If wielded systematically and with perseverance in a campaign extending over several consecutive months, its effect on the morale of the German garrison could be gauged. There were results. It paid dividends.

The waging of this cold war involved risks. The danger of a court-martial death sentence, with its accompanying anguish, was always real and proximate. In the heat of an argument with a German officer, the laying of a restraining hand upon the officer's sleeve was interpreted as 'a personal attack' punishable with death; the raising of an accusing finger close to his face became an insult, a menace; and if it touched his face it was 'an attack' punishable with death.

Happily for the prisoners, there was Lieutenant Alan Campbell, R.A., known as "Black" Campbell. He had been training for the Bar before the war, and devoted himself at Colditz to the defence in court-martial charges brought by the German High Command. Black, the heavy-eyebrowed, black-haired sleuth with the hawk-like nose, gave the German legal pundits no relaxation. When Black himself relaxed, it was to play the piano and write poetry. He had escaped from Tittmoning in broad daylight by climbing over the wire, while twenty-six assistants diverted the sentries armed with machine-guns.

The Germans would not supply him with a copy of their Army Code. He arranged for one to be ghosted out of the Kommandantur. He burnt the midnight oil over this frightening document, written in the heaviest of legal German, a language which, even in its simplest phraseology, lends itself to alternative translations. German is a tortuous language. Its meaning can be twisted, and Black learnt, in time, to make good use of this flexible faculty. He quoted, for the benefit of the German barrister defending, usually a Dr. Naumann, passages of the Code which the Germans omitted to mention, and he shook their confidence by his ability to beat them at their own game of weighting interpretations of text in their favour.

Altogether, he defended forty-two court-martial cases, including thirteen in which the charge was high treason and the sentence death; the plaintiffs being Czech officers flying for the R.A.F. He saved them on a point of International Law. It should be of interest to many, and to legal circles in particular, to read, one day, the story of his long, arduous battle of wits against the German High Command. He fought to ensure that a prisoner had access to his legal advisers in order to prepare his defence. At one period of the war, the number of acquittals he secured on account of his incisive verbal duelling so incensed the Germans at Colditz that they packed him off to another camp—Spangenberg. Within six months he had been caught under a bridge at night, on his way out of his new prison. Sentries shot at him with the aid of spotlights and he was only saved by feigning death. He was returned to Colditz.

Among the many colourful characters he defended was Flying-Officer Peter Tunstall, R.A.F., who, in the course of his sojourn in Germany, underwent five courts-martial with an endless round of appeals and retrials, and paid the price of four hundred and fifteen days of solitary confinement for his convictions with regard to escaping and to the value of Goon-baiting. His last sentence of nine months, for 'insulting the German nation', was awarded too late for him to carry it out. "Pete", a Hampden bomber pilot, was of medium build, fair, with good features and pale blue eyes that had a warning light. His mouth had a humorous curl that could also convey defiance.

In one court-martial, Pete was offered honourable acquittal if he would state that there had been a misunderstanding between himself and the German N.C.O. concerned. The case was one of assault with his index finger! Peter refused to make the statement, adding that the N.C.O. witness for the prosecution was lying. A retrial was ordered and took place at Leipzig. The N.C.O. fainted during cross-examination. Pete quickly seized a carafe of water off the judge's desk and administered it to him, asking the judge, a German general, not to press the poor fellow too hard with awkward questions. Although the prosecution attempted to tamper with the written evidence of defending British witnesses, the court awarded an acquittal. The only spur that drove the Germans to show a semblance of justice was the existence of the Protecting Power —Switzerland—and the threat of 'Nach dem Krieg!'—'After the war!' Black insisted on handing all his briefs to the Protecting Power representatives when they visited the camp towards the end of the war.

Scorgie Price, one of the said British witnesses, went to Leipzig with intentions far removed from the simple resolution to see that justice was done. He went with the idea of making a break. Although the opportunity never presented itself and the expedition was, as far as he was concerned, a failure, it is worth recording what he did.

He wore a standard Army officer's service dress uniform on which had been sewn sky-blue, silver-embroidered épaulettes; sky-blue collar badges and two broad, sky-blue, silver-embellished stripes down the trouser legs. Rex Harrison and Scarlet O'Hara had gone 'all out' to produced a 'variety show' costume. A Frenchman had given him flamboyant, gilded aiguillettes to which he added red tassels. His service dress cap was adorned with silver and blue edging. Over this exotic uniform he wore a simple khaki overcoat.

The German Regimental Sergeant-Major, in command of a heavy guard accompanying the court-martial party, looked askance at what little of the uniform he noticed under the bottom of the overcoat and on Scorgie Price's head. But it was too late to remonstrate. Scorgie had timed matters carefully. The team had to catch a train at the station a mile from the camp. Senior German staff officers would be waiting impatiently at Leipzig. Lieutenant Price was a principal witness in the trial. Besides, the Sergeant-Major was assured that British officers always attended important functions in full-dress uniform—if they possessed it. Lieutenant Price's uniform was the correct ceremonial dress of his regiment, the Gordon Highlanders. The Sergeant-Major could check it, if he liked, but there was the train to catch. . . .

The most important parts of Scorgie's outfit were not visible even when he removed his overcoat. They consisted of the credentials of a high-ranking Hungarian officer on a tour of inspection of frontier patrols. The *pièce de résistance* was a letter of introduction, beautifully forged, complete with the embossed crest of the German Foreign Office and signed by none less than Baron von Neurath, German Ambassador to Hungary.

The *cortège* returned from Leipzig with mixed feelings. The acquittal of Peter Tunstall was a victory, but the return of Scorgie Price was a defeat. Scarlet O'Hara ruefully conceded where his allegiance lay, when he was heard to remark disconsolately, addressing his question to the heavens, "Is there no justice in this God-forsaken country?"

*   *   *   *   *

It must have been the advent of the horse-drawn fire brigade which put ideas into the heads of some of the Goon-baiters. The German Commandant decided to hold a fire practice in the Castle courtyard. It was a ludicrous performance, consisting merely of the entry into the yard, at a hearse-like pace, of a hearse-like fire-engine drawn by two chestnut horses which looked as if they had pulled gun-carriages in the First World War. Hoses were uncoiled. Orders were issued to shut all windows, whereupon weak jets of water rose towards the second floor while the firemen were soaked to the skin by cascading jets which spouted in all directions from the leaking canvas hose.

The rehearsal was quickly terminated. Amid hoots and jeers the fire-engine retired. The prisoners could, obviously, seek no succour in that direction if a fire broke out. The fact that all windows were barred was a little discomforting—but thoughts of fire soon disappeared—ousted by rival and more congenial thoughts of the possibilities of water.

Peter Tunstall was among the first to use the water weapon. An identification parade was in progress in the courtyard one morning, in the chilly early hours, after a major escape. The Dutch were lining up before a table at which sat Hauptmann Eggers—security officer, the official German interpreter, and a *Feldwebel* behind a tall pile of files, card-index forms, paper, pencils, ink, pens and blotting-paper. A bucket of water was poured from a window high up in the wall, behind the seated officials. It drenched the Jerries and left the table a slippery mess of ink pools and sodden paper. Unfortunately for Peter, Hauptmann Priem was also in the courtyard and caught a sidelong view of the face of the culprit. He was 'clapped into jug' and, later, produced for court-martial on charges of: assaulting a superior in the course of his duty; causing a superior to take cover; causing confusion on a roll-call parade, and breaking a prison-camp rule prohibiting the throwing of water out of windows.

A sentence of two months' solitary—to run concurrently— did not prevent him from doing it again. On the second occasion he used an oversize water-bomb. It was high summer and the German Camp Commandant appeared in a spotless white duck uniform, followed by five Germans in the brown uniforms of Nazi politicians, with massive leather belts encircling their paunches, their left arms swathed in broad, red armbands carrying the black Swastika in a white circle. Their shoulders, collars and hats were festooned with tinsel braid like Christmas trees. They were *Gauleiter* from Leipzig and Chemnitz.

The *Gefreite* called "Auntie" ran ahead of them, up the British staircase and burst into the mess-room. Prisoners were having their tea and his shouts of *"Achtung! Achtung!"* were received with the usual compliment of 'raspberries' and rude remarks. Tea continued and his more frenzied *"Achtungs"* were ignored. The Commandant walked in at the head of his procession. He had expected everyone to be standing glassily at attention. Instead he had to wait three minutes—the time it took for the more ardent tea drinkers to note his presence 'officially'.

Benches and chairs scraped, mugs and plates clattered and men rose slowly to their feet, wiping their mouths and blowing their noses with large khaki handkerchiefs in a studied display of insolence of finely calculated duration.

The *Gauleiter* raised their arms in the Nazi salute with their arms bent—Hitler fashion. The salute was returned by the members of one table, including Scorgie Price and Peter Tunstall, in a manner which appeared to please the *Gauleiter*. The prisoners saluted with a variation of the 'V' sign in which the fingers were closed instead of open and the thumb facing inwards. The *Gauleiter*, happy to think that their importance was appreciated, saluted again, and the salute was acknowledged again but with greater vigour. As the procession passed between the rows of men standing to at their tables, the cue was taken up and prisoners everywhere gave the new salute, which was acknowledged punctiliously at every turn by the *Gauleiter*.

They turned, retraced their steps, saluting and being saluted, beaming with smiles at their pleasant welcome and finally left the quarters.

A water-bomb just missed them as they emerged from the British doorway, but spattered the Commandant's duck uniform all over with mud. He shouted for the guard, hurried his visitors through the gates and returned alone. A posse, dispatched upstairs at the double to find the culprit, was not quick enough. Pete was learning; nothing could be pinned on him. The Commandant left the courtyard followed by cries of *"Kellner! Bringen Sie mir einen whisky soda!"*

His exit signalled the arrival of the riot squad. Windows were ordered to be closed; rifles were levelled upwards at those delaying to comply with the shouted commands. Scarlet O'Hara, sleeping peacefully beside an open window, awoke from a siesta in time to hear the tail-end of the shouting. Poking his head out as far as the bars he cautioned the squad: *"Scheissen Sie nicht,* my good men, *scheissen Sie nicht!"*—all to no avail. A bullet zipped through the opening and he closed the window from a kneeling position cursing the ill manners of the "uncouth b——— Huns". The word he had pronounced was *scheissen* not *schiessen.*

The Commandant never appeared again in his white-duck uniform.

*　　*　　*　　*　　*

International games of stoolball between the British and other nationalities had not been popular in the early years of the war. The game had no rules and no referee, and the Continentals were frankly not attuned to such a form of competition.

Then the camp had decided, in 1942, to hold an Olympic Games. Stoolball was not included in the competitions. The Olympics were a great success, and it was thought, generally, a pity that stoolball had not been included.

The upshot was that some British officers conferred together, invented a few rules and produced a referee. British teams were pitted against one another, and the rules modified until they dovetailed with the circumstances and surroundings of the game. Then they were codified and published.

Once more the game was to become international. By that time, however, the Poles had gone, but the French started practice matches of their own with a British referee. Teams consisted of seven a side; scrums were broken up after a few minutes if there were signs of a deadlock and the ball thrown into the air; as before, the ball had to be bounced every three steps or passed in any direction.

A team was composed of three forwards, one half-back, two full-backs and a stoolie.

International matches soon became a monthly feature, and heavy betting took place on the results. For the British, the three forwards were chosen from Peter Storie Pugh, Checko, Dick Howe, Colin McKenzie and Howard Gee; the half-backs from Allan Cheetham, Bush Parker and Peter Allan; the two full-backs from Lulu Lawton, Willie Elstob and Sydney Hall—a Channel Islander, lumberjack and strong-man of Colditz who, with one arm, once lifted an Australian orderly, Archer—a grandfather in the 1914–18 war, by his coat collar and hung him on a peg. The stoolie was usually Bill Goldfinch. Rupert Barry was the recognised international referee. The French team always included Edgar Barras and André Almeras.

The last international match of all, just before the French left Colditz in the early summer of 1943, was the most exciting game ever held in the courtyard. The whole camp, and a large number of Goons, turned out to watch it. The game resulted in a draw at four all. The Jerry spectators were as excited as the rest, some yelling for the British, others for the French.

Although stoolball was the excuse for a 'rough-house', played in a cobble-stone courtyard, nobody hurt himself seriously; Checko is recorded to have once broken a finger during a dive for the stool over the top of a large scrum.

When the French left, enthusiasm for the game waned. It was gradually replaced by basketball—known in Colditz as 'dolley-ball'. It lacked the verve and the rough-and-tumble excitement of stoolball, but was very fast. Bill Scott, a Canadian captured in the Dieppe raid, had represented Canada at basketball in Olympics before the war. He undertook coaching and was the moving spirit in popularising the game. A league was formed. It provided scope for the laying of odds, which the camp bookies, principally Hector Christie and "Screwie" Wright, were not slow to appreciate.

The bars on the courtyard windows saved them from breakage by wide-flung balls during the more hectic moments of stoolball but the Gothic chapel windows were only protected by wire-netting, which was not tough enough for the job. They were consequently often broken. The Germans did nothing about it, preferring to replace the broken panes on rare occasions rather than go to the expense of stronger screens.

One day, shortly after the French farewell international stoolball match, the courtyard gate opened to allow the entry of a little man in grey overalls, known as Willie, carrying a long ladder and accompanied by the usual sentry to look after him.

Peter Tunstall happened to be ambling across the courtyard at the time. He was rather at a loss to know what to do with himself since the Franz Josef escape attempt in which he had been one of the participants. The weather was fine and warm. Spring had turned to summer, and some prisoners had even started sunbathing in the square of sunlight that carpeted the yard at noon.

Pete's normal relaxation, 'Goon-baiting', also seemed to have 'hit a low' since the climax of the water-bombing. He was on the verge of one of those vacuums in a prisoner's life when several months may pass in a procession of painfully slow days, at the end of which the prisoner, waking up, cannot account for the passage of time. There are no signposts, and he appears to have been dreaming through a long, fitful slumber.

Pete sat down absent-mindedly on the stone steps near the canteen and idly watched Willie, an ordinary little workman, carrying a wooden rule, who now slowly climbed his long ladder which he had leant against the wall beside one of the chapel windows. Absent-mindedly Pete's gaze turned to the sentry who stood nearby.

"They're all alike," he muttered to himself, "can't pick out one in a hundred—wonder who thought of the name 'Goons'—just what they are."

Little Willie took measurements, climbed slowly down the ladder again, spoke to the sentry, and walked off towards the courtyard gate.

Peter saw him disappear, wondering vaguely why he had gone away. "Suppose he's gone to fetch the glass." Then his eye roamed once more towards the sentry. The latter was standing stolidly on guard five yards from the ladder and facing the courtyard.

The reaction of a well-trained "Kriegie" was instantaneous. Peter rose; the vacuum had filled. There was a glint in his eye. He returned hurriedly to the British quarters and button-holed the Weasel (Don Donaldson), who in turn shouted to-wards a far corner of the almost empty room.

"Heh!—come over here, you browned-off eagle—I want to talk to you—quick."

Bag Dickenson yawned and slowly rose from a bed in the corner. "Are you addressing me?" he queried, tucking his shirt into his trousers as he walked over. He sat on a bed opposite the other two. "You've upset my sleep quota, you rocky mountain buzzard."

A few minutes later they descended together to the court-yard where they separated.

Don sat down on the cobbles. There was nothing unusual about that. He sat near the sentry, upright, against a wall and facing him. He started playing with his hands. Looking wide-eyed into the sky, he made his hands climb Jacob's ladders; he played churches and people and the preacher in the pulpit; he made his hands into mice which chased each other all over his body, behind his back, round his neck, under his shirt and up his trouser legs; he counted his fingers and started all over again. He not only attracted the gaze of the sentry, but that of a small group of mildly amused spectators whom he had to motion away so that the Goon's view was not obstructed.

In the meantime, Peter Tunstall and Bag Dickenson re-moved the ladder, which they carried into the porch at the bottom of the British staircase, behind the sentry's back. They started to climb the spiral steps but found that the twenty-five-foot ladder would not circumvent the curves.

It became securely wedged. There was only one solution, which did not require much thought. While the browned-off eagle fetched a saw (made out of a gramophone spring) from his tool kit, which was the best in Colditz, Pete returned to the courtyard and signalled the Weasel to carry on. This was asking for something, because Don was not prepared for a long solo act. Pete could see his mind turning over as his eyeballs rolled, following the juggling motion of his hands. He left him to it and went back to the staircase, where Bag and he were soon engaged in an argument as to how much of the ladder should be sawn off. Bag was playing for safety while Pete insisted on running it close. They compromised at five feet from one end.

It took ten minutes to saw through both legs of the ladder, which they did to the accompaniment of generally encouraging, but sometimes very rude, remarks from passers-by navigating the obstruction on the stairs.

Pete was wondering what the Weasel was doing and how soon Willie might return. He was delighted to see, when he descended to the courtyard with a five-foot length of ladder under his arm, that the little fellow had not yet come back and that the Weasel's knot of spectators had grown. Don was finding great difficulty in clearing a view for the sentry, who was genuinely intrigued by his efforts to scratch his left ear with his right foot.

Pete leaned the five-foot length of ladder where the twenty-five-foot one had previously reposed and retired to a distance to view the effect. At that moment little Willie was let into the courtyard again, carrying a large square pane of glass carefully in his arms. Don, seeing that his act was no longer required, stood up with a final handspring and walked off hurriedly to the French quarters. The knot of idlers was dispersing when the new focus of attention presented itself. The sentry and little Willie stood, side by side, gazing incredulously, with jaws dropped, at a transformation of which Lewis Carroll might have been proud.

The prisoners started to laugh. The sentry shook his head slowly from side to side and Willie looked up and down the chapel wall. They faced each other and Willie asked, " *Was ist geschehen?*" A crowd was gathering and the laughter was growing. The sentry answered, shrugging his shoulders and looking frightened as if he had seen a ghost. "*Ich weiss nicht. Sie war bestimmt hier. Ist da vielleicht ein Poltergeist?*"

Little Willie laid the pane of glass against the wall, took out a large handkerchief, mopped his brow and blew his nose to recover his composure. It was not easy. There were faces now at almost every window, and laughter was echoing round the courtyard. He and the sentry were the only figures on the stage, playing before a large audience.

He approached the five-foot ladder, picked it up, turned it over and adjusted it under his arm. The sentry, crestfallen, picked up the glass, fell in behind him and, in single file, they marched forlornly across the courtyard through a gangway formed between cheering prisoners.

CHAPTER XI

THE FLYING DUTCHMAN

ON June 7th, 1943, the Dutch contingent received orders to pack up and leave at twelve hours' notice. This did not perturb them, as they had known of the move for a week through information passed inside the camp. Their contraband was safely stowed in prepared suitcases. One Dutchman packed his suitcase for the last time at Colditz. He had packed it every morning and unpacked it again every night for two years.

The Dutch were bound for Stanislau, in Poland. Their departure would mean the end of a long chapter in the story of Oflag IVC; a story of close collaboration with the British, of unfailing understanding and generosity, of courage and good humour. They would be missed everywhere in the camp. The smartest 'turn out' on parade and in chapel, their divine contempt of the Germans, the Hawaiian orchestra, would be no more; Vandy's inimitable personality would disappear from the Castle and only his ghost would haunt the corridors in the minds of the men who remained. Soon, even those memories would fade, but, for all who knew Vandy and his Dutchmen well, they can never fade entirely. A pleasant aura surrounds them to this day, and an honoured place remains for them in those inner recesses of the mind where narrow distinctions fade but a deep impression rests. As the tracks left by a stream of vehicles which pass along a sandy road twist and intertwine and eventually merge into two great ruts, so the mind recollects an episode, a chapter, an era that has long since passed.

The whole camp turned out to see them off.

"We'll miss you, Vandy," said Dick.

"I'm *rather* sorry to go," replied Vandy, who was obviously deeply moved. "Ve may haf a chance to escape on the vay. I haf many men prepared. Good-bye, Dick. Ve had good times together. In Colditz ve haf shown those Huns how to behave themselves."

"Yes!" said Dick. "It's funny, isn't it, how well they've behaved in Colditz considering the hell we give them?"

"Ach! Dick, that is the secret. You must alvays give them hell. If you do not, you are finished. The Hun, he vill sit on you and sqvash you and bully you to death unless you bully him. He only understands that. I was in camps before I came to Colditz. There I saw vot happened. Germans despised the prisoners and gave them hell. Here it was othervise. You vere all brave men—you had proved it—and you gave them hell from the virst days. So, they respect you and are afraid to bully. It is a simple qvestion of domination by vorce of the character. Do not vorget! Goodbye, Dick . . . and . . . Gott bless England! . . ."

So, the irrepressible Vandy, the officer in charge of all the Dutch escapes but never of his own, departed.

Hardly had Vandy left the courtyard with his men to be searched in the Kommandantur before entraining, than he gave expression to his deep convictions with regard to the Germans. His large suitcase was a maze of secret pockets, and had a false bottom filled with escaping contraband. The Germans took from the open suitcase an Army overcoat, the collar of which Vandy had altered and dyed for civilian purposes. Speaking German fluently and with a fine colloquial vocabulary, equal to that of any *Wehrmacht* sergeant-major, he seethed with indignation, mounted a stool and harangued the whole room. He would not move without his coat. He would lie on the floor and they would have to carry him. How right Vandy was! The Germans knew that he would lie on the floor. They knew that bayonets would not move him. It was 'vorce of character' all right. The major in charge gave in, and his men were sufficiently subdued by Vandy's oratory and by his determination not to look further into his belongings.

The fifty-eight Dutchmen voyaged for four days in two old-fashioned railway coaches, crammed together like sardines.

The Colditz guards, numbering thirty-three, under the command of a Hauptmann, stood at the windows of the compartments and along the corridor. The windows were plastered with barbed wire. On the evening of the second day, near Teschen on the Polish border, while water-bottles were being filled at a stop, Baron van Lynden, a cavalry lieutenant and an aide-de-camp of Queen Wilhelmina, escaped. He was soon missed, and the German captain of the guard, stopping the train at Krakau, refused to continue farther without guard reinforcements from the local garrison. Twenty more guards were piled into the coaches on the third evening and remained with them until they reached Lemberg (Lwow). The party reached their destination, without further incident, at the end of the fourth day.

Stanislau is an industrial town in the province of Galicia, in the south-east of Poland. The camp to which they were conducted was two miles from the railway station. It had once been an Austrian cavalry barracks and later a Polish prison. On their arrival at the station they were met by a German officer with a bicycle. The Colditz Hauptmann flatly refused to escort the prisoners to the camp without adequate supervision; thirty-three guards were not enough. Again reinforcements arrived from the prison. The fifty-seven Dutchmen were then marched, in four squads at intervals, surrounded by a total of fifty-six guards and eight N.C.O.s and led by two officers, along the Adolf Hitler Strasse, the main street of Stanislau. Silent, sympathetic Poles clustered on the pavements in small groups to watch them pass. They arrived at the camp singing patriotic Dutch songs, and were delighted to see Dutch faces at the windows to greet them. They were all officers and cadets of the Dutch forces who had remained in Holland on a bogus *parole* at the beginning of the war. In May 1942 one hundred of them had been shot for underground activities and about two thousand had been transported to Stanislau. Their morale was not good, but the influence of men like Vandy changed the atmosphere of the prison within a matter of weeks.

Vandy had his showdown with the Prussian *Abwehr* officer

of Stanislau immediately on arrival. The latter was showing off in front of the Captain and the guards from Colditz and began browbeating the prisoners. He 'went' for a lieutenant in Vandy's platoon and 'caught a packet' himself for addressing a junior officer in a squad under the command of a more senior officer. Vandy took the opportunity, with righteous indignation on his side, to explode with anger and concluded by appealing in German to the Colditz Hauptmann who was handing over his assignment. The Colditz sentries thoroughly enjoyed the situation.

"Herr Hauptmann, is it not your experience from Colditz that we prisoners have always behaved with correctness and decorum because the German officers have treated the prisoners in the same manner?"

The Hauptmann could only answer "Yes", although he was still smarting under the loss of one of his prisoner contingent.

This collusion left the Stanislau *Abwehr* officer at a loss. Vandy believed in attacking from the start, and never letting go once he had the advantage.

To emphasise the contempt in which the Dutchmen held the Germans of Stanislau, and the *Abwehr* officer in particular, three of the Colditz party escaped from the first floor of the building within an hour of arrival. The windows overlooked a drop of twenty feet and beyond that a garden and the highway to Hungary. The drop was, nevertheless, too much for two of the three, who twisted their ankles in the fall. A window collapsed with a crash of splintering glass at the psychological moment and gave the alarm. Otherwise all the Dutchmen would have disappeared within ten minutes.

The two men with twisted ankles were recaught immediately, but the third, Van Lingen, was free several days before he was recaptured in the Carpathian Mountains, having asked for food at the farm of a *Volksdeutscher* by mistake.

Van Lynden, who had escaped from the train, was recaught after some days at Görlitz, and returned, at first, to Colditz much to the amusement of the inmates. He remained in the cells for a week before removal to Stanislau.

Vandy was soon recognised in the camp as 'Escape Chief'. Among the younger officers, and especially the cadets who had been incarcerated in 1942, there was a feeling that they had been duped, by their seniors in Holland, into betraying their country by giving their *parole*. They had little confidence left in those around them. The advent of the Colditz diehards caused a spiritual rejuvenation among them, and the blood of patriots began to course once more through their veins.

The camp was separated into two halves; the officers being kept apart from the cadets (aspirants). Vandy placed one of his most trusted cadets, Aak Hageman, in charge of escape matters in their barracks. The morale of the whole camp rose steadily throughout the summer and autumn of 1943.

On November 30th three more Dutchmen escaped. One, travelling alone, made his way to Hungary and later to London. The other two, former Colditz men, Charles Douw van der Krap and Fritz E. Kruimink, nicknamed "Beer" by the English, reached Warsaw, where they disappeared into Bor Komorowski's underground. Beer was eventually dispatched to Paris, where he fought with the French Resistance and took part in the relief of Paris.

Van der Krap and an Englishman were stopped by a German sentry one evening on a bridge over the Vistula in Warsaw. He demanded their papers. While he was examining Douw's, the Englishman gave him a right to the jaw which sent him over the balustrade into the river and through the ice. The next day the Germans found the body under the ice and Douw's papers lying nearby. The Poles thought it was time he moved. With typical *sangfroid* they sent him as a fireman on the engine of a German military train which carried him back to Holland. Van der Krap took part in the Battle of Arnhem, and was rescued with the few survivors of the Airborne Division who were helped back to the Allied lines.

Then came the 'big move' on January 10th, 11th and 12th, 1944. It was public knowledge when it came, and was, in fact, considered to be rather late in the day, as the Germans in Stanislau were terrified of a Russian advance long before

January. This time the move was to a huge camp at Neu-Brandenburg in Mecklenburg, a hundred miles north of Berlin, housing Americans, French, Poles and Serbs in different compounds.

Vandy and his second in command, Lieutenant Dames, made the escape preparations and gave Hageman the assistance he needed to organise the cadets. In general, the intention was not to make a break on the journey unless a reasonable opportunity presented itself; the new camp was reputed to have good possibilities. However, before leaving Stanislau there were several escape schemes on hand to be put into immediate action.

Vandy and Dames first concealed twelve men under the floor of their theatre auditorium. Secondly, they equipped six others to re-enact the escape of Douw and Beer in 1943, which had depended on the help of Yugoslavian orderlies. Four of the six were Colditz men, the fifth non-Colditz, and the sixth a Dutch Rear-Admiral. Thirdly, among the cadets, four men, of whom two from Colditz, were also concealed in the camp before departure.

The move was organised by the Germans, in three batches, one on each of three consecutive days.

The cadets departed on the first day. Before leaving, the *Abwehr* officer made a speech. He said that it was no use trying to escape because: (*a*) it was mid-winter with snow everywhere, (*b*) their boots would be removed on the train, and (*c*) he had transported thirty thousand Italians from Italy without a single escape. This incredibly tactless approach was enough for the cadets.

When they arrived at Neu-Brandenburg there were sixty-eight missing. Many more had escaped, but had been recaptured at various stations and put on the train again. A German sentry, who spent hours shooting at the cadets as they escaped, said afterwards that the men leaving the train reminded him of a game of tiddlywinks.

On the second day the senior officers left. One escaped on the way to the station and hid in a culvert. He was seen by a guard who fired twice into the culvert, wounding him seriously. He was transported back to the Stanislau camp.

On the journey, the same guard shot and killed another Dutchman who had made a hole through the floor of his wagon and lay between the tracks waiting for the train to move off after a stop in the open country.

A third officer jumped the train, fell and remained unconscious on the tracks. A train, passing in the other direction, cut off both his legs. In addition, forty-four others escaped.

The next day, the third batch, including the Colditz group, travelled. Thirty escaped. On the way, the third train, like a trawl-net, picked up those recaptured after escaping from the first two trains. The Dutchman who had lost his legs was taken on board. His case was given up as hopeless by German doctors, but a Dutch surgeon attended him in Neu-Brandenburg, day and night for a week, and saved his life.

The move was a major disaster for the Germans. When they counted up the totals at the end of three days, one hundred and fifty prisoners were missing.

A special alarm was broadcast covering Germany and Poland. Hitler was advised of the escape and Himmler's minions were set to their work of extermination. The code name for the order was known to the Gestapo as 'Stufe Drei'.

It was many a day before Vandy could add up the final score of this escape. It went somewhat like this:

1. The twelve who were hidden in the theatre had to give themselves up after a week as the camp remained fully guarded though empty. They followed the main body to Neu-Brandenburg.

2. Of the six who escaped (including the Admiral) two, the Admiral and Diederik Baron van Lynden (ex-Colditz), reached Roumania with identity papers and exit and entry visas supplied to Vandy through his wife from the Dutch underground. They were freed by the Russians and sent to England. The other three (ex-Colditz), including Captain Veenendaal, R.N.I.A., and Lieutenant Donkers, R.N.I.A.,

reached the Dutch border, where they were trapped. The sixth was recaught on the Czechoslovak frontier. They were all later forwarded to Neu-Brandenburg.

3. Of the four cadets who hid in Stanislau before the move: one reached Hungary, was released by the Russians and found his way to England; one was recaught and sent back to Stanislau, where he disappeared; and two ex-Colditz men, Hans van Seydlitz-Kurzbach and Aire Ligtermoet, escaped to Russia, where they were imprisoned along with Germans. Ligtermoet, who died in Odessa in 1947, was awarded a posthumous decoration. Van Seydlitz is still missing.

4. Ten officers, including the officer wounded in the culvert and the cadet from 3 above, were submitted to 'Stufe Drei', and one officer was shot dead under the train.

5. In spite of the snow on the Carpathian Mountains and the absence of boots on their feet, seven men reached Hungary.

6. Three more arrived safely in Holland and two reached Switzerland *via* Vienna.

Totalling up: one hundred and sixty-four men attempted to escape, of whom fifteen made home-runs, eleven were murdered, one had his legs cut off, two died in Russian prisons, and one hundred and thirty-seven were recaptured.

*   *   *   *   *

Within eight days of arriving at Neu-Brandenburg, on January 22nd, the first escape, organised by Vandy and Dames, took place. Twelve men, seven of them from Colditz, disappeared from the camp. One, ex-Colditz, named Fraser, reached England *via* Sweden; one is missing; one was executed, and the remainder returned to Neu-Brandenburg.

These men were incorrigible.

A new block of eleven solitary confinement cells had to be constructed beside the old, rotten, timber-frame barracks in which they were housed in this camp. The cells remained fully occupied into the autumn of 1944.

In September 1944 many of the older officers were moved to a camp at Tittmoning, not far from Salzburg in Austria, owing to the damp, unhealthy conditions existing in Neu-Branden-burg.

The record of Vandy's sixty-four officers and cadets, mostly of the Dutch East Indies Forces, who were sent from Holland in 1940 to Colditz *via* another camp—Juliusburg—is here set down: thirteen made home-runs; two others reached Russia, one is dead, one missing; and, in addition, this company can lay claim to twenty-six 'gone-aways'.

CHAPTER XII

ROUNDABOUT

THE summer was in full course when the French, at last, after
several false starts, received orders to pack in preparation for a
move. They were going north-eastward to Lübeck, where the
Poles had gone. The move was to include the Belgians, but left
behind, temporarily, a second batch of eighty French for
whom there was no room on the first train. The second batch
also included a few de Gaullist Frenchmen who, eventually,
remained permanently.

Shortly after the departure of the main French body, sixty-
five British officers arrived from Oflag VIIB, Eichstätt. This
raised the total of the British contingent to about one hundred
and sixty souls.

The Eichstätt mob, as they were sometimes called, com-
prised the men who had broken out of their camp by tunnel on
the night of June 3rd–4th.

The tunnel was well engineered and was about forty-five
yards long. Unfortunately, none of the sixty-five who escaped
made the home-run.

After completing their bout of confinement, during which
three made another break, they were dispatched to Colditz in
several parties. The three who made the second break were
Gordon Rolfe, D.S.O. (Major, Royal Canadian Signals), Bill
("Dopey") Miller (Lieutenant, Royal Canadian Engineers) and
Douglas Moir (Lieutenant, Royal Tank Regiment). They did
not travel far and soon turned up again at Colditz.

Among those who arrived from Eichstätt were: Mike
Edwards (Lieutenant, R. W. Fusiliers), George Drew (Lieutenant, Northamptonshire Regiment), Charles Forester (Lieutenant, Rifle Brigade), Bill Scott, M.C. (Lieutenant, Essex

Scottish, Canada), John Penman, M.C. (Lieutenant, Argyll and Sutherland Highlanders), and Lieutenant-Colonel C. C. I. Merrit, V.C. (South Saskatchewan Regiment). Captains the Lord Arundell of Wardour (Wiltshire Regiment) and the Earl of Hopetoun (Lothian and Border Horse) were also Eichstätt tunnellers who trickled into Colditz.

Others who arrived at about this period were Charlie Upham, V.C. and bar, the New Zealander; Tony Rolt, the motor-racing driver; and Michael Burn, M.C., *The Times* reporter who had been captured at St. Nazaire.

The opportunity offered by the move of a large party was not lost upon the old hands in the camp. When the Poles had left in 1942, Bertie Moustead had changed places with Count Felix Jablonowski.

Bertie Boustead was tall and thin and exchanged with Felix Jablonowski, who was of small build. Boustead knew no Polish but learnt off by heart his Polish prison number. During the departure proceedings, each time the name Jablonowski was called, he stepped forward and, in reply to whatever the German interpreter asked him in Polish, he said, *"Trzysta pięcdz-iesiąt siedem"* which was Felix's prison number—357. It did not matter what the interpreter asked, he always obtained the same answer. The Germans made a habit of asking for the prisoners' numbers so that Bertie managed to 'get away with it' on the final parade and again in Lübeck, the camp to which he was sent with the Poles.

After a week, Bertie's name was called out at *Appell*. The Germans wanted some information about a parcel addressed to Jablonowski. The interpreter asked in Polish, "What are the contents of the parcel?"

Bertie replied, *"Trzysta pięcdziesiąt siedem."* The interpreter asked him a second and a third time, but always received the same answer: *"Trzysta pięcdziesiąt siedem."* The comedy could not last long. The Germans checked up on Jablonowski's particulars and Bertie had 'had it'.

At Colditz, Felix was soon busy answering a string of awkward questions in atrocious English. He was 'rumbled' and an exchange of prisoners took place causing the Goons much annoyance. Neither Felix nor Bertie managed to escape on the journey, which was the purpose of the whole subterfuge, owing to the number of guards employed—an N.C.O. and two sentries to each prisoner.

This exchange had now passed into history. The only memory which remained vivid was that of Felix Jablonowski sitting up in his bunk on his first morning in the British quarters wearing a hair-net. He had to be told that the practice might make him conspicuous.

When the Eichstätt British arrived, Dick immediately prepared an exchange with some of the French still at Colditz who were due to leave any day. The faces of the 'old lags' were too well known to the Germans, but some of the 'new boys' might be exchanged successfully.

Lieutenant Cazaumayou and two other Frenchmen quickly responded to the idea and three promising-looking British officers among the new arrivals were picked out. They were Lieutenant T. M. Barratt, The Black Watch (R.M.R.) of Canada, commonly known as "Jo-Jo the Dog-faced Boy," who took the place of Cazaumayou, and Lieutenant D. K. Hamilton, R.A., and Lieutenant C. E. Sandback, Cheshire Yeomanry.

These three left Colditz with the last French contingent. They had no opportunities for escaping *en route*. They arrived at Lübeck, where there was a huge French camp, and were soon lost in the crowd. They began reconnoitring for an escape. It was high summer—July. The weather was fine and dry, most suitable for a long trek across country but, within four days, Hamilton and Sandback were unearthed, evidently from the Colditz end. The discovery would have come about through photograph identity checks on the Eichstätt men in Colditz, which were due in any case.

"Peter" Barratt, however, appeared to have a respite. He knew it would not be for long, so he arranged with one of his French colleagues from Colditz to make a further exchange if his name was called. The next day it was. Sous-Lieutenant

Diedler presented himself as Lieutenant Barratt, and was whisked back to Colditz with Hamilton and Sandback.

Barratt was caught a few days later leaving the Lübeck camp under a pile of sacks in a cart. He was escorted to the Kommandantur, where he gave his name as Diedler and was marched off to the cells.

The next morning he was cross-examined about his attempted escape, and the German-French interpreter began to think he was dealing with a moron. Barratt knew well enough how to say, "*La plume de ma tante*", but his French lessons at school had not provided for the present contingency.

He was soon unmasked.

The Germans were confronted with a problem. They had already disposed of a Lieutenant Barratt under the alias of Lieutenant Cazaumayou. Now they had a second Lieutenant Barratt under the alias of Sous-Lieutenant Diedler. They even began to have misgivings as to the seriousness of the name Diedler. It had an ironic, Anglo-Saxon ring. They unravelled the mystery eventually, but it annoyed them considerably, just as it amused the Frenchmen at Lübeck, to know that the prisoners were playing with them.

*   *   *   *   *

The companionship of men like Gigue and Madin, of the French stoolball players, and the French language teachers was badly missed in Colditz, but their memory was kept alive by the wireless-set the French left behind them. Dick took over the control of the secret studio. Lulu Lawton and Hector Christie together organised the stooging teams required for the periods of news reception and the routine camouflaging of the secret entrance to the studio.

Michael Burn, adept at shorthand, became the first news reporter. He was known as 'The Scribe'.

The operation of entering or leaving the studio took five minutes. Stooges were posted on each of the four floors of the building, two more in the courtyard and one at the entrance to the upper attics where the studio was concealed. The last stooge held the key and was responsible for the door through which passed the operator—Dick, the scribe—Mike, and the camouflage-man—Lulu. The three crossed two more attics. Lulu went to work at a point where the roof beams and the attic floor joined. Floor-boards were removed, then a sawn length of timber joist, then a four-inch depth of under-floor rubble and, finally, more boards. The operator and scribe descended into the studio. Lulu replaced all camouflaging as he worked, and then retired. The heavy layer of dust over everything in the attic was a great bugbear and necessitated careful treatment. A knocking signal at the end of fifteen or twenty minutes warned the stooges that the news reception was over. The process would be repeated to extract the two officers from the studio. Mike then retired to a quiet nook, enlarged on his shorthand notes and prepared his bulletin. When this was ready he called together his assistant news reporters from their various quarters, and copies were made from his original.

As the Allied pressure increased from 1944 onwards, news bulletins were demanded ever more frequently and the work became too much for one team to carry out efficiently. The studio operation, in fact, was carried out so frequently that the danger of over-confidence or staleness on the job became very real. The team consisted of no less than eleven officers. Dick decided to institute a second team. He trained Jimmy Yule as operator. Jim Rogers, who had begun studying shorthand furiously as soon as he saw his principal joy in life being taken from him by a news reporter who was proficient in this art, was appointed scribe of the new team, to his intense satisfaction. Norman Forbes undertook the camouflage work; Hector Christie trained a second team of stooges.

In the event of being trapped in the attics or studio, two methods of escape were available, depending on where the Germans were.

When the French tunnel had been discovered, the ropes which had been used by the French for the disposal of their tunnel debris were removed, leaving the long cylindrical sleeves from the top of the tower to the ground-floor empty. There was access to the sleeves from the attic.

In effect, the radio team of three had a fast-descending lift at their service. A piece of iron plate reposed over the sleeves at each floor level. If an alarm was given when all three were in the attic above the studio, they waited until the last moment, in case of false alarms. As soon as they heard the German keys in the attic lock (and having checked that the iron plates were in place!), they dropped, one after the other, down the cylindrical sleeves, using their arms and thighs as brakes. An exit was, nowadays, conveniently provided by the Germans two floors below—they used it for inspection purposes. All three could thus descend two floors in a matter of seconds and sortie by the exit into their own quarters. The safe descent of the sleeves required practice, because if the braking was not sufficient the body accelerated downwards and a heavy fall could result. Of course, if the iron plates were not over the holes there was the prospect of a vertiginous descent, out of control, to the ground-floor.

If the operator and scribe were ever actually to be trapped in the studio, there was a last line of retreat. The studio reposed partly over the solid outside wall, partly over the ceiling of the (now) British quarters. The joists and ceiling lathes were exposed in the studio, and the latter could be broken in an emergency simply by jumping on them. The operators would then fall into the room below. In the event of surprise, they could, at least, save the wireless-set by the emergency exit. Fortunately, this method of evacuating the studio never had to be used. The sleeve self-propelled lift, on the other hand, was frequently employed as the Germans made surprise searches of the attics. Although its existence was known, the whereabouts of the wireless-set remained a secret from the Germans until the end of the war.

The electric power for the receiving set was tapped from the Castle mains. The supply was 220 volts D.C., that is, direct current. The set was manufactured to work on 110 volts D.C., and a dropping resistance had, therefore, to be employed in the circuit. The mains supply was switched off by the Germans at night, but this obstacle was circumvented by tapping the positive lead, using it as supply and by earthing the negative lead to a lightning conductor.

All went well until the R.A.F. and the U.S.A.A.F. set about obliterating the power-stations. Then, for long periods, there was no power at all.

The prisoners had to have their news. Dick and the scribes were in a quandary.

Officers used to mess together in groups of between seven and ten, depending upon how many could be conveniently seated around the various-sized kitchen tables which were provided. A group seldom remained more than a few months together. The petty exasperations that pass in everyday life were liable to accumulate, to combine and become distorted into grotesque catastrophes, causing major upheavals in the stifling conditions of the prison. One group alone is known to have remained constant throughout the war. Its members were Padre "Dicky" Heard, Harry Elliott, Kenneth Lockwood and Dick Howe. They formed a durable nucleus at their mess table around which others gyrated, sometimes attracted, sometimes repelled. It was to be expected that the variety of topics of conversation was gradually exhausted as the war continued until, among the old guard when at table, there was scarcely any object in conversing. It was as if each could read the mind of the other.

Even mannerisms were so well known that their subconscious motivation was understood. Questions could be answered before they were asked. When Dick Howe stroked his nose he was given a cigarette, because that was what he would have asked for in a few seconds' time. If Harry twirled his moustache with one hand and stared momentarily into space, his table companions sat back, wondering which of his many funny stories Harry was about to tell. If he stroked his moustache with both hands, the question was, "Which Goon has got your back up this time, Harry?" because, indeed, that was what he was going to disclose. When Padre Heard coughed gently twice, it meant he wanted "A pinch of salt, please," and he was given it, usually, before the words came to his lips. When he gazed fixedly out of a nearby window overlooking the chapel it was understood by his colleagues that his remarks, in a few minutes' time, would concern the chapel organ and he would relate how the Germans never repaired the bellows nor the missing keys and stops.

The association of ideas—the sequence of thoughts that fill up the mental activity of man—is like the pathway in a labyrinth. New openings and new paths appear at every turn, tempting the mind to travel along them. Concentration is, presumably, the art of not being deflected, or of consciously noting the deflection so as not to take the wrong path a second time.

Dick Howe was certainly not concentrating when he sat, one day, at the mess table mentally bemoaning another power cut that had ruined the whole day's new bulletins. He was staring vacantly in the direction of Dicky Heard who, in turn, was staring fixedly out of the window. Dick was suddenly thinking about organs and then about bellows, then about electric motors and then generators. At this point there must have been a short circuit somewhere in his mind because Dick jumped as if he had been electrocuted and banged the board in front of him with his fist. "I've got it!" was all he said and left the table.

He repaired to the chapel, mounted the miniature spiral staircase that led to the choir loft and examined the electric motor that worked the bellows that worked the organ.

"If the Jerries won't repair the bellows," he thought, "we may as well, at least, make use of the motor."

Electricity supplied to an electric motor turns it. If an electric motor is turned by other means it can supply electricity. Upon this simple principle Colditz wireless news reception was made independent of a mains supply of current. The prisoners built their own power-station!

Dick 'borrowed' the organ motor. It was wired into a closed circuit through the ordinary wiring of the camp in such a way as to feed the radio. The motor, when required, was produced from a hiding-place and bolted on to a firm platform. Bos'n

Crisp provided a rope pulley-belt, fifty feet long, which fitted the 'V' section rim of the motor pulley. A large wooden, collapsible, driving-wheel was manufactured. It was five feet in diameter, made in three segments, bolted together, and it was mounted on trunnions attached to a cupboard which was laid flat on the floor in the dormitory. When not in use, the cupboard resumed the vertical and the wheel was dismantled. The trunnions and wheel segments were transformed into shelves, angle-pieces, back-boards and loose, nondescript pieces of wood.

The wheel was known as the treadmill, and it amply deserved the name, because the reduction gear-ratio to the generator pulley was, as might be expected, not sufficient to provide the generator speed necessary for the current required without immense exertion on the part of relays of the camp's strong men. The power plant worked well. The background interference of the unsmoothed current was noticeable, though not disturbing. Its volume depended on the steadiness of the output, which depended, in turn, on the freshness of the slaves.

After severe bombing raids the slave-gang, consisting of men such as Checko, Charles Lockett and Mike Edwards, was called out for work on the treadmill in order to provide the camp with the news and the Radio Parson's bulletins, precious links with the outside world and with reality. What would the Radio Parson think! What might have been his thoughts had he known, as he came over the air, that men were sweating at a home-made treadmill to turn a chapel organ motor in order to feed a wireless-set so that they could hear the gospel he was preaching! Could he have heard the swearing and the groaning of the perspiring slaves! Could he have seen the glow of the tell-tale lamp in the parallel circuit as it rose and fell, accompanied by the voice of the foreman of the slave-gang—now cautioning "Slower!" then urging "Faster! Faster" and ending with "Steady at that speed!" as the intensity of light indicated the strength of current being produced.

There were several reasons why the men in Colditz went to

such pains to ensure that no news bulletin was ever missed, but it may be revealing to mention one reason in particular. It was imperative that no report of the capture or surrender of any town to the Allies should be overlooked. Large sums of money were involved for the lucky holders of winning tickets in the continuously running 'Town Falling' sweepstake.

CHAPTER XIII

WALLY AND TUBBY

NEWS concerning the men who escaped successfully from Colditz in 1941 and 1942 trickled into the camp slowly, and was sketchy when it arrived, to say the least of it. Nevertheless, when it came it boosted the prisoners' morale considerably. A first wave of elation started about a week after an escape, when, with the continued absence of the escapers and glum reactions from the Germans upon questioning by the S.B.O. as to their whereabouts, it was reasonably safe to assume that the men were out of enemy territory, provided they had not been killed *en route*.

Reliable confirmation arrived by various routes: sometimes a picture postcard slipped through the censor's net, written in a disguised hand from a fictitious character, but leaving no uncertainty in the mind of the recipient as to the meaning of the seemingly innocuous phrases in the text.

Hank Wardle, often called Murgatroyd by Rupert Barry, had thus written to him from Switzerland in November 1942:

We are having a holiday here [in Switzerland] and are sorry you are not with us. Give our dear love to your friend Dick. Love from

Harriette and Phyllis Murgatroyd.

"Harriette" and "Phyllis" with the H. and P. heavily emphasised, were obvious cover-names for Hank and Pat.

The successful exits of Colditz escapers leaked into the camp during the spring and summer of 1943. Details of the escapes never reached the prisoners, and the stories which they would have given much to hear were left untold until years later.

On the other hand, inaccurate reports, rumours and half-truths became rife, sometimes even leading men astray by causing them to concentrate their efforts on doomed escape routes. For instance, one conclusion reached by some of the Colditz escapers in 1943 and 1944 was an unfortunate one, though deduced from a sound premise; sound, in that, as the rate of outflow of escapers from Switzerland across German-occupied France to Spain and England from November 1942 onwards was woefully slow, men argued it was better to seek other frontiers; unfortunate, in that other frontiers presented all the problems of the unknown, whereas, in Colditz, there reposed the secret of a well-documented frontier crossing into Switzerland, which had proved successful on repeated occasions.

Bill Fowler reached Switzerland safely in the early hours of September 13th, 1942. He reached Spain on January 30th, 1943, and was in England on March 27th, over six months from the time of his arrival in neutral territory. Billie Stephens took even longer. He arrived in Switzerland in October 1942 and landed in England a year and eight months later. Men who escaped to Sweden were back in England in a matter of days, but along the escape routes from the camps to Sweden the casualties could be counted in tens if not in hundreds. The old adage, 'Better safe than sorry', was applicable in so far as safety can ever be held to apply to escaping; 'Slow but sure' suffers from the same inexactitude. Perhaps 'Better slow than sorry' is the answer.

Although the escapades of Wally Hammond and Tubby Lister, free in Germany like a couple of Don Quixotes, took place in December 1942, titbits of information concerning their adventures reached Colditz only by the summer of 1943.

Going back a little in time, what happened was this:

One day, at the end of November 1942, Wally asked Dick Howe what he thought was the best remaining way of escaping from the Castle and Dick's reply was of crystal clarity. He answered dryly, "The best way, Wally, is through the main gate." Dick's accompanying grin conveyed an ironical twist to his dryness.

Wally and Tubby were both Engine-room Artificers. The former had been rescued by his captors from the submarine H.M.S./M. *Shark*, on July 6th, 1940, and the latter from H.M.S./M. *Seal*, in May 1940. Wally was small in build, with a barrel chest. He dressed neatly and gave a clear-cut impression. His features stood out distinctly against a sallow complexion of uniform tint from his neck to his deep-furrowed forehead. His eyes were sharp and watchful, like those of a bird. Tubby was very much his opposite: taller, much heavier and inclined to run easily to fat, with a rosy complexion, a big nose and a casual air. He would accept life as he found it, with one proviso—that he never lost an opportunity of improving his lot if it came his way. But he would not go out of his way to find it. Wally provided the initial driving-force and, once roused, Tubby displayed all the ingenuity of a sleuth.

They made a formal application to the German Camp Commandant to be removed from Colditz and to be sent to their rightful camp—they were not officers; they were Chief Petty Officers. Dick engineered a demand from the S.B.O. to the Commandant to the effect that the officers objected to their presence in the camp. An interview took place. They expressed the opinion that they did not want to live with officers.

The Commandant's dictum was:

"You escaped with them—you must live with them."

To which Wally replied, "The only reason we escaped was because we had nothing to do."

In parenthesis, they had been caught in Hamburg with a number of naval officers tunnelling their way out of another camp—Marlag Nord.

"Are you prepared to work for Germany?" asked the Commandant.

"Yes," was the answer.

A few weeks passed. Then, at an hour's notice, they were given the order to move. They were ready: completely equipped by Dick with papers made out for Flemish engineer collaborators, money and a mental picture of the Swiss frontier crossing. They survived the search before departure by the means prescribed at Colditz, which is better left unmentioned. Accompanied by three guards, they set off for a troops' camp at Lamsdorf.

At Leipzig main station they supplied the buffet attendant with Red Cross tea while she, a war-worn blonde, provided the boiling water. Prisoners and guards sat down together to enjoy a brew of good, strong English 'char'. The combined charm and carefree friendliness of the two E.R.A.s was difficult to resist. The Goons, returning hospitality, bought a round of beer. Cigarettes were offered by the prisoners.

The buffet was crammed with German uniformed men of different ranks and services. Many were intrigued, stopping for a moment to gaze upon the unaccustomed sight of men in khaki and field grey chatting together round a table in jovial conviviality. Wally was enjoying himself. Unaccustomed to the sound and movement of a busy hub of life, he sat, for a moment surveying appreciatively the scene before him. He noticed a very old man threading his way amongst the crowd, picking up cigarette butts from the floor and out of the ash-trays on the tables. He wore the medals of the 1914–18 war.

As he approached the table where the prisoners and their escorts were now busy over tall glasses of lager, Wally pushed a newly opened packet of Player's cigarettes, which lay at his elbow, in his direction. The German veteran raised his eyes, poignant with the sadness of a long disillusionment, to look at his benefactor, clad in the uniform of the enemy. Grasping the cigarettes, he came smartly to attention and saluted Wally Hammond. The echo of his heel-click sounded painfully loud in a room where the hum of conversation had suddenly ceased. Eyes turned incredulously towards the scene of an act of treason. But the veteran profited by the pause and disappeared from the restaurant before a movement was made to accost him.

The two prisoners arrived in the R.A.F. section of Lamsdorf prison just at the moment when the P.O.W.s were having their hands tied behind their backs with Red Cross string, in retaliation for the tying of German prisoners taken by our Commando raiders on the Channel Islands. They were thrown into the same compound and suffered the same fate. Thus they remained from 7 a.m. to 9 p.m. daily, with an hour's freedom for lunch.

Within a week, however, early in December 1942, Wally and Tubby succeeded, with the help of a Regimental Sergeant-Major named Sheriff, in having themselves drafted to a working-party in the gasworks at Breslau. One hundred British P.O.W.s were working there, but none had as yet, according to report, escaped.

When they reached Breslau, Wally and Tubby carefully studied the route they travelled—by tram—to the works. Their plans were maturing. They had gathered some useful information about the possibilities of making a break from the gasworks. They were handed over by the Germans to the N.C.O. in charge of the working party, Sergeant Brown, and, wasting no time, they began sounding him to find out his reactions.

He was the right type, as far as they were concerned; enthusiastic, anxious to help and thoroughly knowledgeable as to the routine of the works. He advised them to lie low for a few days and to study the lie of the land while he set about procuring some necessary articles of civilian clothing and equipment for them. In the meantime he allotted them the task of shifting coal from one dump to a second, which was within the reach of an electrically powered rail-mounted grab engaged in loading it into railway trucks. They began their first day of toil amidst the hum of industry. The gasworks was a maze of railway sidings. Shunting engines whistled and belched smoke and vapour, marshalling the clattering wagons. White puffs of escaping steam rose from a hundred points around and above the grime-covered brick buildings.

Every time an engine passed near Wally and Tubby, the electric leads of the grab crane were across the tracks. During the first day's work, to the accompaniment of sparks and sheets of flame, they were mangled out of all possible service.

The evening saw a small heap of coal shifted six yards.

During the second day the heap was shifted another six yards in a direction at right angles to the first move; the crane was out of commission. On the third day the heap was moved a further six yards, again at ninety degrees, and on the fourth day the coal was returned to its original location by this indefatigable team of coal hauliers. Before the fourth day's work was over, an old poverty-sticken couple appeared with a cart drawn by a starving horse. They were old-age pensioners, allowed to appear at regularly defined intervals to remove dross, the only fuel permitted them for heating their homes. Wally and Tubby took charge of the horse. No foreman was in sight. They halted the cart between their coal heap and an extensive pile of dross nearby and loaded the cart with coal. The aged couple stood by, looking on appreciatively, but with fear in their glances. When the cart was full and the coal covered with a layer of dross to pass inspection, they proffered surreptitiously a packet of German cigarettes which the two prisoners accepted. They would be useful camouflage on the forthcoming journey.

The cart trundled away.

Towards the end of the week, after loading the remains of the coal on to a wagon, they were instructed to tidy up, collect the remaining coal-dust together with a lot of rubbish in the vicinity and shovel it on to the existing pile of dross. On Saturday, December 12th, 1942, before knocking off work, they carved out of the slack a long mound representing a newly filled grave. A cross made of two pieces of wood nailed together was placed at the head and in large letters in the coal-dust, plain for the world to see, was inscribed 'ADOLF, R.I.P.'

They planned to move that night. Wally describes their preparations in these words:

> For a Colditz incumbent the getaway was a cakewalk; the filing of a few bars, the cutting of a few wires, the timing of a few patrols, obtaining some civilian attire, and we were ready.
> With the help of Sergeant Brown and two soldiers I gathered together a pair of large brown and grey check flannel trousers, a dark grey jacket and a fawn raincoat with

the initials F. L. inside which I could not remove, so I added a P. to make it P. F. L. as the name I was travelling under was Pierre Lebrun. I also wore one of those caps that grandfather wore, very small, with a button in the centre. Tubby had a dark blue pair of trousers, a heavy woollen jacket and a Trilby hat that had been folded and hidden for years. All the steam in the world would not remove the creases. Later, the rain and sleet improved it. But his coat was the funny piece, a dispatch rider's windjacket, treated with boot polish. If it was not a Saville Row fit, it nevertheless kept the rain out. Tubby carried his toilet gear, boot brushes and food in a small suitcase, and I contented myself with a large-size brief-case, in which I carried, amongst other things, needles and cotton and a small bottle of concentrated cough medicine: the latter in case I might get my smoker's cough at an awkward moment.

We both smoked pipes, of German meerschaum design. Our pouches were filled with Bulwark Strong underneath and covered with a layer of mixed French and German tobacco. We also flaunted the German cigarettes.

But Wally and Tubby had not reckoned with a stooge. On Saturday night, for the first time in two years, a Goon sentry was placed on their projected route. They were undaunted. Packing away their civilian kit, they let it be known widely that the show was off until Sunday night. At the same time they resolved to try an alternative route during the early part of the next day, Sunday. They volunteered for the routine chore of washing out the Sunday dinner soup cauldrons. Quietly they collected their escape equipment and hid it in the cauldrons. They carried these to the wash-house which had an exit into the gasworks proper. They changed their clothes in the wash-house, walked into the works and left again through the manager's garden. They encountered little difficulty and there were no alarms. Taking a tram to the railway station, they bought tickets for Dresden, their first hop to regain the Colditz escape route, and by 9.40 p.m. were trundling towards freedom. Wally's papers were signed by Willy Wants, after the variety artist! They were stopped and questioned on two occasions, but their papers carried them through. Once a police officer retained their papers an unusually long time and their anxiety grew acute. Then the officer returned to them and apologised, saying he had to be on the look-out for escaped P.O.W.s. He added reassuringly that he had caught two the previous day. Wally accepted his apologies and expressed the hope that he would catch a few more before long. "They are a *verdammte* nuisance to the honest hard-working citizen," he said feelingly, in German, as they parted.

They reached Dresden, and then Nuremberg, travelling standing all the way in packed railway coaches throughout Sunday night and Monday. *En route,* at Chemnitz, a sympathetic German soldier bought them each a glass of beer. From Nuremberg their journey continued during another night and day towards Ulm. They were on tenterhooks, because Ulm was the death-trap for many a Colditz escaper before them. It was to be avoided if at all possible, yet, like Rome, all roads seem to lead there. They found, arriving at 9 p.m. on Tuesday evening, that there was no connection for Rottweil until the next morning. They were stuck in Ulm for the night.

They had to make a decision quickly. To remain in or near the station was suicidal. The weather could scarcely have been worse. Sleet had been driving against the carriage windows as they drew into the station; the temperature was now below freezing and a high wind was blowing snowy gusts into the booking hall. It was no night to spend out in the countryside. Besides, Ulm was a big industrial town. They would spend most of the night walking to the country and, to find a sheltered hiding-place where they would not freeze to death was, virtually, impossible in the darkness. Walking anywhere after midnight was dangerous. Police patrols would stop marauders abroad in the late and early hours. They had to find cover somehow and quickly. A cinema was no solution. There was only one answer.

As they hesitated for a moment under the archway at the main entrance to the station, peering into the snow-laden blackout beyond, Wally said in an undertone:

"How about it, Tubby? We're in it now up to our necks. We can't stay here."

"The only sensible place to be to-night is in a warm bed, my feet don't belong to me any more. Our papers are pretty damn good. Why not try a cheap hotel?"

"Our German lingo's not good enough."

"Yes it is. You've managed fine so far, and aren't we Flemish, anyway!"

Wally turned to a passer-by.

"*Bitte, gibt es ein gute Hotel hier in der Nähe—aber billig?*"

"*Jawohl!*" replied the stranger, "*zwei Minuten von hier, links da oben ist das Bahnhofshotel. Es ist nicht teuer.*"

"*Danke schön,*" said Wally as the stranger disappeared into the darkness.

They followed, pressing against the wind and holding on to their hats. They turned left, crossed the road and proceeded slowly looking at the doorways one by one until they saw the sign of the Bahnhofshotel faintly outlined above them.

"Here it is," said Wally, "it's all or nothing now. Once inside, if the Jerries examine our papers and don't like 'em, they'll catch us with our pants down—good and proper—in our beds, as like as not."

"It's a fair risk," said Tubby, "my feet say so!"

"O.K. Here goes!"

They pushed through two pairs of heavily curtained swing doors and found themselves in a long hall furnished in Victorian style with plenty of gilt. A lounge opened out to the right and a staircase ascended at the far end. On the left were the offices, the cashier's desk and the hall porter's lobby. The whole place needed repainting, but there was an air of cleanliness about the floors and furniture.

The weather outside was an excuse for the two men to remain muffled up, concealing their shabby suits. Wally asked for a room in his elementary German and a well-dressed man behind the cashier's desk asked in perfect English:

"Do you speak English! I see that you are not German. Perhaps you understand English?"

Wally was completely taken aback. He was on the point of saying, "Yes, of course," when his wits returned to him. "Just a leetle, speak veery slow, please. I can understand Eenglish a little better than German. Ven you speak fast I understand not."

"Tell—me—exactly—what—you—want," pronounced the man behind the counter slowly and distinctly. He spoke in an educated manner with an air of authority. Wally accepted him as the manager, which he was.

"*Ach!* that ees good. Vee weesh one small room with two—*zwei* beds—vone great bed eef not, yes?"

"Yes, I can give you a room with two beds."

"How much, please?"

"Seven marks fifty with fifteen per cent. *Ablösung.*"

"Vee shall take it," said Wally, relieved. At eight marks to the pound he had expected the price would be higher.

"Fill in these forms, please," said the manager politely. "Here your name, here your occupation, your nationality, where you come from, where you go to; and your reason for travelling."

"Vee are ingineers—diesel—nationality *flämisch*, go to Rottweil, vee come from Stuttgart. Vee haf important reparations to do in Rottweil." Wally reamed it out slowly in pidgin English as he wrote his particulars down.

He noticed Tubby spelling 'engineer' with an *e* in the English way and nudged him meaningly, pointing with his pen to the word on his own form. Tubby dropped a blot of ink on the *e* and started again with an *i* in the Continental fashion.

The manager looked up the railway timetable and confirmed that their Rottweil train left at 10 a.m. the next morning. Being Flemish workmen, though not understanding a word of that language, Wally and Tubby felt it appropriate to exchange a few broken sentences in Maltese, which they knew in a scrappy fashion. This made a good impression on the manager, who smiled and said:

"I will give you room fifty-two. Let me have your papers, please."

They handed in their identity papers, which were pinned to the forms they had completed, and they were escorted upstairs. The lift was not in use. Two comfortable beds in a warm cosy room greeted them.

"Do you wish for anything to eat or drink?" asked their conductor.

"Noting, *danke*," replied Wally—with Tubby echoing the words a split second after him. As the door closed, Tubby went to a basin in the corner and turned the taps. After a minute he exclaimed, "Hot water, by G——!" and began stripping off his boots and socks as fast as he could.

Within ten minutes they were fast asleep, tucked into their beds between clean sheets, enjoying more luxury than they had ever had since they left their submarine base in 1940.

They awoke next morning thoroughly refreshed but with hunger gnawing at their vitals. They had not eaten for nearly forty-eight hours. It was now Wednesday morning. Tubby produced German bread, margarine and sugar from his suitcase and they sat up in their beds chewing in silence. The evening before, they had not felt so hungry. That was the effects of weariness after the severe nervous tension. Fatigue alone, if sufficiently intense, can suppress the pangs of hunger. Two major primitive forces seem incapable of taking possession of the human frame both at once. One or the other is uppermost and claims the whole consciousness until it is satisfied. The hackneyed expression tired *and* hungry is inaccurate unless the sufferer is neither very tired nor very hungry.

As the pangs of hunger ebbed, nervous anticipation began to assert itself. Their pulses quickened as thoughts came unchallenged and their hearts pounded. Wally expressed their mutual anxiety:

"Do you think we'll ever get our *Ausweise* back?"

"They're probably examining them with magnifying glasses at the police-station at this moment," said Tubby with nervous jocularity. "If they're not downstairs I'm not waiting for them."

"We'll never get far without 'em," said Wally. He jumped

out of bed and went to the window, pulling back the curtains. Outside the snow had turned to sleet again and the roofs were glassy grey under a sombre sky.

They shaved and dressed hurriedly and packed their belongings.

"All set?" asked Wally, opening the door of the bedroom. Tubby nodded. Then they noticed a beautifully polished pair of military high boots reposing outside a door on the opposite side of the corridor.

The anxiety of the moment faded into the background and a gleam of devilment came into Tubby's eyes. He glanced at Wally and met his gaze.

"No! not that," whispered Wally. "Just plain water. Fill the chamber-pot." Tubby was back in the room in a twinkling, filling his bedside pot with water from the basin tap.

"Steady!" said Wally, as Tubby appeared again with the brimming pot, "don't spill it near our door for hell's sake."

Gently they tipped the water into the boots.

"Not enough," said Wally; "quick, another!"

The corridor was empty. No sound issued from the other side of the door. Quickly another potful was tipped into the thirsty boots, filling them, and a faint trickle of water appeared from underneath the soles. They closed their own door quietly and walked downstairs. It was 8.45 a.m.

At the cash desk, Wally asked for the bill and the identity papers. The manager was obviously short of staff. He was in his shirt-sleeves and had been cleaning the lounge, but his grey hair was carefully brushed and he had shaved. He asked if they had had a good night and "Will you not have breakfast?"

"Vee haf no coupons," said Wally, biting his lip and feeling he would like to run straight out through the swing doors.

"You must have some coffee then—*ersatz* coffee. It is very cold out this morning," said the manager, almost forcing them towards a small table in an alcove of the lounge. They sat down. Then, suddenly, rose in their seats ready to take off. A German officer was coming down the stairs and he was not wearing jack boots.

He passed them with a *"Guten Morgen"* and did not stop at the desk. Wally and Tubby relapsed into their chairs, sighing audibly.

"What the hell made you do it?" whispered Wally hoarsely.

"It was your idea," said Tubby, "you distinctly said water!"

"My godfathers! now we've got to sit here for half an hour drinking filthy coffee." Wally grimaced and resigned himself to fate. What they had done could not be undone. Their papers were not yet forthcoming. The *ersatz* coffee seemed to be waiting for the acorns to grow and, at any moment, screams of rage would issue from the stair-well. They fidgeted uneasily in their chairs.

After an agonising wait of ten minutes the coffee arrived in two large, steaming mugs. More sighs were followed by sub-dued curses. The coffee was far too hot.

"We've got to drink some of the blasted stuff," said Wally, eyeing the staircase. Tubby promptly poured most of his mug into a flower-pot of aspidistras, where it formed a cloud of vapour around the plant.

"For crying out loud!" said Wally, pouring half the con-tents of his mug into Tubby's empty one. "Let's get out of here quick before the place blows up."

Together they vacated the alcove and approached the desk again.

"Tank you—*danke schön*," said Wally to the manager, now seated behind his desk. "Ze bill, if you please. Vee must hurry."

"But your train does not go until ten o'clock, you have plenty of time!" said the manager with exasperating accuracy.

"If you please, vee vish to buy zom tings bevore," Wally replied with painful care. He was hypnotised by the stairs and could not keep his eyes away. He spoke now, deliberately facing the staircase, ready to turn about and run at the first bellow from above. "Hurry please, and do not vorget the *Ausweise, bitte*," he murmured as beads of perspiration appeared on his forehead. Almost in a trance he noticed Tubby edging towards the swing-doors.

At last the bill was ready. Wally fumbled—much too nervously, he thought—for the German notes in his wallet. He paid the bill; still no shouts from the direction of the staircase.

"The *Ausweise* please?" he questioned. He could see them nowhere on the desk.

"*Ach* yes! of course, forgive me. Here they are," said the manager apologetically, bringing them out from under a counter.

"Good-bye! *Auf Wiedersehen!* Tank you!" Wally said, clutching the two papers with soaring relief registering on his countenance. "I 'ope vee shall kome again zoon to visit Ulm."

Tubby repeated "Good-bye, tank you!" and opened the swing-doors.

Outside, they both gasped as heavy sighs filled their lungs with cold air. They quickly disappeared into the crowd hurrying towards the station. They muffled their coats around them as they scurried along, and the first streaks of a storm of sleet carried on a biting wind stung their faces.

In the shelter of the station they paused for a moment to recover their breath and their composure.

"Phew! We're well out of that," said Wally.

"I 'ope the R.A.F. vill kome again zoon to visit Ulm," mimicked Tubby, grinning. "Vone German officer kan use his boots to put out ze fires—*nicht wahr?* I'd give a lot to go back and see the fun, wouldn't you?"

"Sorry, Tubby, we've not got time—let's telephone the manager from Switzerland instead. Come on! we've got to get the tickets to Rottweil. There may be a queue. The train goes in half an hour," said Wally, and they headed for the booking office.

There was a queue, and they waited nervously for fifteen minutes before their turn came. Wally did not wait to be asked for his *Ausweis*; he pushed it in front of the girl issuing the tickets saying, "*Zweimal, dritter Klasse, Rottweil, bitte,*" and tendered his Reichmarks at the same time. The tickets and change appeared without a word.

They hurried off to the train and found the platform without difficulty. Seeing a *Raucher* (smoking) third-class carriage, they climbed in and were soon smoking their pipes with evident satisfaction and more at ease than they had felt since they awoke that morning. Several other passengers entered the carriage just before the train departed.

As it gathered speed, leaving the grey windswept atmosphere of Ulm behind, Wally noticed that one middle-aged unprepossessing female passenger was obsessed with Tubby's dispatch-rider coat. Tubby had finished his pipe and was feigning sleep. Wally saw her curiosity growing and spreading as she gazed up at his crumpled hat, then studied, it seemed, the texture of his coat, and continued downwards to his boots. There was only one answer to this. Wally stared at her—long and intently—with his sharp eyes. It was not long before she became visibly self-conscious. He continued the grilling until she was so confused that she forgot all about Tubby. He kept it up until she reached her destination half an hour later. She left the carriage blushing crimson as she stumbled over Wally's feet to reach the door, still followed by his burning and pseudo-lecherous gaze.

They arrived at Tuttlingen at 4 p.m., where they broke off their journey to Rottweil. This was the Colditz route as followed by the author and others from the Castle before them. Tuttlingen was only fifteen miles from the Swiss frontier, whereas Rottweil, reached by another line, changing at Tuttlingen, was much farther away, and for that very reason a less suspicious town to be heading for. A wait for the Rottweil connection gave passengers a legitimate excuse to leave the station. Wally and Tubby took the precaution of drinking water from a cast-iron fountain in the station before they walked past the barrier, showing their tickets.

Before they had walked half a mile, they encountered a police patrol. They were ready. The officer questioned them and searched their wallets, their pockets and Wally's brief-case, all the time with one hand on his pistol. He said:

"*Warum fahren Sie nicht nach Rottweil?*"

"*Wir warten auf den Zug nach Rottweil um sechs Uhr fünf*

und dreissig," answered Wally. "*Wir sind seit zwei Tagen im Zug—wir machen jetzt einen kleinen Spaziergang. Können wir irgendwo ein Bier kaufen?*"

Wally continued volubly. His German vocabulary soon exhausting itself, he carried on in broken German with words of Maltese, pidgin English and some French thrown in. He and his mate were going home to Belgium for Christmas when the order came for the rush, breakdown job at Rottweil. If the police officer did not believe them he only had to telephone the *Arbeitsführer* (works foreman) at Rottweil. They would be quite happy if the police officer could put them up for the night, provided he 'phoned the *Arbeitsführer*.

The officer was slightly taken aback by this frontal attack. He said simply, "*Komm,*" and they set off together, not as a party of prisoners with their gaoler, but amicably, side by side. After twenty minutes they reached a large house standing back from the road. They followed the officer inside and discovered that they were in a 'pub'.

There were a dozen country-folk and two soldiers in the saloon, and the officer told one of the latter to keep an eye on the two strangers while he went to the telephone. The officer was calling their bluff. They looked around casually but with their eye on the door. A 'getaway' might be managed, but Wally had plenty of fight in him still. He could continue to bluff in spite of the 'phone call. Within five minutes the officer returned; handed them back their papers; led them outside and told them how to find their way back to Tuttlingen station.

Wally said in German, "But we have had our walk. Now it is time we had a drink."

"*Ach so!*" replied the officer, "then go back and have your beer and return to the station afterwards. *Gute Nacht!*" and he left them standing at the pub doorway.

Tubby and Wally looked at each other. A sly smile spread over Wally's face and Tubby winked. They re-entered the pub and ordered beer. They drank one each quickly and ordered seconds. The other occupants of the bar were friendly and talkative. A large flabby-looking man with a bald head and staring pale blue eyes approached them asking, "*Sind Sie Flamen?*"

"*Jawohl!*" they answered with mock gusto.

The large man then recounted what seemed to be a long story in a language they had never heard before in their lives. At last Wally and Tubby were listening to the throaty tones of the language of their adopted birthplace! So this was Flemish, they thought and exchanged bewildered glances. They were definitely 'up against it'.

The large man stopped, smiled jovially and fixed them with his glassy eyes. For a second there was stony silence. Then, with one accord, Wally and Tubby started to laugh. They laughed loud and long—not forgetting to drink their beer between guffaws. The large man began to laugh, too. This gave them a chance to stop. When he ceased, they began again. Their beer finished, they put down their empty glasses and, still roaring with laughter, they shouted "*Gute Nacht! Gute Nacht!*" to the Flemish linguist and the assembled company and backed out of the room as quickly as propriety allowed.

"Phew! Lumme!" said Tubby, as they stepped outside, "that was a near one. Who would have expected to hear that lingo on the Swiss frontier. Do you think it really was Flemish? Perhaps he was having us on and that's what all the joke was about!"

"He was speaking Flemish all right, or perhaps Dutch. I could pick up a word here and there," said Wally, and added as an afterthought, "that was two near ones, not one! You've forgotten about the policeman and the 'phoney telephone!"

"He seemed quite happy about it. We must be expected at Rottweil after all! What was your next move going to be, Wally? I was ready for the door, if he'd come back looking glum."

"If he'd come back suspicious," Wally answered, "I would've told him to 'phone again and let me speak to the *Arbeitsführer* about the diesel breakdown job. That would've stumped him long enough for us to think up the next one."

They walked quickly, continuing along the road they had

come, then, approaching some woods, they left the road, skirting along the fringe of the trees. They travelled by compass all that night and the next, making very slow progress across country, and lying up in the daytime in dense woods. In the early hours, after the second night's tramp, in spite of the walking, they began to feel the cold. They were stopping frequently to check their direction and at such moments the sweat on their bodies chilled and made them shiver. They came upon a woodman's hut. The door was locked. By climbing on to the low roof and removing a few tiles they were able to drop inside. They made ready to spend the day there with suitable precautions. Wally detached the lock on the door and held it shut with a piece of string while Tubby cut out knots in the pinewood boards of the walls with his jack-knife, providing spyholes in all directions.

They found some boards in a corner, spread them out on the floor over the damp earth and slept fitfully until morning. From dawn onwards they took turns at the spy-hole watch. They were in a clearing and would make a run for it if anyone approached the cabin.

During the day they reviewed their trek of the previous night, established their position with a fair degree of accuracy and made plans for the frontier crossing. At midday they ate the last of their food. They suffered badly from thirst, and during a rainstorm they tried to collect water in a bowl under the hole they had made in the roof. The rain did not last long, but they captured a few drops which they lapped up like dogs. It no more than moistened their tongues.

Not a soul approached the cabin all day. At dusk they departed leaving a five mark note under the broken lock which they placed carefully in a tool cupboard in the hut. They walked, at first, due west along a railway line in the forest until they reached open country. Then they turned south, skirting the trees for an hour before hearing the sound of traffic using the road they were heading for. They lay down near it and began timing patrols.

At this point, about five miles west of Singen, the road

passed within half a mile of the frontier. Across the road were fields inclined to be marshy, and the bottom of a wooded hill sloping towards the east beyond the fields was their target. A deviation of two hundred yards to the right or left of the bee-line from where the men lay to the edge of the wooded hill would find them back in Germany and probably into the arms of a sentry.

By midnight they were ready for the 'off'. The moon was shining brightly and had been helpful so far. Now, for the last lap it would be a hindrance. It would help others to see them when they least wanted to be visible. There was a low ground mist, on the other hand, which would be useful if they chose to drop suddenly at an alarm.

They waited for a motor-cycle patrol to pass with flashing headlamps, counted three minutes and crossed the road. Wally went about twenty yards in front of Tubby. They timed the crossing well, as a large cloud began to cover the face of the moon. They carried jack-knives in their sleeves. After twenty-five minutes of fast going, with the mist enveloping them up to their waists, they approached the trees at the bottom of the hill. Suddenly a torch was flashed on Wally before he had time to drop, and there was a shout, "*Halt! Wer da?*" He approached the sentry in a roundabout way. Tubby had dropped and had not been seen. Wally forced the sentry to turn with him as he advanced until his back was facing the direction where Tubby lay. The moon reappeared, bathing the scene in an unearthly light. The sentry had not unslung his rifle. It was a good omen. Then Wally distinguished the outline of his Tyrolean-style cap, and his button gleamed showing up the Swiss cross. He looked beyond the sentry and saw the form of Tubby appearing out of the ground mist. He was much nearer than expected and Wally caught the glint of his knife as he moved noiselessly like a shadow. "Stop! Tubby, for God's sake!" he shouted over the guard's shoulder, "he's Swiss."

Tubby masked his knife and fell on the astonished sentry's neck as he turned. Keyed at one moment to the pitch of killing his enemy, Tubby was so overcome at the next that he found himself hugging the sentry shouting, "Swiss, Swiss, good old Swiss!" The sentry accepted the greeting good-humouredly. He spoke a little English and contented himself with establishing that they were prisoners of war who had escaped, accepting their statements at face value. He shouted to another sentry in the darkness of the woods and then escorted them, talking cheerfully all the way, to the village of Ramsden. They were handed over to the commander of the guard post, who promptly produced bowls of soup and sent them to bed with four army blankets each in the 'off-duty doss-down'. The time was 2 a.m. on Saturday, December 19th.

They arrived in Berne for Christmas and for a reunion party that will long be remembered by the participants. The others were: Ronnie Littledale, Billie Stephens, Hank Wardle, Bill Fowler and the author, all ex-Colditz inmates who had escaped during the autumn.

*   *   *   *   *

The Colditz group in Switzerland was growing into a colony. The escapers were packed off by the Military Attaché for a time to Montreux, then to Wengen and later to Saanenmöser in the Bernese Oberland. They all learnt to ski on the comparatively deserted slopes, first of the Kleine Scheidegg and then of the Hornberg, and in a matter of two months had regained much of their former strength and energy.

The invasion of North Africa in November 1942 by the Allies and the subsequent entry of the Germans and Italians into Vichy France upset all the recognised ways of travelling to Spain. With the Germans present, new and much more clandestine 'tourist' routes had to be organised.

Bill Fowler and Ronnie Littledale were the first of the colony to leave. They crossed the Swiss frontier into France on January 25th, 1943. Bill set down his record of the journey to Gibraltar on his arrival in England and it is reproduced here as he wrote it—a straightforward account fresh with vigour and the simplicity of understatement which was so typical of this fine airman who, as his companion Ronnie too, was to meet his end before the war was over.

On the 25th of January, 1943, Ronnie Littledale and I went to Geneva, where we were given French identity cards and introduced to a Belgian called Jacques. We were told that our journey must be left entirely to him.

We were taken then by car a short distance, to a point near the French frontier, west of Annemasse. Here we waited in a yard while Jacques made a reconnaissance. In a few minutes he came back and told us to follow him, so we walked till we came to a small stream, where we were joined by a French girl about twenty years old. We crossed the stream, which was shallow, and were helped out of the water on the other side by a French customs official in uniform. We waited hidden behind a wall for a few minutes, and then Jacques led us down a deserted road into Annemasse village. He took us to a house where we dried our clothes, had some food and met a man in a ski-ing suit, who, Jacques told me, would be our guide for the next part of the journey. He and the French girl left us.

We went to bed and very early next morning, with our new guide, we walked to a garage, passing some Italian soldiers on the way. The guide left us here, arranging with a man to drive us in a car to La Roche, where we arrived at 8 a.m., and went to a hotel. We slept most of the day in a corner of the lounge, interrupting our dozing to eat a good lunch, at which our guide rejoined us.

At 4 p.m. he led us to the railway station, where he gave us a hundred francs each and told us to book separately to Chambéry. We boarded the train—arriving at Chambéry at about 9 p.m., where we changed. The guide bought tickets to Perpignan, where we arrived, after an all-night journey, at 9 a.m. on the 27th of January. We took a tram to the Hôtel St. Antoine. We spent the 27th and the 28th very quietly in the hotel, only going out once to have our photographs taken for our fake identity papers in the back room of a small shop close by.

On the 29th of January our guide handed us over to a

Spaniard and then departed. We took a bus to Elne, arriving there in the evening. The Spaniard insisted on our buying our own tickets and sitting separately in different parts of the bus. At Elne we met a French boy about nineteen years old who said he was coming with us.

Darkness descended upon us as we walked along the railway line southwards and crossed the River Tech by the railway bridge. We continued across fields until after an hour's trek the guide said he was lost. I directed him towards the south by the stars and we eventually came to a goat track which the guide said he recognised. We followed this and arriving at a cave, we lay down and slept for some hours. At 6 a.m. the following morning (30th January) we set off again. We marched the whole day, reaching the La Junqueras–Figueras road at 4 p.m., and, while crossing it, we were arrested by Spanish soldiers who were patrolling the district in a lorry picking up the numerous refugees in the neighbourhood. They seemed familiar with this routine and were not even armed.

The lorry took us to La Junqueras, where we were locked into a cell. We were not searched. Later we were interrogated in French by a Spanish officer who said he supposed we were Canadians. We told him we were British officers who had been captured in France (following our instructions). I gave the name of John Parsons, while Ronnie gave his name as Bighill (opposite of Littledale). The military authorities then handed us over to the jurisdiction of the civil police.

Our guide was put into a separate cell, and the police telephoned to Madrid about him. They found out that he had been a Red in the Civil War and beat him up properly in the next room, apologising afterwards to us for the nuisance caused, saying that the man was a 'Red murderer' and deserved all the treatment he got. While waiting in the cell, we burnt our papers. The police searched us and questioned us again. The Chief of Police promised to treat us well and to send us to an hotel. He asked us what we thought of General Franco and what was our opinion of the Bolshevists. We said we thought Franco was a grand fellow and that we admired the Russians, who were our Allies. At every opportunity we demanded permission to see the British Consul and always received the answer, *Mañana*.

On the 1st of February we were marched off to a central prison in Figueras, where our heads were shaved and we were inoculated under dirty, unhygienic conditions (I was tenth in line for the same needle), and thrown into the filthiest gaol I have ever seen in my life, and I have seen quite a few! All that has been written in the war about Spanish prisons is correct. We were jammed in with fourteen other men; some of them criminals, mostly Spanish, and two of them awaiting death sentences, in a disgusting, dirty hole, measuring four yards by two. In this cell we spent twenty-three days without blankets or even straw, sleeping on the damp stone floor huddled together like sardines and crawling with vermin. The only window was bricked up leaving a six-inch aperture, and as it was mid-winter long hours were spent in total darkness. The cold was intense. For all natural functions, a pail was placed in the middle of the cell and removed once every twenty-four hours. It made the atmosphere so foul that prisoners were sick intermittently all day long. Two men died during our incarceration and their bodies remained propped up in the corner for two days before the guards removed them. A tureen of gruel a day was all the food we were given. The only hope of maintaining life was to pool valuables and to buy, at exorbitant prices, extra food from the guards. My only asset, a wrist-watch, went.

We were visited, once, by a representative from the British Consulate, and, as a result, on the 22nd of February, a Spanish Army sergeant conducted us to Barcelona, where we reported to the British Consul and were sent off to an hotel.

We were given civilian clothes and stayed there till the 18th of March, when I parted company with Ronnie.

A Spanish Air Force officer took me to Alhama de Aragon, where I met several men of the R.A.F. and U.S.A.A.F. We were well treated here, and, on the 24th of March, I set off with six R.A.F. personnel, mostly Canadians, to Madrid; and thence to Seville, where we spent the night. The next day we motored to Gibraltar, stopping on the way at one of the principal sherry towns, where the British Consul, a Spaniard, happened to be a wine merchant. He conducted us over his cellars. We sampled varieties copiously and, on our departure, he presented each one with a bottle of sherry 'for the road'. One of the Canadians admired the Madonna lilies in his front garden so the Consul pressed an enormous bunch on him. The sherry lasted us as far as La Linea, on the north side of the neutral zone separating Spain from Gibraltar. Here the Canadian with the lilies climbed on the bonnet of the car, swearing he would kiss the first British citizen he met in Gibraltar. At the north gate of Gibraltar, a sentry challenged the convoy, whereupon the Canadian climbed unsteadily from his perch, solemnly kissed the sentry on the cheek and presented him with the huge bunch of lilies. The party was escorted to the guard-room, led by the Canadian. The sentry, carrying his rifle under one arm and the Madonnas in the other, followed. He seemed to regard the incident as an everyday occurrence, evidently accustomed to the arrival of service 'tourists' from captivity.

CHAPTER XIV

THE GHOSTS

DICK HOWE, in his capacity of Escape Officer, played an important rôle in the black days of Colditz, in the darkness before the dawn. Always encouraging, never despairing, he fostered, cajoled and counselled.

*   *   *   *   *

When Scarlet O'Hara was allotted a bed in the first floor quarters over the parcels office where the French had formerly resided, he browsed around the rooms for several days and then took to measuring. What he carried out was a miniature trigonometrical survey. It was certainly three dimensional, and soon wound itself up around the spiral of the staircase in the turret leading up to his dormitory.

Between the first floor and the ground-floor, beside the spiral, he calculated there was an uncharted space sealed off from all directions. He set to work, and in a matter of six weeks of patient toil he had worked through a couple of feet of masonry and found his secret chamber. He quite expected to find some treasure, hidden there centuries before, but there was nothing. Dick helped him to build a camouflaged entrance weighing a hundredweight and turning on pivots like the French tunnel entrance.

Then Dick left Scarlet to his own devices, to choose his own team of workers and carry on with the job. The job, of course, was tunnelling downwards through the stone, mortar and concrete of the massive staircase foundations.

The point in favour of Scarlet's scheme was that he could tunnel in almost any direction. The Germans might hear his sledge-hammer at work—in fact they did—but for a long time they could not find his working.

His team consisted of senior officers, none below the rank of major, which accounts for the title conjured up by Don Donaldson. 'Crown Deep' was the name and it stuck like glue.

Tunnelling continued for many weeks. The dull thuds of hammer blows reverberated up the stairs, rivalling the sounds of heavy excavation that used to emanate months earlier from the nearby French tunnel. The Jerries listened and probed and searched in vain.

Scarlet approached Dick periodically.

"I want you to come and have a look at the working," he would say, and both of them would descend through the hinged opening into his chamber. Scarlet would light up his lamp.

"I've been driving a heading in this direction, see?" and he would point to a depression in the foundations about the size of a small hip-bath. "That represents three blasted weeks' work! It's heading in a good direction, out between Gephard's office and the chapel. It starts off fine and dandy and then it gets tougher and tougher. It leads you up the garden path good and proper and lets you down good and proper."

Both the scene and the occasion were familiar to Dick, and he would look wistfully round the chamber at the other holes. One after the other, as his gaze travelled round, he recollected Scarlet's grumbling phrases. Grudging defeat, painful susceptibility at his own impotence, dogged refusal to accept fate, and a nonchalant sarcasm that veiled the suffering.

"And where do I go from here?" Scarlet would ask pathetically, kicking the rubble under his feet in a fruitless gesture as he followed Dick's gaze.

"Why not try heading inside towards the courtyard, you might pick up the drains again," or "Have a go over there towards Monty's hole. He's heading for the old French tunnel and two different entrances would have many advantages."

Dick's counsel always encouraged Scarlet to start off again and the familiar thud of his working would waft up the medieval turret once more. It was a reassuring sound to the men who climbed, daily, up and down the winding stairs. Comments passed from mouth to mouth.

"Crown Deep's at work again."

"Yes, never heard it last week. Couldn't think what was different about the place."

"Life's not the same without it!"

"It's like a heart. When it stops throbbing, there's a death in the house."

The Germans were bound to react violently eventually. Their sound recorders must have been working overtime. Crown Deep never had a real chance. As they could not find the entrance, in desperation one day they brought in their own team of navvys and set to work on the staircase. Their action savours of the rival mining operations that were carried out between the German and Allied trenches during the First World War. In this case, fortunately, Scarlet had no high explosive or he would certainly have used it. The Germans wielded their pick-axes, sledge-hammers and wedges and discovered his concealed chamber. Crown Deep passed into the catalogue of Colditz failures. Only the name survived; an epitaph without a grave.

*   *   *   *   *

It is one thing to be incarcerated alone in a stone cell like the Count of Monte Cristo; to have only bare hands with which to hammer against the walls and finger-nails with which to scrape away the mortar. To have company in such a situation is another matter. It is a mixed blessing.

Prisoners can commiserate together, they may also grow to hate each other. They can help one another and they may be wildly jealous of each other. There can be order or anarchy; an outstanding character can seize the helm and hold the course; moral weakness and the absence of leadership breed bad blood and lasting enmity. The elemental forces in man's nature are scarcely veiled; they lie under a veneer of civilised custom which grows tenuous. They can burst into fury as a spark becomes a roaring furnace. All the physical constituents, the infinite monotony; all the mental anguish, the panoply of tyranny and the atmosphere for revolt, are present.

The stage was set for heroism or violence in the stifled community life which existed behind the walls of Colditz. The majority of the inmates lived for escape. The decision, for most of them, taken long ago, was irrevocable. It was too late now to turn back, There was no road behind them. Instead, if they turned, beneath them was a yawning chasm. They stood giddily on the brink. It was the pit of despair, threatening to engulf them in a mad, suicidal fall. Scarlet O'Hara's Crown Deep was an instance of men beating their fists against walls of solid rock. Monty Bissell's hole was another, and the glider, in a different sense was, probably, the last. Here was resolution for its own sake. This way lay sanity for active, courageous men who were determined not to look back.

A few, very few, attained Nirvana; they deliberately faced the yawning chasm, gritted their teeth, steadied their swaying minds, clung to the edge and slowly stepped backwards into tranquillity and resignation.

*   *   *   *   *

The ghosts were in a bad way. In spite of all the tender care that Monty Bissell expended on them, they were definitely wasting away. Like a mother hen looking after its chicks, Monty saw they were fed and kept warm before he ever thought about himself. But their trouble was disturbing. It was not so much physical as mental. Their morale was at rock bottom.

Not that their chains were heavy. They did not have long sessions of clanking; on the contrary they were quiet ghosts. Their job was to be silent and to be inconspicuous. In fact, they were not supposed to appear at all. Naturally, under such conditions the morale of any ghost could be expected to go to pieces.

The reader will remember that the ghosts, two of them, were hidden in Monty's hole in the chapel. Their appearance or disappearance—take your choice—had coincided with the escape of Rupert Barry and his French companion down the theatre light-well in November 1942. Dick had decided, on that occasion, to be reasonable as to the number. Volunteers were called for, and Jack Best and Mike Harvey had been chosen.

Monty Bissell, at the time, was busy digging a tunnel under the steps leading to the pulpit.

Jack Best thought that, by becoming a ghost and going to ground, he would be free to help Monty and to work to his heart's content, and Mike Harvey thought so too.

Monty looked after them well. They were his first, and almost continuous, charge to the exclusion of other activities. He attended to their every need, brought them their food and all the titbits he could muster. He saw that they were warm, regaled them with news of the activities of the camp and of events taking place in the world outside. The ghosts for their part repaid Monty's care and attention by tunnelling quietly and leisurely forward.

They had a few tins of Red Cross food laid in as a reserve, but Monty thought it would be a good idea to lay in a stock of staple diet for them as well. Bread would go mouldy in a day. There was nothing else save potatoes; they were better than nothing and, thought Monty, they would prevent starvation. Thus, if the chapel was closed by way of a reprisal for some 'offence against the Reich' for a month or longer, the ghosts would survive long enough for Dick and Monty to evolve a plan to extract them and at the same time obviate their disclosure. Dick thought this a wise precaution and set about obtaining the potatoes.

He went to the mess kitchen in the British quarters one Sunday afternoon to find Goldman, the cockney Jewish orderly. Goldman was there, seated at the kitchen table, poring over a letter he was writing home. His blond, curly hair fell over his forehead and a pencil protruded from the corner of his mouth. The table was littered with postcards and letters, on paper of many different colours.

"Goldman," Dick said, "I want to talk to you."

"Yes, Captain 'Owe," said Goldman standing up and transferring the pencil from his mouth to behind his ear.

"Could you scrounge me a small sack of potatoes?" Dick continued. "I want them for the ghosts. They must be absolutely sound—no bad ones—because they may have to last some time."

"Why, Captain 'Owe, that ain't so difficult, and you know I'd do anything for you, anyway. Come along wiv' me. De Jerry cook and me, we're pals. 'E's comin' to visit me after the war an' see de family."

They descended the stairs to the courtyard and headed for the cookhouse. The door was locked. It was two o'clock and a Sunday. Cooking for the day was finished. Goldman was not deterred. He opened a small serving hatch near the door, stretched his arm through and slipped the lock of the door on the inside. Dick and Goldman walked into the kitchen and shut the door quietly after them.

Silence reigned in the deserted cookhouse, but from around a corner, in an alcove, wafted a sound of gentle snoring. The German cook corporal was sprawled over a desk fast asleep, with his head on his folded arms. Goldman crept over to him, then bawled at the top of his voice, "*Achtung!*"

The German N.C.O. came to his feet as if a thousand volts had been shorted across his terminals and stood rigidly at attention before Goldman's cheery "Wat yer, cookie!" brought him to his senses and relaxed his galvanised frame. Goldman grinned airily at him. "That's right, cookie, you can stand at ease now, but don't go to sleep on dooty again, see!"

The German, a comparatively young man, retired from the Russian front on account of wounds, was, rather naturally, in a surly mood. He and Goldman wrangled for several minutes. Finally the grumbling ended with Goldman showing the corporal all the photos of his family in Hackney, in return for which extraordinary favour the Jerry felt it his bounden duty to hand over thirty pounds of potatoes. Goldman and Dick turned to leave the cookhouse with the sack hidden under a jacket. The

German, as docile as a lamb, accompanied them to the door and closed it politely after them.

"You see 'ow it is, Captain 'Owe. It gets you anyfink you want."

"What does?" asked Dick.

"Charm," replied Goldman. "It's charm what does it."

The ghosts now had their reserve of potatoes.

Three weeks of confinement in a black hole under a chapel are not warranted to lift morale, and the ghosts, in spite of Monty's nursing, began to wilt. The atmosphere was not of the best, either physically on account of the curious smell which could hardly be described as the odour of sanctity, or spiritually, because of the indefinable proximity of the dead. The dead had died many, many years ago, but their spirits seemed not far removed from their decayed coffins under the chapel floor. It was ironical that the ghosts should be so affected by the company of their elders, if not their betters. The fact is, the chapel was 'plain spooky' in the dead of night.

After three weeks it had become obvious that the ghosts should be relieved of the strain and given some fresh air. The excitement and hubbub of the light-well escape had died by Christmas 1942, and it was considered safe to let them out of close hiding provided they were protected by stooges from being seen face to face by a German who might recognise them.

The French tunnel was discovered within two months of their taking up residence. Work had to cease completely for a time. Then they began once more in a new direction, with a view to connecting up with the French tunnel and making use of it again.

Sound detectors were known to be installed all around the chapel. They had to proceed at a snail's pace.

By the summer of 1943 work on the chapel tunnel had to stop. Monty and his ghosts had reached the French tunnel, but the Germans had laid a trap. Sound detectors must have been left hidden in it. Every time the British tunnellers entered it the Germans appeared to know, and a squad would enter the chapel, search it and leave a sentry posted there for twenty-four hours (relieved, of course, periodically). Progress came to a standstill.

Grismond Davies-Scourfield made a break during the summer. He was 'gone away' for seventeen days before recapture at the Dutch frontier. His story cannot be told here, but during his absence Mike Harvey stood in for him on *Appells*, with the result that when the German Commandant was informed by long-distance telephone of the recapture of a Colditz prisoner he replied, "It can't be so. We had an *Appell* two hours ago and the count was correct."

Mike promptly went back into close hiding until the tangle was sorted out!

For the period of less restricted confinement, Monty, still looking after his brood like a mother hen, instituted the stooging system that made it safe for his chicks to sortie at all times, except, of course, during roll-calls, when they went to ground again. He had a team of stooges working for him, including Keith Milne, known as the 'City Slicker', one of the most charming, unassuming and gentle characters it is possible to imagine, and handsome, dark-haired and black moustached into the bargain. Be that as it may, he was noticed late one evening at his look-out post by Lulu Lawton.

"What are you up to, Slick?" he asked.

"Stooging for Monty's ghosts," came the reply.

Lulu said nothing, but it was eleven o'clock and he suspected something. He searched high and low for Monty and could not find him. Then he happened to pass Monty's bed, and there he was tucked up nicely, fast asleep, with only his forelock showing. Lulu shook him.

"Huh! . . . Hm! . . . Oh! . . . What? No! What the hell do you think you're doing?"

"What time did the ghosts go to ground?" asked Lulu.

"Hours ago. Has anything happened? Are they all right?"

"What time did you put them away?"

"Six o'clock. Why? What the devil's up with you, anyway, Lulu?"

"Nothing, nothing at all, Monty! Only the City Slicker's going to be a bit browned off."

"By the holy Saint Patrick!" shouted Monty, leaping from his bed. "I forgot to lay him off." He looked at his watch, "That's five hours ago," and he rushed in his pyjamas to release the faithful sentinel.

Stooging hit a low spot at that moment, but Monty could be said at least to have erred on the right side. Stooging also had its high spots, and reached a peak in Dick's plan for the escape of Bush Parker and Mike Harvey.

The Australian airman and the English sailor had a notion that a door in the wall of the Castle, half-way down the first causeway, led somewhere. The door was marked *Luftschutz-raum*—air-raid shelter, and was being used fairly frequently these days for its allotted purpose. Although it was impossible to estimate with certitude—as the door was not visible from the prisoners' windows, frequent observation during air-raids gave the impression that there was a second way—in or out—of this air-raid shelter.

Bush Parker was determined to find out and he wisely chose Mike Harvey as his partner for the attempt. Mike, being a ghost, was at the top of the escape roster.

Together they buttonholed Dick about it.

"Mike and I," he said, "have been watching the causeway during air-raids now for a couple of months, and we are as certain as we can be that there is a second entrance to the *Luftschutzraum*."

"How do you make that out?"

"We've counted the bodies going in and then the bodies coming out. They never agree."

"H'm, where have you watched from?"

"From the window in the *Saalhaus* [theatre block] on the second floor which overlooks the causeway and is immediately above the air-raid shelter entrance."

"But you can't see the door from there," said Dick.

"No, I admit that, but by looking downwards from the top of the window there's only about a yard of the causeway which is blind. We can't be absolutely certain, but we're nearly certain. If there's a second exit, it's beyond the sentry on the second gate. Once past this gate, we have a good chance of bluffing our way past the others. It's worth a try, Dick, if you'll O.K. the idea and help us."

"Wait a minute, now, what's the rest of the plan?"

"Well, Mike and I drop from our *Saalhaus* window by rope right in front of the door. I can bring some keys which I know will open it. I've studied the lock carefully every time we've walked by the door going down to the park. We get into the cellar, kit and all, and find our way out."

"With three sentries looking at you all the time!" commented Dick.

"No!" replied Bush. "Only two for certain. The third would not worry us very much if properly stooged."

"I reckon all three will have to be properly stooged. It's just about impossible, Bush. Look! where have you got to put your stooges to cover the beats of the three of them? . . . You see? They have to be miles apart in different rooms. So you'll need a string of supplementary stooges to pass on the signals. That means seconds wasted, and I can see right now this is a job of split seconds. You're in the direct beam of searchlights all the time."

"Once I can get into the air-raid shelter doorway," interrupted Bush, "I've got some deep shadow to help me. It's about nine inches inside the wall face. If I hug one side I might get away with it for a few minutes while I open the door."

"That's a fair risk, I agree," said Dick, "but the stooging is the trouble. You'll need all the stooging, in any case, while you cut the window bars. That'll take you ages. No! you go away, Bush, and have another think about it. I will too."

Dick kept his promise and produced what he christened 'the electric stooge'. Five stooging posts were necessary to follow the movements of the three sentries directly concerned and also stray patrols. Dick manufactured five 'make-and-break' press-button switches. These he fixed at the five stooging posts, connecting them all in series through the Castle wiring along with a tell-tale shaded lamp installed at the corner of the window where the 'job' was to be performed. When all buttons were pressed down the light went on. This signal meant work could proceed. If one stooge only saw danger, he released his button and work stopped instantaneously.

The cutting of the window bars by Bricky Forbes took many days of the most patient labour. Absolute silence was essential. The saw used was made, as usual, of razor blades. By the time the window was ready, however, the even more hazardous operation of letting the two bodies down in the full searchlight glare within the vision and easy hearing of the three sentries, one only fifteen yards away, could be tackled with some confidence.

Incredible as it may seem, Dick and his colleagues succeeded in letting Bush and Mike down to the causeway where Bush picked the air-raid shelter lock. As he did so a sentry saw Mike, fired at him, missed, and ran to the alarm bell. Bush and Mike disappeared through the door, which was not solid but made of wooden slats. As a posse of Goons dashed out from the guard-house, Bush put his hand through the slats, relocked the door and removed his key. The two men disappeared down a long flight of stone steps into the recess of the air-raid shelter.

The Jerries searched the area for an hour, but never thought of unlocking the door of the air-raid shelter. However, Bush and Mike were unlucky. There was not a second exit. They were in a cul-de-sac. The escape was, to all intents and purposes, from the moment of that discovery, doomed. Although dressed in German fatigue overalls, they would have to walk out of the air-raid shelter doorway into the glare of search-lights and in full view of three sentries. Not only that, they had, within ten yards, to ask one of the sentries to open a locked gate, which required a password. If an air-raid had occurred while they were in the shelter they might have had a chance, but they could not budget for an air-raid in advance, and that night there was none. The two men therefore remained hidden in the shelter until the next day. They then tried to pass the sentries, but were trapped. . . .

Months of difficult work for nothing; the escape was a failure and a complete anticlimax.

The same evening over their supper, Dick's table were holding an inquest on the escape. Harry Elliott said it reminded him of a story that his uncle George used to tell. Twirling one end of his moustache, he began:

"This old uncle of mine, you see, lived for a long time in India. Uncle George was his name. He always talked about snakes as serpents, and he had a habit of telling stories without any point at all. There was one story of his in particular which we, as children, always loved, and we could always be certain of getting it by asking him, 'When you were in India, Uncle George, did you ever see any snakes?' to which he would reply, 'Serpents, my boy, serpents! Well, as a matter of fact I did see one, very close to. When I was in Poona and your Uncle Edward was staying with me, we were walking together in the compound when we saw a serpent of the species *cobra de capello* coming towards us. It came to within a few feet of us and then disappeared down a hole.

"'I clapped my hands and the servants came running. I ordered chairs to be brought and had them placed one on either side of the hole. Your Uncle Edward sat in one chair and I sat in the other, and though we waited there for several hours, we never saw the creature again.'"

The ghosts had doubles. Mike Harvey's double was Lieutenant Bartlett (Royal Tank Regiment), who looked rather like him. As soon as Mike was caught, he posed as Bartlett and Bartlett went into hiding. Unfortunately, when Mike set off to the solitary confinement cells the German sergeant in charge looked at him closely and said, "You are not Bartlett!"

He could not make out who the stranger was, but he put him in the cells, nevertheless, for safety. It took the Germans two days to sift out the mess this time. A security officer came to Mike's cell with his correct papers and that was the end of Mike as a ghost.

Iack Best carried on.

CHAPTER XV

THE TERRACE

DICK was sun-bathing on one of the rare occasions when he found time to do so and during that short period of the day when the sun stared almost vertically downwards into the deep pit of the courtyard. It was sultry August weather. Roughly a third of the yard reflected the dazzling white glare of the sunlight, while the shadows deepened to black around the sides.

He lay on a blanket stretched over the cobbles, naked, except for a pair of pants, and was deeply engrossed in *Gone with the Wind*. His eyes followed the printed words and his thoughts soared on the magic carpet of fiction, upwards and outwards, far beyond the walls, beyond the horizons. Over the blessed gardens of oblivion he floated happily setting his course towards the mountains of the past. What a godsend books were— like cool water upon the fevered brow, like the caress of a loved one!

Dick was brought back to earth through the sudden covering of his open page by a blanket which descended seemingly from nowhere. He looked up.

"Sorry, Dick," came a cheerful voice as the blanket was whisked away and spread more carefully beside Dick's own. It was Gordon Rolfe, the Canadian. The sunlit patch of cobbles in the courtyard was filling up with bodies. Soon no cobbles would be visible as row upon row of sunbathers formed up for an early afternoon siesta.

"Getting like Coney Island around here," said Rolfe.

"Palm Beach!" protested Dick. "Put on your rose-tinted spectacles—look at those two lovelies—just flown in from Hollywood this morning." Dick nodded towards two particularly skinny, angular, almost nude figures wending their rickety way amongst the recumbent forms.

Rolfe grinned and sat down cross-legged on his blanket.

"Dick," he said, "how about you taking me for a Cook's tour around the Castle? It'll save me a hell of a lot of time. I'm trying to find a way out the same as everyone else, but if I can build on your knowledge I might, with a new pair of eyes, hit on something that hasn't yet been thought of."

Dick thought for a moment before replying.

Among the Eichstätt tunnellers there were many outstanding escapers, men who had broken bounds more than once before but who had not made the home-run. Gordon Rolfe and Dopey Miller; Frank Weldon of the R.H.A. and J. Hamilton-Baillie, R.E., the two leading tunnellers of Eichstätt; others like Hugo Ironside and Douglas Moir of the Royal Tank Regiment, and Tom Stallard; Phil Pardoe and Tony Rolt of the Rifle Brigade.

Dick said, "The Old Lags have looked out of the same windows for so long that they've got permanent squints. I'll take you round all right with pleasure, but if it's to be a Cook's tour how about half a dozen of you new chaps coming along together?"

Dick mentioned some of the names he had thought of.

Gordon Rolfe agreed:

"I'll get hold of them, Dick! they'll be only too glad. What's the best sort of time? We don't want to look like a bunch of tourists."

"Oh, some time in the evening is probably best. How about after the five o'clock *Appell*?"

"I'll fix it—sorry for interrupting your reading." Rolfe sprawled over his blanket and Dick returned to the realms of the Southern States and the time of the Civil War.

They met again in the cool of the early evening after the roll-call. Rolfe had gathered quite a party, including Dopey Miller and Tony Rolt. He led them, first of all, once the *Appell* guards and N.C.O.s had retired, through the doorway opening from the cobbled yard into the corridor leading to the sick ward. He walked over to a small window in the north wall of the ward beside a round turret at the north-west corner of the Castle, and beckoned the others to look out and downwards, pointing:

"Have a look down there," he began. "Through this window —you can see where the bars have been repaired—Bush Parker did his stuff with Mike Sinclair, Hyde-Thomson and Lance Pope in the Franz Josef escape. . . ." He went on, describing to them how the escape had been engineered. He told them how Mike had hung on, trying to get the second sentry to move, how the two Franz Josefs had faced each other and how Mike had been wounded. At the end Rolfe asked:

"Why didn't Mike make a break with his two men—he should have, don't you think—instead of hanging on?"

"Many people have asked that question," said Dick, "to be quite candid I've taken the can back for it. I left the final decision to Mike himself instead of giving him a specific instruction to quit at the slightest sign of obstruction. What some chaps argued afterwards was that, knowing Mike, I should also have known that he just wasn't the type who would quit, and I should, therefore, have given him an order."

Walking back once more into the corridor he pointed to Gephard's office and they looked through the window at the end of the corridor down on the sentry footpath. "Six men went out there to the right, from the building known as the clothes store, starting off with a hole underneath Gephard's desk. They were dressed as German N.C.O.s and Polish orderlies. Two of them—Bill Fowler and a Dutchman—got to Switzerland. Underneath where we're standing is the cellar where the French tunnel started; it ran under the chapel towards your right heading for the park."

They returned to the courtyard. Dick stopped outside the doorway, looking up at the clock tower. "The French used the tower," he explained. "Their entrance was at the top and they hid fifty tons of stone and rubble in the attics, mostly over the chapel. In the chapel at the moment," he went on, "there is a working run by Monty Bissel. We're hiding a ghost in it. Don't do any snooping in there without letting me know first."

The party walked casually across the courtyard and into the dentist's room on the east side of the Castle. Dick gathered them once more at a window and pointed out through the bars. "You see that buttress over there to the right. Well, it's hollow —it was a medieval lavatory. Vandy and half a dozen Dutch and British got down to the bottom of it from the third floor. It was on rock. They tried tunnelling but were caught. Just round the corner, beyond the buttress and above us, is the window where we had the team ready to go out if the Franz Josef bluff had worked." He led them through several small low-ceilinged rooms, unlocking two doors on the way with his master key.

They found themselves in the barber's shop. "Under this floor there is still a whacking great hole left by Pat Reid. The Jerries have never found it. If anyone has ideas for starting up work again here, they're welcome. There are several snags but nothing is impossible. You might have a think about it." He led them next to the canteen in the south-east corner.

"This area's vulnerable," he explained, "and may give you something to think about. We had a tunnel here in 1941 which led out under the canteen window and under the grass lawn beyond. Fourteen of us were caught. Several efforts have been made by Poles and Frenchmen to get out of the window—unsuccessful. Up above, there's a sealed room which we reached by a snow tunnel. It connects with the German quarters. On another occasion a team got into their quarters through a hole in the German lavatories which backed on to one of our dormitories. There's hope of doing something up above on the roof —it might be possible to have another crack at breaking through the gable of the Kommandantur and entering the German attics . . . let's go and have a look at the cookhouse."

Germans and orderlies were still at work and they could not approach the windows overlooking the German courtyard to the south. Dick contented himself by standing inside the doorway and explaining:

"This is where Reid, Ronnie Littledale, Hank Wardle and Stephens got out into the courtyard, then over the sentry's beat into the Kommandantur and out to the moat and away; four home-runs. Above the kitchen, Frenchmen have tried the roofs and chimney-stacks, so has Peter Storie Pugh. It might be tried again, but it's not a cakewalk. Don Thom and Donaldson have had one shot also along the lean-to roof just under the stacks—you've got to be an acrobat to get there because it's an overhanging roof, though nearly flat, once you're on it."

Someone asked 'out of the blue': "Why don't you ever try to escape yourself, Dick?"

"I suppose because I'm a b—— fool," was the response, "but you can't do my job and try to escape as well. The two just don't add up. I know everybody's plans. It would be too easy to pinch someone else's idea and use it myself. Even if I had an idea of my own—nobody would believe me. I might have retired some time ago and asked someone else to take on the job—but now—at least I can't do it until you fellows are well stuck in. Then one of you might take over."

In the courtyard again, he showed them the de-lousing shed. "In one corner of the shed," he said, "there's a tunnel shaft— it was found by the Jerries but the working has been used again. The Poles, before they left, made a tunnel, from their quarters over the canteen—which were once ours, too; joining up with the drains. The drains run just beside that corner of the de-louser and they linked up. They continued outside the courtyard, under the main gate. The escape is in hand at the moment and Duggie Bader's in charge of it. He could do with help—it's a stinking job—every cut festers."

They next trooped upstairs to the theatre where Dick told his audience the story of the light-well escape. Then pointing to the stage, he said:

"Four men got out from under the stage—Airey Neave was one. They went through a narrow corridor, over the main gate, into the German guardhouse and walked downstairs and out— in German uniforms, of course. Two made home-runs to Switzerland. A couple of Poles also got into the guardhouse from the building opposite this theatre block, by walking along a four-inch ledge forty feet above the cobbles. They made too much row climbing down their rope on the outside. A Jerry officer popped his head out of a window. They were only then about a hundred feet above the rocks at the bottom, hanging on to the rope. The Jerry pointed a pistol at them and shouted 'Hands up!' I'm told the Poles laughed so much they nearly let go."

Looking downwards from one of the theatre windows facing due west he showed the group where Bush Parker had dropped in the searchlight beams on to the causeway. Finally, the tour ended in the British quarters overlooking the terrace which also faced westward and were situated just to the south of the turret where Dick had begun.

"Some weeks ago," he told them, "Don Thom took the bull by the horns. He's an Olympic diver, incidentally. He's as tough as nails and a bundle of springs. I think he was browned off by all the effort we put into Bush Parker's escape which fizzled out. We've got another job on hand at the moment, too, and I'd ask you chaps to leave this area alone until it's over. If I tell you of Don Thom's effort you'll see that we're up against a very tough proposition."

"Have you a large-scale plan of the Castle?" Gordon Rolfe asked. "I'd like to study it for a while to get my bearings."

"Yes, there is a plan," said Dick, "it's a series of plans really. It gives the state of the buildings from about the seventeenth century onwards, as a matter of fact. The one thing I can't tell you is how we got it. I'll show it to any of you who want to examine it. Lulu Lawton will get it out of its hide after dinner."

"What happened to Don Thom?" Tony Rolt asked.

The group had relaxed. Some were lolling on the beds, others were looking out of the window down upon the terrace. The bars prevented them from having a clear view directly below them. Nobody was in a hurry.

"Don Thom's escape was a Douglas Fairbanks showpiece," Dick began. "Don first of all earned himself a month in the cooler—that was easy. Then, during the hour's exercise on the terrace you're looking at below you, he just leapt for it. It's the most daring escape recorded here and more death-defying even than the park escape of Mairesse Lebrun, the French cavalry officer. Mairesse at least had the assistance of one other officer and was exercising in the park under guard. There have been many escapes from the park, incidentally, which you'll hear about. Don Thom dared four sentries in broad daylight, one of them—you can see from that window—with a machine-gun. I know exactly how he must have felt because I'd never have the guts or suicidal courage—call it what you like—to do it myself.

"The men in the cooler inside the Castle are usually taken out under guard to the terrace through the guardhouse itself. They come out through that small doorway at the south end. The terrace wall drops, from the outer balustrade, forty feet to the garden below. The far edge of the garden is protected by the low parapet wall which you can see, and by the nine-foot barbed-wire fence. On the far side there's a precipitous drop which descends into a welter of rocks and concertina wire about fifty feet below. The cliff then levels out into the back-yards of a few houses alongside the road which borders the river.

"Bag Dickenson, Van Rood and Don were all doing solitary together. One morning, the same as any other as far as soli-taries are concerned, the three of them were escorted for their daily exercise, one sentry in front, one behind—regular daily routine—through the courtyard gate, into the guardhouse, down a few curving steps, and out on to the terrace.

"A sentry went first, and Bag next, through the little door-way into the open air. Dom Thom was third. As he passed the door, he took off his jacket, dropped it in the corner, and vaulted the parapet; a clear forty foot drop—just like that! Don's tough, but still, forty feet is not the kind of jump to be contemplated when rifles and machine-guns are going to open on you as soon as you land. As he dropped, he gripped the bars of two windows, one under the other, to break his fall. You can't see the windows from here, they're below the terrace in the guardhouse wall. He was seen by four sentries, including the one following Van Rood, and the fifth—the sentry in front of Bag—turned round when his mate shouted. Five sentries tried to hit him as he ran. Bag and Van Rood jitterbugged into their two sentries on the terrace and managed to upset their aim. But a machine-gun post in a pagoda and two other sentries opened fire without hindrance.

"Don Thom ran to the fence. He probably saved his life by turning to the right when common sense dictated he should go to the left. He scaled the nine-foot wire with the bullets whizzing around him. He was forced to slow up by the climb. Then he dropped out of sight down the cliff below; hit or un-scathed nobody could tell. He wasn't yet out of danger. Two sentries, who could still see him, potted away. He must have been moving fast at the bottom, tearing his way through a weak point in the concertina wire. But he couldn't make it. His clothes were ripped to pieces and he got tangled up; he had to put up his hands and they stopped firing. The nearest bullet took a piece out of his scalp."

There was a long pause when Dick finished the story. Then Tony Rolt asked:

"Did you say, Dick, that another escape was being planned from the terrace?"

"Yes, Mike Sinclair and Jack Best are going to have a crack, at dusk though, not in broad daylight. They have to start inside the Castle, of course. The only other way to get out on to the terrace is to do what Don Thom did and that means a daylight job."

There was a long silence. It was broken by the sound of a raucous voice in the corridor shouting: "Char up! Char up!" As if waking from a dream, the men rose and ambled out silently one by one to the mess-room.

*   *   *   *   *

Jack Best, of the R.A.F.V.R., the boy from Stowe, the Empire-builder with a farm in Kenya, was becoming desperate. He had been a ghost for almost a year. The tables were turning upon him and he was beginning to look like a haunted man. Jack, at thirty years of age, had the patience of Job. It was the reason why he had been accepted when he volunteered for the unenviable task of becoming a ghost. But it was plain that the job was beginning to tell on his health. Don Donaldson had, not without reason, christened him the 'unfledged eagle'. Now his downy feathers were drooping; his hair was looking thin and bedraggled, ready to fall out in a high wind. His long beak of a nose was losing flesh. The bridge was standing out prominently and the tip would soon meet his chin as his mouth receded. His dark eyes, with the fire of the eagle within, were more sunken than ever, and looked like two coals burning into his skull. His tall angular frame was hunched. The protruding shoulders and arms looked as if they should sprout feathers at any moment.

The only way by which he could break the vicious circle in which he found himself and retain his self-respect was by escaping, because he was no longer officially recognised as a prisoner. He had escaped, but into another prison inside the prison instead of outside. If and when he escaped properly, another officer could take up his ghostly manacles. If he made a home-run the arithmetic would, in his case, be simplified; it would have caught up with him. From the German point of view, the sum would add up correctly. But if he was recaught the Germans would have to use algebra, beginning with "Let X be the officer who escaped in November 1942. . . ." If Best was recaptured after some days of freedom there was one series of possible solutions. If he was caught at the camp, there were other solutions, including the possibility that he was entering the Castle—gun-running—a possibility not so far-fetched as it might appear at first.

Although Jack had a tremendous sense of humour, he lived on his nerves. He had seen the funny side of living like a mole underground at Sagan—Stalag Luft III—while he tunnelled himself and his friend, Bill Goldfinch, outside the wire to mark up a 'gone-away' and earn them both a place at Colditz. He could still see the funny side of being a ghost—up to a point, but by November 1943 the joke was wearing thin.

Mike Sinclair was planning his next escape. A duel of wits

of his own conception was to take place on an old battle-ground: the terrace where Don Thom had sailed gaily over the parapet as if he had been performing in the high jump at his annual school sports.

Mike selected Jack Best as his partner for the break.

The time at which the perimeter searchlights were switched on was tabulated and graphed as a matter of routine. What Mike was looking for was a short blind interval at dusk; blind in two senses: firstly, on account of the approaching gloom and, secondly, coinciding with a change of the guards, taking them from their points of vantage. He posed the problem to Dick Howe and indicated when he thought the short interval of time might occur.

Regularly, over a period of four months, Dick, Lulu Lawton and Mike watched the changing of the guard in the terrace area; in the pagoda; on the cat-walk; in the garden (an orchard), and in the corner turret. Jack Best could not help them in this, being a ghost!

A machine-gun sentry post, an outsize crow's-nest, situated on an elevated scaffolding, reached by a ladder, in the garden beneath the terrace, commanded the whole wall face of the prison on that side, including the outer wall of the German guardhouse It was known as a 'pagoda', and was manned day and night. Another type of scaffold, providing a long elevated corridor with timber balustrades, was known as a 'cat-walk'. One such was built close to the outer wall of the guardhouse where the garden narrowed, and at one end it jutted out over the precipice below. The sentry post at ground level in the garden and the machine-gun post in the turret under the prison walls was only manned at nightfall, when it became difficult for the machine-gun post in the pagoda to command the walls fully, owing to deep shadows cast by the searchlights at certain angles. The garden sentry also replaced a sentry on the terrace itself, who was useless at night, standing direct in the glare of the searchlights.

The turret sentry and the garden sentry came on duty at the nearest regular guard change coinciding with nightfall. With this pinpoint of knowledge, culled by simple observation, Mike Sinclair opened an oyster.

The first essential that the three watchers deduced was that, between the time when the pagoda sentry left his post at dusk and was replaced and the first turret sentry had gained his position, there was a blind spot of sixty seconds duration. The second essential for the escape was the seasonal advent of a period when the searchlights, governed, as was discovered, by a routine schedule depending mainly on the time of year and hardly at all upon the state of the light on any particular day, were switched on just after a regular guard change. 'Just after' was the important point, so that the sixty seconds coincided with the maximum darkness possible. Not until the end of November 1943 were all the conditions favourable for the attempt to take place.

Sixty seconds! Perhaps seventy seconds. Perhaps only fifty! Dick, Mike and Lulu were not prepared to argue over ten seconds either way. The job to be performed was one that would require the services, under peace-time conditions, of a team of workmen for a day with long ladders and several tool kits; an industrial safety inspector, and a merger of Lloyd's insurance brokers. Mike Sinclair and Jack Best, dispensing with the anomalies of peace, reckoned to do the job in sixty seconds.

The bars of a window in the British quarters on the second floor of the Castle, thirty feet above the terrace, had to be cut by way of an opening gambit. This was done in the same manner as for the Franz Josef attempt.

Bos'n Crisp prepared no less than ninety feet of the best rope he had ever made from strips cut out of the blue check cotton sleeping-bags and tested at every splice.

The civilian clothing, the maps, the money, the home-made compasses and the identity papers were forged with minute accuracy.

Mike Sinclair selected his wire-cutters. He preferred the pair made by Bill Goldfinch to the factory-made pair smuggled into the camp.

The four of them discussed the launching ramp.

"You'd better use the long table," said Dick, "and give it a thorough rub down with sand-paper. The long one will take the two of you lying flat, end to end, and you can be shot straight through the window opening, holding on to the rope."

Mike said, with a curious air of finality, "I want you two, Dick and Lulu, to do the launching; nobody else. I don't want anyone else to do it."

"Mike will go out first," Dick explained, "with the wire-cutters strapped to his leg When he's dropped to the terrace he takes the rope end with him and jumps over the balustrade, Don Thom fashion. Now, Jack, if you don't hustle after Mike, you'll find yourself suspended in mid-air over the terrace when he takes the rope with him over the second drop. Everything's got to move together. Lulu, you must let the rope out as fast as Mike needs it, but keep it fairly taut all the time. Jack, you've simply got to be on the terrace by the time Mike goes over, so you must slide down the rope following Mike like streak lightning down a moving escalator. Get me?"

Jack intervened "What about the brief-case and the second length of rope all attached to the end of the main rope?"

"When you've finished with the main rope, that is, after the second drop, unhitch them both—they'll be on a slip-knot—and carry on. Now, Lulu, this is where you come in. As soon as the tension is off the main rope you must haul in like mad! Jack, don't forget to keep a firm hold on the rope or you'll find your food and kit disappearing upwards. Let go only when everything is clear. After that, the rest is up to you and we can't do much more for you."

When the two escapers reached the bottom of the second drop they would have to run thirty yards diagonally across the garden, cut a gap in the barbed-wire perimeter fence, tie the second rope to a post and drop down the rocky cliff below, a matter of fifty feet. This was the cliff over which Don Thom had thrown himself, clinging to jutting crags as he hurtled down in broad daylight with rifles blazing at him. On the new assault, Mike and Jack hoped to tie their rope and disappear over the edge before they were seen. To this end, of course, silence was invaluable.

At the bottom of the cliff they had concertina barbed-wire to deal with before they were finally 'gone-away'.

*　　　*　　　*　　　*　　　*

The stage is set for the escape of sixty seconds. It is a cold afternoon at the end of November 1943, with sleet and a biting wind which augurs well for a murky evening. The day wears on. The two bars of the window have been cut by Bricky Forbes and Bill Goldfinch. The stooges are placed as the gloom of evening begins to creep over the Castle and their intercommunicating code system is checked. The signal 'all clear', will come from the accordion of the master stooge at a window directly above that at which the operation is about to take place. Dick will give the final order, 'Go'. . . .

Zero hour has arrived and zero minute will soon be here. The wind has dropped, which is a pity. Mike and Jack will need all the self-control they can muster to avoid making a noise and giving the alarm on the last lap.

In the dormitory there is silence as the shadows deepen. Along the smooth table the two escapers lie. Jack Best is dead still. Mike is fidgety. The cutters strapped to his leg are uncomfortable. They may give trouble. Dick is readjusting them.

High up in a corner, sitting on the top of a wardrobe, is John Watton, the camp artist, with his drawing-board, pencils and chalks. He is working furiously in the gathering dusk, his hand and brain alive to the terrific tension as he tries to translate the suspense of the moment on to the flat medium of paper. He stares downwards. His eyes gleam in the fading light and his hand circles upon the paper.

"Three minutes to go," says Dick in a hushed voice, "providing the sentries behave themselves. Keep dead calm. Remember it's a cinch. Go quietly as you drop and move."

The two men lie still, stiffening against the fierce heave that will project them along the table out into the twilight one after the other, like rockets from a launching ramp; that will shoot them out of the window in a headlong swoop which they must check before landing. The rope is laid out straight beside and behind them. Mike holds it coiled around his right arm.

All the actors on the stage who may approach the window have blackened faces, and the two escapers, in addition, wear long dark stockings over their shoes. Their two forms lie stretched, like beasts on a sacrificial altar, ready for the moment when the high priest will raise his arm aloft and pronounce the words of doom.

"One minute to go," Dick intones in a low voice, clear for all to hear in the grim silence.

Two strong men stand rigid beside the window, waiting, ready to grip the bars and twist them out of the way at the signal. The whites of their eyes flash out of their blackened faces.

Derek Gill and Mike Harvey stand by the rope, to pay it out, to prevent it tangling and to take the weight of the descending bodies.

Dick and Lulu, the priests, stand over the table while Dick leans towards the window, listening intently, peering downwards.

Mike is jittery. He is complaining the cutters are too tight around his leg. Almost like a child, he is whispering to Dick, "They're too tight! They're too tight! I must have them looser —help me quickly—looser—quick—— No! Dick, there's no time now. It's too late. There's not enough time, stop."

The accordion starts to play.

Dick looks at his watch and raises his arm, counting audibly, "Four—three—two—one," and then drops it at "Go!"

The two strong men at the bars clench their teeth and heave with the strength of devils, twisting the bars inwards and sideways in a slow, quivering movement fraught with the tautness of muscles and the wracking of sinews. Hell breaks loose. The spirit of action like an unholy demon takes possession of the room.

Lulu and Dick grip Mike bodily, one on either side, and hurl him through the window feet first. He shoots horizontally outwards. Another tremendous heave and Jack Best slides forward, rockets out and disappears from view. Gill and Harvey feel the rope tearing through their hands. They let it out to the first marker knot, lean back, take the strain with the rope twisted round their forearms. There is a tremendous jerk, followed by a thump. The rope holds. The two are down on the terrace, thirty feet below.

The rope pays out again, uncoiling like a cobra, weaving, snatching and turning, as Mike races across the terrace.

Dick, at the window, raises his arm again in signal. Gill and Harvey take the strain once more on the rope. Mike and Jack are over the terrace and dropping down the second forty-foot descent.

The guardhouse door is opening. A shaft of light breaks through the gloom along the terrace. A German N.C.O. walks out, advancing slowly along the terrace. He seems momentarily blind.

"They must free the rope!" hisses Dick. "Good God, he can see it! It's straight in front of him. For Pete's sake, Derek! heave it in, heave like mad!"

As he speaks the light blue rope slackens. The German leans on the balustrade. He looks over the parapet. At that instant the rope whistles past him, upwards, not a yard away. He has heard something; he whips out his revolver, but seems not to have seen the rope. He shouts: *"Hallo! Hallo!"* There is no answer.

A scurry above, as the rope is hauled through the window, makes the German look upwards for a moment, puzzled. Then he turns towards the garden as a distinct 'ping' is heard from the direction of the wire below. Another loud 'ping' and the German shouts again, *"Hallo! Hallo! Was ist los?"* and peers into the shadows below, shading his eyes with his hand, and with his revolver cocked.

Mike has crossed the garden and is cutting the wires underneath the pagoda where the new sentry has taken up his position. Mike appears to take no notice of the guard who has come out on to the terrace. He has not seen him. The sentry above him answers the N.C.O.: *"Ich weiss nicht."*

Jack is in the shadow under the terrace wall. He can see the German above him and dares not move. He cannot warn Mike. A third 'ping' is heard clearly by Dick and Lulu in the window high above.

The German walks slowly along the terrace near the parapet, looking outwards. The night sentry in the garden has reached his post and is standing fifteen yards away. This is Jack's chance; he creeps to the end of the wall and then across the garden among the fruit trees and the deeper shadows to where Mike has already fixed the rope for the last drop. Mike drops over. Jack follows, but lies on the edge of the drop, trying to close the wire gap behind him. He looks up and sees the German on the terrace staring straight towards him with his pistol at the ready. That is enough. He drops out of sight, sliding down the rope over rocks and bushes, fifty feet, to the bottom. The N.C.O. turns slowly away.

There is more barbed-wire below—coils upon coils of it.

"We can't get through there," whispers Mike hoarsely; "we must crawl along to the end."

They do so, slipping and stumbling on the steep incline, ripping their clothes on the wire at every move until they reach a narrow path.

Here Mike tackles the wire again: 'ping! ping! ping!' Bill Goldfinch's home-made, five-to-one lever wire-cutters do their work. They crawl through.

But a woman in a nearby cottage has heard the scrambling and comes to the window, looking out. *"Was ist los?"*

Silence! as the two men lie prone, their hearts pounding, she moves away and they are off again.

They are dripping with sweat, winded and breathing painfully. Their civilian clothes are badly torn. Seventy seconds ago they were prisoners in the impregnable fortress. Now they are free. . . .

*   *   *   *   *

As they moved off into the countryside at a slow trot, Dick stood motionless at the window high up in the Castle.

The German N.C.O. had returned to the guardhouse, walking slowly with hesitant steps, frequently turning round, obviously worried and uncomprehending.

Dick gazed outwards over the fast darkening countryside, out into the gloom towards the river where he knew his two men were heading He was tingling all over with nervous elation. Then, as he peered, he felt his legs weaken under him and he gripped the window-sill to steady himself. Gall rose in his throat and a sudden revulsion turned his stomach. His eyes misted over. He closed them quickly, gripping the sill tightly. The nausea continued for a couple of minutes as he fought against the urge to vomit. . . . The crisis passed slowly and he opened his eyes.

The searchlight came on with a blinding flash around the Castle and all beyond turned as black as pitch.

"They've gone-away! They're safe by now!" said Dick thickly, turning to Lulu and the others, and mopping his blackened brow with the flicker of a smile spreading over his face. There was silence again. He glanced at his companions, noting at once he was not the only one whose stomach had turned over. After the fever of the past two minutes they were stunned. For a few seconds they had all been escaping with the two who had disappeared. Now they stood silent, wondering, almost inexplicably, why they had not gone, why they were still in the room within the oppressive walls. There were no words that they could say.

Watton climbed down from his perch, shaking with the excitement of the action. "Fantastic, simply fantastic!" he shouted, waving his drawing-block wildly round his head.

"I'm glad you like it," said Lulu dryly. "I'll appreciate a signed copy of the result, if you don't mind."

Dick said simply, talking to them all, "Thanks for a pretty piece of teamwork. You've made escaping history to-night— I think." And as they went about clearing away the signs of the escape, Dick turned once more to the window, staring out into the blackness beyond the searchlight beams.

He stood, motionless, with the reflection from the blazing arcs outside accentuating his worn, haggard features, still streaked with black theatre paint; the strong chin, the drawn lines of the skin and the sunken eyes. His thoughts had suddenly been turned inwards. He was trying to answer the questions that had flashed through all their minds when they stood silent and perplexed a few moments before. "Why were they still there? Why had others gone?" There seemed to be no general answer. "Many are called, but few are chosen," he thought, "might not be far off the mark."

It was more than a question of plain guts. For this kind of escaping a man required a will of iron and a calculating, cold-blooded courage that was not commonly found. There was a deep sense of duty behind it all, too—but that applied to all of them.

"All over the world," Dick thought, "men are fighting and falling. To be impotent—a prisoner—helpless and unable to help, is a degrading state, hard to bear."

At least these men were doing something. They could hold up their heads and keep their self-respect. They were thinking of the future and not necessarily of their own. They had not Milton's excuse. 'They also serve who only stand and wait' was not for them. They were not blind.

For several minutes Dick stood at the window, then, turning slowly, he came out of his reveries.

"I thought Mike was a bit jittery to-night, not quite his usual self," he said to Lulu. "I wonder why the Goon chose to come out on to the terrace at that precise moment?"

"Most inconsiderate of him," was Lulu's comment as they walked out of the room together.

CHAPTER XVI

CHINA TEA

TONY ROLT was one of the sixty-five Eichstätt tunnellers. From the day they had arrived, in July 1943, these tunnellers had been known as 'the new boys'. The name clung to them and, the English being a conservative race, they were still new boys at the end of the war, by which time they had been indistinguishable from their blood-brothers, 'the old lags', for nearly two years.

In self-defence the 'new boys' invented 'the men of spirit'— a term which they applied to any and sundry among the 'old lags' who, either by innuendo or direct attack, tried to inculcate in them a sense of inferiority. They were not to be browbeaten and the sarcasm behind the appellation had its effect.

Undertones and rumblings, disturbances from the intrusion into Colditz, echoed around the camp and slowly died away. Like the spilling of one lake into another when the weir gates are raised, the two waters clashed, shot up in spray, sent waves dashing to the shore, swirled in eddies, rippled, merged and gradually subsided into one, still, homogeneous pool, deeper than before.

The new boys were under a disadvantage: the disadvantage suffered by all new boys throughout the world. They did not know the ropes, they did not know the old boys, they were in strange surroundings and sometimes at a loss—humiliating under any circumstances. But they brought with them some new ideas which the old boys eventually acknowledged— grudgingly to begin with—and later with enthusiasm. The scorpion's lash of 'the new boys' lost its sting.

Tony Rolt was one among the many whom the old boys would have liked to claim towards the end of the war, as one of the 'men of spirit'. This term also, like an old, well-worn, ugly pair of shoes, became 'cosy' from long usage.

Rolt, in his early twenties, was an amateur motor-racing driver who had achieved fame before the war. He was a lieutenant of the Rifle Brigade. He was tall, dark and clean-shaven, almost streamlined, like one of his cars, and he had a serious yet lively nature; at one and the same time painstaking yet bubbling with enthusiasm.

He could not drive a delicate, highly-tuned racing car out of Colditz; even a heavy tank would not have gone far. He used to lie for hours on his bunk, exasperated by the frustration, stung by his own impotence and goaded to action by the blackness of the escaping outlook. He wondered how some highly technical *flair* could be brought to bear on escaping; there was any amount of scientific talent in Colditz. It was clear to him that only the most desperate action would succeed in these days. The last two escapes which had put British prisoners outside the perimeter wire were cases in point. When men were taking to leaping over forty-foot walls in broad daylight, braving the machine-guns, rocketing out of windows attached to ropes, weaving between sentries in mad, second-splitting escapes, it was time to be original, and in a big way. To Rolt's way of thinking there was no hope of success for anything in the least mundane. The Jerries had all that taped, tied up and sealed irrevocably.

He brought together and crystallised the gleanings of weeks of cogitation one day in December 1943. He sat brooding over a morning cup of acorn coffee, made palatable with powdered milk and a saccharine tablet.

Rumours were abroad that Mike and Jack Best had been recaptured. Pessimism was on the prowl again, looking for victims.

He spoke first to Bill Goldfinch, who was sitting opposite to him munching a piece of German sawdust-bread thinly coated with the remains of a Canadian Red Cross butter ration.

"Quite a tribute, I thought, the way Mike Sinclair took your home-made wire-cutters in preference to the factory-made variety. You're a bit of a wizard with your hands, Bill. Where did you learn it?"

It was not a coincidence that he should be talking to Bill Goldfinch. It was part of his thinking—this morning, it seemed, everything had come to a head. Bill Goldfinch was sitting there. The time was ripe.

Bill was speaking.

"There's nothing to it, Tony. I just got the habit of tinkering when I was a kid, ever since the family went out to Rhodesia. My old man was an engineer. I suppose that had something to do with it. He sent me to work in the Salisbury City Council engineering department. I'm not happy unless my hands are at work."

"What made you join the R.A.F.?" Rolt asked.

"I got mad keen on flying and aircraft design. That sent me into the R.A.F.V.R. when I was twenty-one. It must have been about 1938. That's how I'm here now. I got called up when war started and was trapped in the Greek evacuation. My Sunderland flying-boat crashed at Kalamata. If I hadn't been spitting blood I'd've been evacuated. Instead they operated on me—found nothing wrong—only mouth bleeding. But before my operation wound healed I was a prisoner. I met up with Jack Best in the hospital."

As he listened, Tony was thinking: "This is the man all right. I'm sure he'll do it. . . . I bet he will." Aloud he said, "Bill, I've got an idea. I'm going to tell you something that'll make you think I'm going round the bend. I'm not though—not yet."

"Go ahead, I'm listening," said Bill quietly, in a reassuring voice. He was like that, reassuring, with a touch of kindliness. His fair complexion, his mousy hair and his pale blue eyes made up a picture of an unassuming, even shy nature. His inner strength, the peculiar tough fibre which has nothing to do with physical strength, but a lot to do with mental equanimity, only made itself felt after long contact with his personality. He was the type of man who would survive alone in a lifeboat after weeks of exposure, long after all the other occupants had gone overboard.

"I'm not an engineer, you see, Bill," Rolt continued, "but I know enough about mechanics and, I think also, enough about aerodynamics to imagine that what I'm thinking about is not complete nonsense.

"I seriously think a glider could be built that would be able to take off from one of the roofs of this castle. Don't think me crazy yet—listen—let me finish. I've been thinking about this idea for months. There's a long roof overlooking the river—the one over the old French quarters. It's so high that the ridge is completely out of sight from all the sentries below. In fact, you can only see the ridge if you go down into the town or away over the river. Look!" Here Rolt produced a piece of paper from his pocket. He unfolded it and spread it before Bill Goldfinch.

"You see—there's a cross-section of the castle to scale with the sentries at their posts. Their lines of vision run from the roof gutters straight up, skywards. They can't see anywhere near the roof ridge. We could make a flat launching ramp like a saddle, built in sections, to sit on the roof ridge. It's twenty yards long."

"You mean," interrupted Bill, who was becoming curiously excited in spite of himself, "you mean, the glider would be catapulted then?"

"Yes, that's it. I've already got some ideas for the catapult, but let me finish. The glider would have to be built in parts, with dismountable wings. I don't know how many persons it could take. That's where you would begin to come into the picture. What do you think, Bill? I can't do this myself, but with one, or even two, professionals I'm sure a glider can be built. I'll do all the donkey-work, everything I can possibly do, but I don't know enough about aerodynamics, and I'm not a highly skilled craftsman."

"A glider isn't so very hard to build, you know," said Bill, becoming involved and beginning to fall for the idea. "What it requires is tremendous patience. I only wish Jack Best was around. He's just the man for this. He's got the patience of Job. A glider consists of literally thousands of parts, all the same—like the wings of a bird—thousands of feathers all the same shape. If I made a few prototype parts and some templets, you could carry on."

"Does that mean you'll seriously think about the idea?" asked Tony.

"Yes," said Bill. "I'll think about it," and that was all Tony Rolt could extract from him at that sitting.

During the next two weeks Rolt continued to badger Bill Goldfinch until he had the latter sitting down in front of a home-made drawing-board with pencils, paper, rulers and rubber. From that moment Bill Goldfinch was lost. He found himself starting upon a course which would lead him he knew not where, but quite likely to a 'sticky end'. He was at the top of a steep hill, sitting astride an infernal machine of his own making, without brakes—or engine. He was gaining momentum, out of control, and the end of the hill was just round the corner.

*　　*　　*　　*　　*

While the new boys were still new, it goes without saying that they had their legs pulled.

Harry Elliott was recounting to a few of the newcomers, some time after their arrival, the history of the several continental contingents which had come and gone from Colditz. He talked glowingly of the Poles; humorously of the French and Belgians; warmly of the Dutch, and, to make sure that he lost nothing in effect, he reminded his listeners of the Yugoslav officers, the Indian doctor and the North Africans, and introduced them forthwith to a Bedouin sheik who was, at the time, a resident in Colditz. Nobody quite knew, and least of all the Bedouin himself, how he had filtered down to Colditz. He had been mixed up in some mêlée in North Africa and had been captured. Nobody understood what he said, and he could not understand what anybody else said. One misunderstanding led to another, until the smiling sheik, with the features of an Oriental king and the character of a humorist in perpetual adversity, arrived at Colditz, where it seemed he would not have much opportunity to strike his tent or silently fade away.

"What a collection of nationalities!" exclaimed one new boy in respectful admiration. "What a pity there are no Chinese!" said another with a slight hint of sarcasm.

It was enough for Harry. He would shake them.

"Oh! but haven't you met the Chinese naval officer?" he said.

"No! Where is he? Do introduce us. This is terrific!" The hint of sarcasm had gone. Now there was only astonishment and unconcealed wonder.

The Chinese naval officer was in the sick-bay, explained Harry. He was not very well but he would try to arrange an introduction for the next day.

Harry lived in the sick quarters himself at that time. He was working hard at his own escape plans. His jaundice had given place to duodenal ulcers. These were having marital complications with a genuine form of arthritis, which he was nursing successfully into a galloping paralysis. He had, unfortunately, failed to discover an appropriate disease that was highly infectious—one which would help him back to England quickly and not into a 'Klimtin'.

Two Dutch colonial officers, one of them a naval lieutenant, had remained behind in the sick ward long after the main Dutch contingent had departed. They occupied beds near Harry. He confided to them that he was committed to produce a Chinese naval officer on the following day. They agreed to carry it off with him. The Dutch naval lieutenant was sallow-skinned with an Asiatic type of head and definitely Oriental eyes, which, of course, accounts for the mental vision that had goaded Harry on. This Dutchman would be the Chinese officer; the other Dutchman, Steenhouwer by name, would be his interpreter. They would speak 'Chinese'—in reality Malay, and hope none of the British would understand.

Harry returned to the charge next day, telling the new boys that his Chinese naval officer friend was feeling well enough to pay an official call on the British in their quarters. He suggested

237

after tea that day as an appropriate time, and explained that the Chinese officer could, of course, only speak Chinese, but that, fortunately, a Dutch officer in the sick ward knew a smattering of that language and had kindly offered to act as interpreter.

Tea-time arrived. The senior ranking officer of the quarters, Captain Lord Arundell, posted himself near the door as he heard the visitors mounting the stairs. There were thirty officers scattered around the large room, some sleeping, others reading, smoking or studying, others seated round the tables chatting over empty tea-mugs. They had been warned of the arrival of the visitor. Harry entered the room first and spoke to John Arundell, who called the room to attention, announcing the arrival of 'a representative of our brave Allies, the Chinese'. Harry whispered his name as the Chinaman and his interpreter came through the door and Arundell repeated in ringing tones: "Lieutenant Yo Hun Sin of the Chinese Navy." Arundell stood his ground, while the Chinese lieutenant advanced, bowing towards him and towards the company in turn. He was wearing a dark blue naval uniform with brass buttons and anchor insignia. An exchange of greetings took place—the Dutch officer interpreting in Malay for the benefit of Arundell.

The occupants of the room began to lose interest. A hum of conversation arose. Arundell called for silence. Attention turned towards the party again, and the Chinese officer gabbled a few sentences of Malay, in a song-song voice, at the assembled company. Steenhouwer, the 'interpreter', translated:

"The Chinese officer sends greetings and wishes of long life to his English friends."

Then the Chinese officer bowed slowly and stiffly down to his waist. The Dutchman followed suit, but not quite so far, and a few of the Englishmen, rather self-consciously, thought they had better do something, so they bowed too.

Arundell said: "Please give our greetings to the Chinese officer and say we are glad to welcome him as representing our staunch Ally."

Steenhouwer translated. There were more bows and then

some handshakes also, for good measure. The Chinaman spoke further phrases, which were interpreted as:

"Great honour to be fighting as Ally of British people, China and England, together, are invincible and will win war, perhaps, after many years."

This piece of laconic Chinese realism, rather shaking to British P.O.W.s, was received with pained smiles.

John Arundell then asked the visiting party to join him at his table. Cigarettes were produced. Officers began to gather around, and the interpreter was inundated with questions.

"Ask him if he knows Chiang Kai-shek."

Malay sentences passed between the two; then beams and smiles and much nodding of heads.

"In case you do not know, Chiang Kai-shek is a great general," was the reply.

"Good Godfathers! what does he think we are!" was the English reaction.

"I say, ask him if they've got heavy tanks in China."

More sentences in Malay, then out came the answer:

"Yes, they have got very heavy tanks in China."

"Ask him if they have finished the Burma Road yet."

"Where was he taken prisoner?"

"How is the Chinese Navy doing?"

"How did he get to Germany?" Questions were reeled off and the two were hard put to it to keep up with their Malay.

The answers were repeated into the crowd who had gathered in the background.

"I say, did you hear that, they *have* got heavy tanks in China."

"The Burma Road is nearly finished."

"He blew up a Jap warship and then got blown up himself."

"The Chinese Navy has a secret weapon."

There was a pause and the Chinese officer seized the opportunity to rise to take leave. He spoke some more words in Malay. The interpreter recorded faithfully: "The Chinese naval lieutenant wishes, before departure, to sing his National Anthem."

Unfortunately, many of the prisoners, by this time, were back at their private occupations. John Arundell had to call for order again—banging on the table.

The Chinaman was standing with his hat on his head, looking very solemn.

An awkward moment of embarrassment followed—the British not knowing whether to stand or remain seated, to put their hats on or stand at attention without them.

The Chinese officer began in a pale, quavering voice, snatches from a Malay fisherman's song that he happened to know.

The British stood stiffly to attention and, when the Chinaman saluted at the conclusion, they acknowledged the salute—a little sheepishly.

Someone said: "Hadn't we better sing *God Save the King?*"

With doubtful enthusiasm and some self-consciousness officers persevered with the lines, and finished the anthem with a major effort.

The Chinaman now bowed in all directions, moving backwards slowly towards the door, followed by his *cortège* who had to edge out sideways, so as not to get in front of his bows.

The door closed behind them, and the curtain dropped upon the incident until the next day, when the new boys spent the morning telling the old boys what the Chinese naval officer had told them. "They've got heavy tanks in China. Got it out of that Chinese naval officer—decent type, I thought," and the old lags would say:

"What Chinese officer? We've got 'em all colours, but take me to a Chinese!"

Then someone began to smell a rat and soon the story was all over the camp. The new boys took a few days to live it down. The man who enjoyed it most, of course, was Harry, who laughs to this day when he talks of it.

*   *   *   *   *

Harry Elliott may have had an even earlier cue for his practical joke about the Chinese naval officer. In fact, he was not the first in the Chinese field and the Colditz story would not be complete without the episode (it happened in 1942) of the British officer who taught Chinese to a Pole for several months.

Cyril Lewthwaite, of the Royal Warwicks, was an unforgettable character. He hailed from Bromwich and was one of the first escapers of the war. On a solo effort from Laufen, Oflag VII C, in October 1940, he escaped in the middle of the pig-swill cart. On reaching the off-loading place, Cyril rose out of the swill with a scream as he received, in the fleshy part of his leg, the full force of a sharp fork aimed at a recalcitrant heap of rotting potatoes under which he grudgingly reposed. Within a matter of minutes he had the whole village of Laufen chasing him in full cry. He ran gamely in two senses of the word, and then found himself cornered in a sharp bend of the River Salzach. He took to the water in the style of Walter Scott's stag with the hounds baying behind him, but, unlike the stag and coming from the Midlands, he had forgotten in his youth to learn to swim. He was soon up to his chin and going deeper. At this tragic point he was recaptured and marched back to the prison. He was escorted by the whole village in a pitchfork procession in which, as the chief object of veneration, he made a sorry spectacle, dripping from head to foot, filthy, with the slime of half a ton of pig-swill upon him and smelling to high heaven as he slopped along the village street accompanied by the jeers, hoots and screams of a population that had nearly tasted blood.

When Cyril arrived in Colditz, he became involved in languages. He had only one language to sell—that was English. He wanted to learn French, German, Italian and perhaps Russian also. He could, of course, select a different teacher for each language he required, and teach them, each in turn, English. But English bored him stiff. He could speak it, but he could not, for the life of him, explain how he spoke it or why. He would have preferred Latin for that. His best French friend had already another English teacher. It was all rather difficult until he found the way out. Then it was plain sailing. He was talking, one day, to a Polish officer who was a barrister. The Pole recounted a story in which a Chinese business-man had fared very badly at the hands of the Polish law-courts because nobody in the country understood Chinese. The Polish barrister spoke French well. Cyril seized upon this and suggested filling the gap in the Polish legal fence by teaching his friend Chinese. The Polish barrister took the bait, hook, line and sinker; gave up teaching French to his other pupils and agreed to concentrate on Cyril alone, in exchange for Cyril's Chinese.

Cyril did not know a word of Chinese, but he was undaunted. He started his lessons quite simply on classical lines. He outlined the notions of Chinese declensions; he said there were twenty, thinking that would give him plenty of breathing space. He spoke of the various tenses and emphasised that the Chinese, living as they do without much reference to time, and the passage of history, spoke of everything in the present tense unless it was about a thousand years old, in which case it went into various forms of imperfect, ultimately ending in the perfect past. As for the future, unless it would take place after a thousand years it was also in the present. This paved the way for Cyril. He was able to explain with graphic illustrations why it was that the Chinese always spoke that peculiar tongue known as pidgin English. He would then quote an old story he knew, about a Chinaman who fumed at a railway station cloak-room attendant searching for his luggage, screaming as his train left without him: "Pretty damn seldom how my bag go. She no fly. You no fit keep station than God's sake." He would explain: "You see, everything is in the present tense unless it's very, very old."

He continued with conjugations and thought it wise to have lots of those, too, Chinese being an ancient language.

He started the Pole off with a Chinese version of *amo, amas, amat*. It was *mo, mao, maoto*, pronounced in a decidedly Oriental manner. Cyril thought he ought to change the meaning, so *mo* meant 'I eat', and so on. He gave him a few other simple verbs to learn as well.

To increase his vocabulary, as the declensions, Cyril said,

were so complicated, he would teach him the first declension and with the nouns of other declensions he would permit his pupil, for the time being, to speak pidgin Chinese. It would increase his 'word power' rapidly. He gave him the equivalent of *mensa, mensa, mensam* . . . to study.

It went like this: *Soya, soya, soyo*. . . . It meant, a bean. I eat a bean: *mo soyo*.

The Pole made progress. In fact, he was much too quick, because Cyril found that, instead of learning any French, he spent his homework hours trying to keep up with his frighteningly assiduous pupil. He struggled on for several weeks until, one early morning, when he was on mess orderly duty, as he queued up in the grisly dawn outside the German kitchen, wooden clogs on his feet, his head swathed in a long balaclava, bare legs showing beneath his dressing-gown, a tattered French khaki cloak, he suddenly heard a voice beside him.

"Hokito tao yen yosh inko?"

He knew the voice only too well. He could bear it no longer. Besides he did not know what on earth the man was saying, and to be caught out like this, at an early hour, was just the last straw—speaking Chinese in his underpants! Cyril prided himself on his military turn-out, and rightly so. In the normal light of day, he was one of the smartest looking officers in the camp.

"Yoshinka yen?" continued the voice solicitously. *"Mao cha pani undu yoyo."* It was the *yoyo* that finally choked Cyril. He remembered teaching some quite fantastic participles, which ended with *yoyo*, weeks before. Only a prodigy could have remembered its meaning now. With a weary sigh he pulled himself together and looking his pupil in the eye, he said solemnly, placing his hand over his stomach:

"Mo chu la beri-beri suyu."

To which his pupil replied, *"Munchi sunya! munchi sunya!"*

Between them there was a bond of perfect mutual comprehension. Cyril fled upstairs and his pupil gazed touchingly after him before returning to the copybook over which he diligently pored.

That was the last Chinese lesson Cyril ever gave.

CHAPTER XVII

THE WRITING ON THE WALL

WHEN Mike Sinclair and Jack Best had escaped over the para-
pets, Dick Howe had no ghost to cover the absence of Sinclair
at the evening *Appell*. He laid on the 'rabbit' instead. An air-
raid that night also gave Dick the opportunity to repair the
window bars while the searchlights were extinguished. He expected that the Germans would notice the hole in the wire and
the dangling rope in the morning. His fears proved groundless.
The hole, hidden under the structure of the pagoda, remained
undiscovered for two days.

Upon the discovery, Lieutenant Barnes, who was Jack Best's
double, went into hiding. At the *Sonder*—i.e. special—*Appell*,
Mike Sinclair and Barnes were declared to be absent.

At this point there were no more volunteers to undertake the
unhealthy job of being ghosts. Jack Best had been haunting
the Castle for just one year!

Mike Sinclair was missing. The '*Rote Fuchs*' had escaped
again! Military and Gestapo telephone wires began to hum.
Heads began to swim and a special inquiry was set up. The
German Commandant appeared before the High Command at
Leipzig, where he had to make the ignominious confession that
he did not know when the escape had taken place.

The two escapers had ended up their hair-raising descent of
the east cliff wall, on that fateful evening, with their clothes
ripped to pieces by the barbed-wire. They found a small path
at the bottom of the cliff, and followed it. In the friendly darkness of a wood, half an hour later, they sat down to repair their
damaged clothing, threading their needles by the light of a
burning cigarette.

Three days later they were captured by civil police in the

small town of Rheine, twenty-two miles from the Dutch frontier.

On this occasion they had not headed for Switzerland. The trouble was that men who escaped to Switzerland had been filtering much too slowly out of that country, with the result that escapers were tempted to try other routes with the chance of a quicker repatriation to England. Knowing the Colditz route by heart, they should have had a much better chance of crossing safely into neutral territory. It was a pity they were biased by information which, though correct at the time, should not have been allowed to outweigh their better chance of freedom.

An astute police officer at Rheine thought he recognised Mike from a photograph published in a police broadsheet circulated daily throughout Germany. At the same time he did not like the look of Best. "Not Germanic enough," he said later. The police officer arrested them both while they were walking together along the main street of the town.

The two men were escorted back to Colditz by an N.C.O. and four soldiers—a small tribute to the esteem in which they were held.

The German High Command were in a quandary. The Red Fox had escaped at an unknown date. Positive evidence as to the Fox's presence in the camp went back several weeks. They were bewildered and angry. All they knew was that there was a large hole in the perimeter wire and that, in the hours of darkness, prisoners might have used it as a rabbit-run. How many had gone out? How many had come in? Nobody really knew. The Colditz inmates were playing hide-and-seek with them. The High Command had to consider the possibility that the Allied secret service might be at work, that the wire had been cut from the outside—nobody had been seen cutting it inside—and that prisoners were being removed or exchanged *ad lib*. The Commandant was made to look very foolish, and his senior officers let him feel the whip of their scorn. The Germans were convinced that the British were up to no good. Mike was a dangerous man, known to have had contacts in Poland before he came to Colditz. A veritable underground movement was forming under their noses. They could not keep the scandal away from the Gestapo, who, as far as the prisoners' intelligence service could estimate, took charge of Colditz men, recaptured while escaping, from that day forward.

Jack Best, immediately upon recapture, knew his part and posed as Barnes. On his return to the Castle he was allowed back into the camp pending his sentence. The question then arose: should Barnes or Jack continue as the ghost? Jack thought he himself should because Barnes, at least, could then remain Barnes, though he would have to do a month's solitary for Jack! Jack, on the other hand, would always be in difficulties roaming the camp as Barnes. However, it was decided the other way.

The Dr. Jekyll and Mr. Hyde comedy continued for several days. But the Germans, under the prodding of the Gestapo, were forced to probe the mystery of the Red Fox's escape. They must have reflected upon the case of Mike Harvey and his double.

A long-drawn-out identity parade was held at which Jack appeared as Barnes, but the Germans pondered a long time over his record sheet. They suspected he was not the man whose photo was before them, but they let him go.

The next day they pounced again. Jack was removed and his finger-prints were taken. They were not those opposite the name of Barnes!

The game was up. Jack continued to bluff until he saw that the Germans suspected he was Flight-Lieutenant J. Best. They were awaiting his records which had gone to Berlin when Jack confessed his real identity.

The end of this story is that Jack was sentenced to a month's solitary for escaping and to a further month for . . . "being absent from one thousand three hundred and twenty-six *Appells*, including three Gestapo *Appells*."

Lastly, Dick found out, months later, how it was that a German N.C.O. had opened the guardhouse door and walked out on to the terrace at the same moment as Mike and Jack dropped from the parapet. Jack, climbing over the balustrading, had accidently pressed an alarm-bell button which had immediately summoned the N.C.O. to the very spot where the escape was taking place!

CHAPTER XVIII

THE YANKEES ARE HERE

AMERICANS were trickling into Colditz in 1944.

Colonel Florimond Duke of the U.S. Army was taken prisoner in Hungary. He had been parachuted into that country on a special mission and had, after some weeks of activity, been captured by the Gestapo. He was treated according to the Gestapo routine, travelled in chains to Colditz, and was released into the Castle more dead than alive. A brave man, who fought in the U.S. Air Force in the First World War, nothing could keep him away from the hazards of the Second, and he 'stuck his neck right out'. He was handsome with a dark brown military moustache, stood over six feet in height and was a quiet retiring individual, with a consoling personality. In civilian life he was the advertising manager of the magazine *Time*.

A member of Colonel Duke's team who ended up at Colditz was Captain Alfred Suarez of the U.S. Army Engineers, commonly known as Al. He was another who loved adventure and, being originally of Spanish descent, he had volunteered and fought for the Government Forces during the Spanish Civil War in the thirties. After this episode, it came about as a natural sequel to his career that he found himself parachuted into Hungary. He was a gay daredevil with a great sense of humour.

Another member of Duke's team was Colonel W. H. Schaefer, U.S. Army, who was less lucky than his two colleagues. Although he reached Colditz, he was kept there in solitary confinement pending court-martial. He was sentenced to death and remained isolated while appeals were made continuously on his behalf up to the time of the liberation of the Castle. This happy event saved his life.

None of these Americans had any opportunity to escape. For

Schaefer, even the most recalcitrant Colditz convict would have admitted there was not a hope. As for Duke and Suarez, there was another very good reason why they should not 'stick their necks out' any farther than they had already done. Their necks were, metaphorically, hanging on to their bodies only by the thread of sufferance. A queer twist of the Gestapo mind had saved them from extermination. Even these brave men realised that they had had their day.

*   *   *   *   *

The *Prominente* were a class of prisoner set apart by the German High Command for special treatment in Colditz. They consisted of prisoners who had connections with important personages on the Allied side by virtue of birth or of fame, either their own or that of antecedents. By the same token they possessed special value for the Germans. It became plain to all, as the war progressed in favour of the Allies, that they would ultimately be used by Hitler as hostages, and this is, in fact, what Hitler, through his lieutenant, Himmler, attempted to do when the time of the great holocaust approached.

Such prisoners were not maltreated. On the contrary, they were allotted small cell-like single bedrooms giving them some privacy and elementary comfort. But they were most closely guarded. During the day they could mix with the other prisoners. At each roll-call they were counted separately. At ten o'clock each evening they were escorted from the general quarters to their rooms by special sentries and locked in.

A guard was maintained oustide their cells all night. They were only released again at breakfast time in the morning. The door of each cell had a shuttered spy-hole fitted in it, and the sentry patrolled regularly throughout the night, flashing a torch through the open shutter to see that the prisoner was up to no mischief.

There was Giles Romilly, Winston Churchill's nephew, a young man with a misleadingly sulky expression because he was unfailingly cheerful with a kind disposition. A wave of dark hair flopped over his forehead; he had strong features

249

and he had heavy-lidded blue eyes and was small and stockily built. He had left England with the Narvik expedition, in 1940, as a newspaper correspondent and had been captured by the Germans. He tried, once, to escape from Colditz, without success. At the end of the war he tried again and succeeded, but more of that anon.

Captain the Master of Elphinstone, a nephew of Her Majesty the Queen (now the Queen Mother), arrived in Colditz in 1944. He had been captured near Dunkirk in 1940.

Other *Prominente* who arrived earlier from Eichstätt, most of them having escaped from its famous tunnel, were: Captain the Lord Arundell of Wardour, Wiltshire Regiment (already mentioned); Captain Lord Haig, son of the Field-Marshal; and Lieutenant Lord Lascelles, nephew of King George VI; Captain Michael Alexander, cousin of Field-Marshal Alexander; Captain the Earl of Hopetoun, Lothian and Border Horse (already mentioned), a son of the Marquis of Linlithgow; and Lieutenant Max de Hamel, a relative of Winston Churchill.

Charlie Hopetoun was one of the three star theatrical producers of Colditz. He produced *Gaslight* by Patrick Hamilton in October 1944, which played to overflowing houses in the Colditz theatre and later he wrote a play which received quite an ovation.

While on the subject of theatrical productions, which became an important part of camp life in 1944, it is worth recording the versatility of Dick Howe, who found, in conditions of semi-starvation, the energy and the time to carry through major theatrical productions, run the escape nerve-centre and control the wireless news service of the camp.

Dick produced *George and Margaret*, which had run in England before the war, in June 1944, and *Jupiter Laughs* by A. J. Cronin in November of that year.

The third outstanding producer, and the peer of the trio, was Teddy Barton. He produced *Pygmalion* in February 1943; *Rope* in January 1944; *Duke in Darkness* in March 1944; and *Blithe Spirit* in April 1944, with Hector Christie of the

Gordon Highlanders acting superbly the part of Madame Acarti. Other leading lady parts were excellently performed by Alan Cheetham, a Lieutenant of the Fleet Air Arm. In May, the theatre was closed by way of reprisal for an offence against the Germans; in June 1944, Teddy produced *The Man Who Came to Dinner*. *Hay Fever* and *To-night at 8.30* followed, and several Noël Coward compositions occupied the theatre until the end of 1944, when productions ceased.

The scenery for the theatre was painted mostly by the master hands of John Watton and Roger Marchand on newspaper glued to wooden frames. Roger Marchand was a French Canadian who had somewhere in his travels picked up a 'Bowery' accent. He was asked one day what he was painting and his reply was, "A'm paintin' a scene for dat guy Ot'ello."

Dresses were manufactured out of crêpe paper. There was plenty of Leichner make-up provided by the German Y.M.C.A. A carpenter's tool kit was accepted, on *parole,* but the prisoners soon dispensed with it, preferring to use illicitly manufactured tools, equally good.

Hugo Ironside was invariably stage manager. The electricians were: a Dutchman, Lieutenant Beetes and later Lulu Lawton, who performed wonders in lighting effects. And the litany would not be complete without mentioning the manufacture of stage props, such as a highly polished concert grand piano for *George and Margaret*, an ugly-looking brass-festooned coffin for *The Man Who Came to Dinner*, made from old Red Cross boxes by Hugo Ironside, Mike Edwards and George Drew.

The superior productions of 1944 were a far cry from the early days when a handful of British gathered together in their quarters on Christmas Day 1940 to hear Padre Platt sing:

Any old iron, any old iron, any any any old iron!
You look sweet, talk about a treat!
You look dapper from your napper to your feet,
Dressed in style with the same old tile

And your father's old green tie on,
And I wouldn't give you tuppence for your old watch chain.
It's iron, old iron!

Let it be said that our popular padre sang it with an unforgettable *éclat*. His false teeth took off from his mouth at the crescendo enunciation of the finale 'Tuppence' and clattered to the floor amidst roars of laughter from the boorish audience.

The possibility of a general reprisal on the camp theatre was always uppermost in the minds of the theatre actionaries. Until the curtain rose on the opening night, nobody could ever be sure a production would take place; there was so much clandestine activity in progress that might be unearthed at any moment, and the closing of the theatre was always among the first acts of retribution carried out by the Jerries.

A cinema show once came to Colditz, but only once; that was in 1943. Scarlet O'Hara remarked loudly after the performance, and in the close hearing of Hauptmann Eggers, who understood English well, "If that's the b—— sort of film the Jerries put up with, no wonder they're losing the war."

His remark closed the theatre for a month and no more films came to Colditz.

No 'privilege' lasted long. Two games of Rugby took place on the Colditz village green in the winter of 1943–4. On two occasions in the summer of 1944, a batch of prisoners was escorted down to the river for a bathe. On one occasion a party of officers went to the cinema in the village. These outings constituted 'privileges'. They were all *parole jobs*, that is to say, prisoners had to sign a promise not to make an attempt to escape during the excursions.

Privileges were extremely rare. Suspicion was mutual. On the one hand, the Jerries thought that frequent repetition would ultimately prove to the advantage of prospecting escapers. On the other, *parole* savoured of the thin end of the blackmail wedge, and the Colditz inmates were nothing if not diehard. The number of prisoners willing to sign *parole* passes dwindled remarkably after the first outing.

Douglas Bader, the air ace, indulged in a different kind of *parole*. He demanded *parole* walks on the grounds of his inability to exercise properly in the Castle precincts owing to his physical disability—namely, that of having both legs missing. The very ludicrousness of a legless man demanding *parole* walks is reminiscent of the defiance of this great airman.

During the summer and autumn of 1944 he had his way. He gave his *parole*—promising not to make any attempt to escape or even to make preparations to this end. What he did not promise to eschew was the continuation, outside the camp, of the cold war campaign which he relentlessly carried on against the Germans inside the camp. He would continue to break German morale by every means in his power.

So, insisting that he had to be accompanied on his walks, in case his tin legs gave trouble on the hills, he usually obtained permission for Dick Howe or another to go with him. Together they would load themselves with Red Cross food. With internal trouser pockets elongated to their ankles and filled to the brim and with their chests bursting outwards, they would set off to demoralise the country folk with food and luxuries they had not seen for five years; English and American cigarettes and pipe tobacco, chocolate, tinned meat and ham from the four corners of the earth. Bader and Dick gave generously, asking for little in return—a few eggs, maybe, or fruit or lettuce. They naturally started this campaign on the accompanying sentries. When they had the latter in their pay by the simple process of bribery followed by blackmail, the way was clear for the major offensive. At first lone farms were visited, then the attack approached the fringes of the town of Colditz itself. The enemy fell like ninepins for the subtle, tempting baits. German morale in the countryside bent under the attack.

CHAPTER XIX

MUTINY

As early as the autumn of 1941, Harry Elliott had studiously learnt the symptoms of a common and unnerving stomach trouble—duodenal ulcers, and had applied carefully the lessons he learnt. He complained of pains. He lost weight. He had warning prior to being weighed, so he started off with bags, full of sand, hanging down inside his pyjama trouser legs, supported at his waist. Thereafter he lost weight regularly by off-loading a few pounds of sand at a time. He painted the skin round his eyes with a mixture of carbon and yellow ochre so regularly that it became ingrained and would not come off with washing. Harrowing pains and the loss of two stone in weight succeeded in sending him to a hospital. Elsterhorst, in February 1942. Here he found two stalwart Indian doctors captured in Cyrenaica in 1941 who 'fixed' blood in his various medical samples. All was ready for a breakout with his Belgian confederate, Lieutenant Le Jeune, when the night before the 'off', the latter's civilian clothing was found.

The Germans were nothing if not radical and, knowing the Colditz reputation, they acted judiciously. The whole Colditz contingent at Elsterhorst was returned, lock, stock and barrel, under heavy guard by the 4.30 a.m. train the next morning, to their natural home.

Harry lay low for a while, then started a chronic jaundice. By 1943, Harry's back began to trouble him—the result of a fall when he was trying to escape in France, after his capture in 1940. Arthritis set in and showed on X-ray plates, but Harry had cooked his goose as far as hospitalisation was concerned. Nobody would take any notice of his serious and troubling complaint. He was becoming a cripple.

"If the Goons won't swallow it one way, they'll jolly well have to swallow it another way," thought Harry. He decided to start up his duodenal ulcers again. This time he had to travel far to make the grade. Already as thin as a rake, he had to lose two more (sand) stone. After several successive weighings he ran out of sand and still the Jerries would not transfer him. His face was the colour of an ash heap at dawn, but the German doctors were unsympathetic. Harry decided he had to starve. He ate nothing for a week, could scarcely stand upright and the Germans gave in. He returned to Elsterhorst hospital.

There were several English doctors working in the hospital, including a radiologist, whom Harry made his particular *confidant*. The result was some really juicy ulcers on an X-ray plate which had his name attached to it. All this time Harry was suffering the real pangs of arthritis, which was turning him into a crippled 'old man of the sea'.

Harry's ulcers flared up and died down in the traditional manner of the really worst type, and the X-ray plates showed the legitimate and pitiable arthritis mingling with cleverly transposed awe-inspiring, if not terrifying, ulcers in such a picture of blended medical misery that expert opinion considered he was at last ripe to appear before the Mixed Medical Commission.

Harry was returned to Colditz as an incurable case with not long to live and a ticket of recommendation for interview by the Commission.

The Mixed Medical Commission was a body formalised by the Geneva Convention for the examination of sick and wounded prisoners of war with a view to their repatriation. It was composed of medical officers divided equally between nationals of one belligerent power and nationals of the Protecting Power of the other belligerent. The Mixed Medical Commission which, at intervals, toured around Germany consisted of two German doctors and two Swiss doctors. Doctor von Erlach was the best known of the Swiss delegates. Although the war had been going on for over four years, the Commission had never been allowed to put its nose inside the gates of Colditz.

Now, in May 1944, the miracle happened and the new Senior British Officer, Colonel Tod, was informed of the forthcoming visit of the Commission to the *Sonderlager* of Germany. Germany was surely losing the war! Colonel Tod had recently taken over as S.B.O. from Tubby Broomhall of the R.E.s, who in turn had taken over from Daddy Stayner in 1943.

Harry realised it was all or nothing. The Commission was due next day. He and another officer, Kit Silverwood-Cope, who had thrombosis in one leg, spent the night walking up and down the circular staircase leading to their quarters—a matter of eighty-six steps—at twenty-minute intervals. They were still alive when the sun rose and took to their beds in the sick ward as bona-fide stretcher cases.

Unfortunately this was not the last ditch. The Gestapo had the final word. Silverwood-Cope had been loose, too long for the Gestapo's liking, in Poland after an escape, and knew much that they would like to know. They had already submitted him to torture in a Warsaw prison without success, but were not courageous enough to go the 'whole hog'. At the same time, in the camp records, he had a red flag opposite his name: '*Deutschfeindlich*'—an enemy of the Reich. It was almost certain they would not let him go.

The other cases submitted for examination included: Major Miles Reid, an M.C. of the First World War; Lieutenant "Skipper" Barnet; "Errol" Flynn and Dan Halifax of the R.A.F.; in addition, two French de Gaullist officers. De Gaullists, captured fighting in various parts of Europe, were now arriving in Colditz, replenishing the French fire which had added much to the spirit of the prison through the earlier years.

The camp as a whole was resigned to the rejection of the case for Silverwood-Cope. But when, at the last minute, the High Command, through the instigation of the Gestapo, began quibbling over the repatriation of the two Frenchmen, they came up against trouble.

The names of those to be examined by the Commission for repatriation would be called at the morning *Appell* and the Gestapo decisions would then be known.

The roll-call sounded and the officers paraded. After the count had been checked by Hauptmann Eggers, Hauptmann Priem read out the verdict of his High Command.

Major Miles Reid, Captain Elliott, Lieutenant Barnet, Flying-Officer Flynn and Flight-Lieutenant Halifax were named, and after that . . . silence. The silence continued, palpitating ominously, fraught with meaning. *"Danke!"* shouted Priem in a forced stentorian voice. This was the German signal for the British S.B.O. to dismiss the parade. No order was given. Nobody moved.

Then something happened which under other circumstances would have caused chuckles of laughter in the ranks. But another mood had gripped the waiting men. They had seen the incident, funny but pathetic, often enough. At this moment, its occurrence spoke worlds more than any words. An officer, who had gone round the bend and who should have been repatriated long ago, appearing from nowhere, advanced towards the German officer in the middle of the open space in front of the parade. He was dressed in a tattered blue tunic, his bare legs protruded from beneath a dirty pair of khaki shorts and on his feet were old plimsolls. He wore a paper cap of his own design like a French *képi* on his head. It resembled, vaguely, the headgear of a French Foreign Legionary. A white handkerchief trailed from the back and the hat was coloured red and grey. Slanting over his left shoulder he carried a long piece of wood—his rifle. He came to attention in front of Priem, saluted smartly with his rifle still at the shoulder, then fumbled in his tunic, produced a piece of paper and handed it solemnly to the German. Priem unfolded it, turned it over and held it open, loosely, in his hand. It was blank on both sides—a helpless, mute appeal. The French Legionary saluted again and marched briskly along the stationary ranks, reviewing the parade before returning to his place in the rear.

"Why was his name not on the list too?" the silence shouted, echoing the unspoken question and, of course, there was no answer. The Germans did not explain their actions in the mad-house of Colditz.

Eggers, speaking in English, addressed Colonel Tod, the S.B.O.:

"Parade the walking cases in front at once, Herr Oberst. Stretcher cases will be inspected later."

The tall, grey-haired Royal Scots Fusilier, standing alone in front of his men, replied coldly: "Herr Hauptmann, this action of the German High Command is despicable. It is dishonest, unjust and cowardly. The Frenchmen must go. I will no longer hold myself responsible for the actions of my officers. The parade from this moment is yours. Take it!" And with that he turned about, marched back to the ranks behind him, turned again, and stood at attention—at the right of the line.

Eggers, speaking in English, started to harangue the parade:

"British officers, you will remain on parade until those ordered for examination by . . ." His further words were lost as, with one accord, the parade broke up in disorder and men stamped around the courtyard, drowning his voice with the shuffling of boots and the clatter of wooden clogs on the cobbles.

This was mutiny. Priem hurried to the gate and spoke through the grille. Within seconds the riot squad entered the courtyard. The two German officers, surrounded by their men with fixed bayonets and followed by three N.C.O. snoops with revolvers drawn, forged into the crowd before them in search of the bodies. Their scheme was to identify and seize the men approved for interview, take them out of the courtyard by force, bang the gates behind them and leave the prisoners to nurse their wounded feelings in impotence.

The German officers and their snoops peered, now to the left, now to the right, into the sullen faces around them. Suddenly there was a shout and a pointing finger was levelled.

"*Dort ist Oberst Reid, schnell! nehmen Sie ihn fest!*" Four guards charged at the man, surrounded and held him fast by the arms and shoulders, awaiting further orders. "*Sofort zur Kommandantur! Rechts um! Marsch!*" Reid was frogmarched out of the courtyard, the posse forcing their way with jabbing bayonets through the swarming, obstructing prisoners, shouting as they went, "*Los, los! Weg da! Los!*"

The search continued, but the other walking cases could not be found.

The *mêlée* in the courtyard continued for fifteen minutes. The Swiss members of the Commission were in the Kommandantur waiting for the proposed repatriates. They became impatient and demanded to be allowed to see the Senior British Officer. The courtyard was by now in an uproar with jeering, booing, catcalls and singing competing for the maximum volume of sound. The Swiss could hear the riot in progress. The Camp Commandant was spotted from a window giving orders outside the gate. He dared not enter. Priem left the courtyard for several minutes, then returned. He sought out Colonel Tod and spoke to him. Tod mounted the steps of the *Saalhaus* and raised his arms, calling for silence. There was an immediate lull. He announced:

"The German Commandant has agreed that the de Gaullists shall go forward for examination."

The whole camp broke into a tremendous cheer. Within a few minutes, the two Frenchmen were produced and, together with the rest of the walking cases who appeared also, as if from nowhere, they were escorted out by the German guards, marching through a lane formed by the cheering mob.

The German capitulation was complete and Allied solidarity, aided by the Swiss Commission outside, had won a memorable victory. The German arrogance of 1941 and 1942 was changing, and from this day in May 1944 onwards, the prisoners in Colditz began to feel solid ground once more beneath their feet.

The episode was an important turning-point. The prisoners knew that Hitler and his minions intended to use them as hostages in the hour of defeat. Here was a gleam of hope. The Camp Commandant would have to square his action over the de Gaullists with the Gestapo, but the fact remained he had countermanded their orders, obliged to do so by the combined pressure of the prisoners and a neutral Power, and was evidently prepared to cross swords with them. What had been done once for two de Gaullists might be repeated. In the hour of Germany's defeat, the sign-post for action pointed towards defiance.

The Mixed Medical Commission passed for repatriation all those they examined, including Harry. They took one look at him and wrote his name down on the list.

*   *   *   *   *

Most of the repatriates, including Harry, remained in Colditz until July when, one evening, they received orders to pack, and the next morning at 5.30 a.m., in the grey light of dawn, they bade farewell to Colditz for ever. The departure arrangements were so sudden that Harry, as he walked through the gates, thought he was dreaming. It was difficult, almost impossible, to believe that he was, after four years, really on his way home, that he would not wake up and find himself lying on his palliasse inside the walls and the barbed wire. A curious feeling took possession of him. A few heads popped out of windows as they filed out, hands waved and voices shouted good-bye. It was all a dream. He had seen it happen before. He would wake up soon. Another part of him felt suddenly guilty; he was disloyal to the men who were shouting those pathetic good-byes behind the bars; and, more peculiar than anything else, was the sensation of tearing himself away from something that had become a part of him—the Castle itself. Could he be having regrets? Yes! He was feeling sorry. Something was being wrenched from him. He was hugging his chains, and would feel lost without them in the strange world of freedom.

The repatriates marched down to the station with the German guards and, as the dawn came, Harry looked back over his shoulder and upwards to the towering outline of the Castle showing pale and faintly luminous in the first light. Only then did he realise he was not dreaming. A sudden fear gripped him and his skin contracted. He was, indeed, outside the walls, but they were reaching out to seize and envelop him again. Now that he could see the Castle's forbidding exterior, the ghostly horror of its greyness, fear came upon him—he wanted to run from the loathsome prison before he was trapped.

The party arrived at the station and boarded the train. Only as it steamed out of the station did Harry begin to feel safe. He was filled with a great exultation and a surge of revengeful elation; he cursed the Castle, as it faded, growing paler and paler in the morning haze, cursed it again and again in a queer uncontrolled frenzy. . . .

He had defeated his bitter enemy, the Castle; he had escaped from Colditz. Those who remained, facing nearly another year behind the bars, would talk about his exploits and his humour until the end of the war, and long afterwards too. They would never forget his 'Battle of the Dry Rot',[1] which was waged unceasingly until the day he departed. They would miss his excursions up the stairs, into the attics, with his faithful band of followers carrying buckets of water—water which they thereupon poured through cracks in the floor until the ceilings seeped, dripping upon the occupants of the rooms below. How the Dutchmen swore when they returned to their bunks at night to find soaking pillows and blankets below the weak spots in the ceiling! They never found out where the water came from. For years they thought it was caused by leaking water-pipes and holes in the roofs. They used a different staircase, and consequently never saw Harry at work. His 'razor blades in the pig-swill' campaign [1] was over. There would be no more Chinese officers; no more sand-bags jettisoned along the road of the years; no more ulcerous landmarks on the patient uphill climb which eventually led him out of Colditz. He had reached the top of the hill and looked once more over the sunlit plains of freedom. He was going home again to his beloved England. He would be missed back there, behind the grim walls, where a

[1] Described in *The Colditz Story*.

gay heart and an unquenchable spirit were like sunshine in the early spring.

*   *   *   *   *

"Dopey" Miller (Lieutenant W. A. Miller, R.C.E.), a Canadian and a born escaper, who thought of nothing else all day long, escaped from Colditz in June 1944, at the time of the Normandy invasion. His was a lone effort. The route out of the Castle was the beginning of that route used by Ronnie Littledale, Billie Stephens, Hank Wardle and the author in 1942. Dopey and his helpers cut a bar in the window in the camp kitchen facing the outer courtyard. On a favourable night, during an air-raid, he climbed out of the window, over low roofs and dropped to the ground in a dark corner. He hid underneath the chassis of a lorry that was parked every evening in the outer yard. During the daytime, the lorry was used on haulage work for the camp, in the village and the surrounding districts.

Early the next morning, the lorry driver started up his engine and drove out of the camp. Dopey was hanging on, underneath. There were no alarms at the outer gates.

He was never heard of again. It is assumed that he was recaptured and that the Gestapo submitted him to '*Stufe drei*'.

Within the camp, of course, none of this was known or thought of at the time. It was hoped that Dopey had chalked up another 'home-run' from the escape-proof fortress. As the days passed into months, however, and there was no news of him, uncertainty as to his fate left an uneasy feeling in the minds of those who knew him. He was not the kind of man who would leave the camp in ignorance if he had succeeded in reaching the Allied lines.

CHAPTER XX

THE RED FOX

As the autumn days of 1944 shortened and the Second Front in France settled down, the prisoners of Colditz gritted their teeth once more to stand another winter behind the bars, hoping for relief in the spring. The prisoner contingent numbered about two hundred and seventy at this time, of whom two hundred were British, the remainder French de Gaullists and a sprinkling of every other Allied nationality. They had hoped for freedom in the autumn, but it was too much to expect and they knew it. An air of sadness and depression spread over the camp: the eternal optimists had little enthusiasm left for the victory that was always 'next month' and 'just around the corner'! They were nearly played out. The winter of 1944–5 was, for Colditz, the grimmest of all the war winters. The incarcerated men had made what little contribution they could to the war effort. They had done everything possible behind the bars and had given of their best. They had pinned down a German battalion. The *Landwacht* were afraid of them. They had made Colditz a byword in the offices of the German High Command. The Gestapo loathed the mention of the name.

Patience in the camp was at the sticking point. As runners, reaching the last lap of a marathon, feel their hearts being torn out of their bodies, unable to drag their legs another pace, yet knowing they must still race hundreds of yards before they pass a finishing line which, in the mist of perspiration before their eyes, they despair of ever beholding, so the escapers of Colditz struggled in a motionless marathon of the mind to retain their equilibrium to the end. The last lap was the toughest endurance test of all.

In such an atmosphere Mike Sinclair decided to try again. His indomitable spirit could not be tamed. He would finish the war in harness. The Red Fox had to be free.

This time he planned a lone and desperate break. Surprise was the essence of it. He would repeat the escape of the Frenchman Pierre Mairesse Lebrun who, in 1941, had been catapulted over the barbed-wire fence in the recreation pen in the park beneath the Castle. Mike planned the break alone so that no other man could be blamed if a hand or foot slipped or the timing went wrong. Lebrun had dared the sentries to shoot him, dodging as the bullets whistled past and jumping to safety behind the park wall with a volley as a send-off. Dick Howe would not have to take the blame on his broad shoulders this time. He would not have to 'take the can back' as he had done for the Franz Josef affair. Mike was seeing to that. He told nobody.

On September 25th, 1944, Mike went down to the recreation ground and walked the well-trodden path around the periphery inside the wire with Grismond Scourfield.

In half an hour the guards had settled down. They suspected nothing. This hour of recreation would be the same as the hundreds that had gone before it.

At the most vulnerable point in the wire, Mike stopped suddenly, turned and shook hands with Scourfield. "Good-bye, Grismond," he said quietly. "It's going to be now or never."

He was ashen-pale. Even the gigantic courage of his spirit could not conceal from his own brain the awful risk he was about to take. The subconscious reactions of the nerves and cells of his frail body rebelled and would not be controlled. His hand trembled as he grasped surreptitiously the hand of his friend. His whole body seemed to quiver. His eyes alone were steady and bright with the fire of a terrible resolve.

In the next instant he was at the wire, climbing desperately, climbing quickly, spreadeagled in mid-air. To those nearby, his progress seemed painfully slow, yet it was fast for a man mounting those treacherous barbed strands. He had reached the top and was balanced astride the swaying wires when the

264

Germans first saw him. They began shouting: "Halt! Halt!" and again, *"Halt oder ich schiesse!"* came echoing down the line of sentries.

He took no notice. Freeing himself from the top strands he jumped down to the ground and stumbled at the nine-foot drop. He picked himself up as the first shot rang out. There were shouts again of "Halt!" and then a fourth time "Halt! Halt!" He was running. The hill was against him. He was not travelling fast. He dodged once, then twice, as two more shots rang out and he ran straight for the outer wall. But the Germans had his range by now and a volley of shots spattered around him. He dodged again. He could still have turned and raised his hands. He was nearing the wall but he was tiring. Another volley echoed among the trees of the park and he fell to his knees and a gasp of horror rose from the men watching behind the wire. Then, slowly, he crumpled forward amongst the autumn leaves.

He lay still as the sentries rushed forward, swooping on their prey. He did not move when they reached him. A sentry, bending down, turned him over while another quickly opened his shirt and felt with his hand over the heart. He was dead.

The Red Fox had escaped. He had crossed the last frontier and would never be brought back to Colditz again a recaptured, spent, defeated prisoner. He had made a 'home-run'. He was free.

*   *   *   *   *

Seven months later, the Castle was relieved and Mike would have been freed—alive. That freedom would not have been of his own making, nor to his own liking. He had reached that stage in the humiliating mental struggle of a prisoner of noble stature when, to desist from trying and to await freedom at the hands of others, would seal his own failure, scar his heart and sear his soul. His duty would have remained unfulfilled.

The sermon that follows was delivered by Padre Platt at the memorial service in the Castle.

"Mike came from an Ulster family living in England. He

was at school at Winchester, went up to Cambridge, and joined the 60th just before the war. He fought at Calais, was taken prisoner, was sent to Laufen and then to Poland. There he made his first escape in which he crossed the frontiers of the General Government, Slovakia, Hungary, Yugoslavia and was caught getting into Bulgaria. He tried to escape on the way back through Czechoslovakia, was recaptured, held for a time by the Gestapo, and finally sent on here two and a half years ago.

"Since then his life has been practically one attempt after another to escape. On different occasions he has got as far as Cologne,[1] the Swiss Frontier, the Dutch Frontier. You know better than any congregation in the world what that means. About a hundred of you have got right away from a camp once, only about twenty more than once—let alone a frontier—and this is the 'Escapers' camp.

"He didn't himself take foolhardy risks, but when he went with others and risks were unavoidable he took full share—and more. You remember his escape as Franz Josef. And in his last and riskiest attempt he went alone. Whenever the story of escaping in this war is written, Mike Sinclair's name will be there, high up on the list. And he deserves it because he had qualities that really ultimately matter.

"When he'd made up his mind upon a thing he was absolutely determined to carry it through. He made mistakes, as we all do, but he learnt from them and had a conscience about them. Most people's reaction to failure is to wipe it out of their memories and be comfortable. Mike's was NOT to forget it—and at times it made him very depressed—but to go on trying till he'd made up for it. That is the kind of character that really matters in a soldier—the kind of quality that made Wellington and Sir John Moore great.

"On at least two occasions while he was here, he made escapes that any soldier would be proud of. When he and Jack Best went through the line in the orchard, the scheme—and it was largely Mike's scheme—was about the most brilliant

[1] An escape carried out from Colditz early in 1942.

there's been here. It came off, so we took it for granted, but it was a grand piece of work. The other occasion was on his earlier 'Franz Josef' escape, then he was nearly killed by a guard losing his head. Mike took the lead in the preparations and the escape itself—he spent three months on it. With two or three people it was a 'certainty', with the members he agreed to include—well, not likely to succeed. At one stage in the escape it was clear to Mike that to get the main body out was going to be a much more dangerous and difficult job than expected, but that, by forgetting about them, he, Lance and Hyde-Thomson could walk out and get clear away. That's a testing moment for a man's character, and we know how unhesitatingly he chose the unselfish way.

"Finally, Mike was a believing Christian, and one who'd known suffering and turned it to use. That's why, although his death is a tragedy for his parents, it isn't just a wasteful tragedy of a life. We say in our Creed that we believe in the Resurrection of the Dead and WE KNOW that Christ's promises are sure. Mike was the kind of man who wouldn't be confident about himself, but we, who knew him, know that he is all right, and that he's met up with his younger brother, who fell at Anzio, and the countless others who, in their country's service, have gone before us on the way that leads through death, but comes out in a brighter eternal world."

CHAPTER XXI

THE GLIDER

BY the autumn of 1944 the construction of the glider was under way in a secret workshop. Assembly had not yet begun, but tall piles of wing sections lay carefully stacked and docketed ready for the great day when they would be threaded on to the spars.

Jack Best had long ago been incorporated in the team; a fourth member, stooge Wardle, the submarine officer, had also joined them.

Jack Best had come out of solitary confinement after the terrace escape in the early spring of 1944. By that time, Bill Goldfinch and Tony Rolt had made a little headway with the glider plans. Tony had remembered Bill's remark, when they first discussed the glider, about how useful Jack Best would have been on such a scheme. Jack was only just out of solitary when Tony took the bull by the horns and proposed he join them.

"It's asking something I know, Jack," he had said, "you've probably had a bellyful of escaping and solitary just recently and want nothing more than to be left alone for a while.

"Tell me some more about it," Best had said.

"We've already started making parts," Tony explained. "Bill has a lot of drawings and whatnots. He has plans, elevations, sections and detail part drawings and he's made some templets. I've been working on the manufacture of parts using the templets; but we need help. The going is slow. You're the chap we need. You're good with your hands and some of the parts are going to require a lot of workmanship and patience, more than I've got."

"Have you mentioned the scheme to Dick yet?"

"No, I think it's time we did. If you'd agree to join us, that would count with Dick too, and I think he'd see we got all the help possible."

"Show me the plans and some of the parts you've made," said Jack.

Tony had led him over to the corner of the dormitory where his miniature workshop, consisting of a small table and a cupboard were situated. He spread some engineering drawings out on his bed and showed him bits of wood already taking shape as wing ribs. He had a pot of glue, and a primitive wooden press weighted with bricks.

"How long have you been at this?" asked Jack.

"Over a month."

"You'll never get anywhere at that rate," Jack had said. "It's all too cumbersome. Where do you melt your glue? Where do you hide the parts? You must have a proper workshop—you need space to build a glider. It can't be built on a bed."

"I know that only too well," said Tony. "What about it?"

"Let's have a talk with Dick," said Best. "We need room and a place where we can work undisturbed."

"I'll find Bill Goldfinch, and we'll tackle him together."

So Jack Best had fallen for the scheme and Tony had again won his way.

Bill Goldfinch had been working for a long time on the design when Jack Best joined them. He was beginning to wonder whether the machine would ever materialise or merely remain a dream child—perfect on paper.

Tony's introduction of Jack Best into the scheme gave him new zest and enthusiasm for the work.

Dick was tackled and listened, incredulously at first, and then with growing interest as the three men laid before him the details of the plan. What sounded preposterous to begin with became feasible in Dick's mind as he looked over the drawings and realised that the entire machine would be constructed from wooden bedboards and floorboards, cotton palliasse covers, and a large quantity of glue. Goldfinch and Best were, probably, the two finest craftsmen in the camp.

Jack Best had manufactured, years ago, a complete tool kit of tempered chisels, saws, planes, augurs, bits and brace. The two men had infinite patience. They were meticulous and persevering. If anyone would ever succeed, they would, thought Dick, and Tony Rolt could be relied on to whip up the necessary enthusiasm among the stooges and recruit unskilled help when required.

He gathered together the sheaves of paper on which Goldfinch had drawn his stress diagrams and made his aerodynamic calculations.

"Have you checked these?" he asked.

"I've been over the figures three times," said Bill, "but they should be checked by someone else. Lorne Welch could do it. He's a gliding expert."

"Right! Get him to run through them carefully and give them back to me afterwards. I'll have a third opinion also, and, if all three agree that it will fly, then go ahead, and we'll find a proper workshop for you.

"I suppose the dumb cluck who wins the toss will have to take off in it?" he remarked as an afterthought.

"The glider is designed to take two passengers," said Goldfinch calmly.

Dick turned to him in astonishment, "Blimey O'Reilly! you'll need some catapult to launch that weight safely!"

"Yes," said Goldfinch, "we'll need a bathful of concrete."

"Go on," Dick chuckled, "what then?"

"As I see it," continued Goldfinch, "we'll fix a pulley at the far end—the launching end—of the runway; you know—the flat tablelike pieces saddled astride the roof ridge. The glider will be pulled forward on its skid by a rope passed around the pulley returning the full length of the runway underneath it, passing over a second pulley at the starting end, and there attached to the weight."

"Do you mean," intervened Dick, "the bath filled with concrete?"

"Yes. The bath will have to be free to fall a distance equal to the length of the runway, that is sixty feet."

"How do you release the rope from the glider?"

"Simple enough. We'll use the same type of automatic release hook as all towed gliders use. It's foolproof. Better still, we could make a light trolley for the glider to sit on and fix the rope to that."

"Provided the glider calculations are O.K. and it's airworthy," said Jack Best, "I'm sure the take-off will be all right. Holes will have to be made in all the Castle floors, as far as I can see, down to ground-floor level. That should give the full sixty foot drop required for the bath."

"I propose," said Goldfinch, "to use the bath tub, you know the one, on the third floor under the attics. We can suspend it over the holes and let it go when everything's ready. You've got plenty of cement, Dick. Will you let us have enough to mix up and fill the bath?"

"Yes, if you ever get that far," said Dick. "There's tons of sand and gravel and rock up in the attics from the French tunnel. You can mix that with it and make a respectable concrete. Where are you going to build the glider?"

"Ah! now this is where I come in," Tony interrupted. "Jack Best says we've got to have a proper workshop where we can work undisturbed. I'm afraid I agree. Otherwise it'll take years. I've only made a few parts, so far, to Bill's designs and it's taken me ages. It's not so much the actual work, but all the alarms and the hiding of parts and the stooging and so on that wastes the time. If we could fix up our jigs on benches and not have to dismantle them; if we had a permanent stove handy for the glue-pot; if the tools did not have to be hidden all the time—then we could get somewhere."

"Well, there you are!" exclaimed Dick. "You've posed the problem that I was just going to raise. What are you going to do about it?"

"I've been thinking about it a lot," said Rolt, "and I have an idea. We might be able to wall off completely a section of the top attic over the chapel without the Jerries being any the wiser. If it was done, say, in one night and made to look exactly like the original wall at the end, they might never notice the shortening of the attic. It's long enough as you know."

"What do you think, Dick?" said Bill and Jack together.

"Quite canny," Dick agreed grinning, tickled at the prospect of the Jerries regularly patrolling the attic with torches to see there was no monkey business going on while a whole workshop was set up under their noses. "The French tunnel debris is going to be put to good use, I see! Let's go and have a look at the attics."

The four of them, together, examined the uppermost attic carefully. The west end of it was ideally situated for the workshop because it abutted the roof ridge above the old French quarters along which it was proposed to launch the glider.

If this end of the attic were sealed off, the machine could then be constructed and assembled where it would be used. When ready for launching, a large hole could be pierced in the west wall just at the level of the roof ridge outside. Unseen by prying eyes, the saddles would be posed and interlocked forming a runway two feet six inches wide; the machine taken through the hole; its wings attached outside; the rope fixed around the pulleys and the machine would be ready for the take-off.

The attic was long and dark. There was no ceiling; only the timber-roof trusses and the boarded floor, and the faintest glimmer of light entering between the layers of tiles.

A properly constructed false wall, built to look like the existing end wall, immediately under one of the trusses would give no clue as to the existence of a space beyond, unless measurements were taken to check the lengths of the floors at different levels.

The four men agreed the idea had a fair chance of success.

"The problem as I see it now," said Dick, "is to get the wall built and camouflaged to look like the old one before a Jerry interrupts us. That means it's got to be done in one night. Can you see it being done?"

"I think so," said Tony Rolt. "If you'll give the O.K., we can get enough volunteers. With about a dozen men working

272

all night it should be possible. We'll make a sketch of the old wall and reproduce it again in three-ply and cardboard as near as damn it. We can prepare the wall in sections beforehand."

"That'll do as a foundation," said Dick. "What you want after that is to tack canvas on to the wall; you can use the palliasse covers from the beds in one of the unused dormitories and apply a coating of plaster on to the canvas. I'll show you how to prepare it. The French used it on the tunnel doors very successfully. It turns out exactly the right colour when it's dry. To be expected—I guess—as the original plaster was obviously made from local ingredients. You sift out of the tunnel debris a fairly fine grit about one eighth of an inch diameter—no more. You mix that with the clay and sand from the tunnel— there's tons of it round the corner—and make a puddle. You smack this on to the canvas about a quarter of an inch thick and let it set. We'll try a sample out right away and check it. How about the framework for the wall?"

"There's some good floor-boarding around here," said Tony. "It's thick stuff—a good seven-eighths of an inch and five inches wide, that should do. It's what Bill proposed to use also for the main wing spars of the glider."

"How long are the wings to be?" Dick asked, beginning to pace out the width of the attic.

"Each wing is sixteen feet long and five feet wide," said Bill, "but that includes the aileron—fourteen inches."

"Good," said Dick, "they'll just fit nicely into the width."

"Just a minute—" interrupted Bill, "the fuselage is longer. It's eighteen feet without the tail wing and rudder."

"Well, I make the width thirty feet," said Dick checking again, "it should be ample, even allowing for dead space where the sloping roof meets the floor."

"That'll do," said Bill, "the tail and rudder are separate and fit on afterwards."

"Good! Now, what about the width of the room—where shall we build the wall? About twenty feet should do you. That brings us"—Dick said breaking off his sentence as he measured again—"That brings us just under the second truss. What do you think?"

"Twenty feet should do," Bill replied, "if we take too much the rest of the attic will look suspiciously short. We've got to squeeze a bit. We can always break a hole in our own wall to help push the fuselage out, if necessary, on the day."

"The next thing you want is lighting, leave that to me," said Dick. "Lulu Lawton and I can fix up a branch circuit from below. We'll do that when the wall's finished. Now, about getting in and out? How about that corner over there, where the flooring's already off? You could get in by ladder from the lower attic and we could make a trap-door. Yes," Dick ruminated, "let's go down below and have a look at that corner."

They left the upper attic, locking the doors as they went and descended to the lower attic which was unoccupied and lit by dormer windows. Dust was everywhere as it had been above, but at least there was daylight and some pretence at turning the attic into a room had been made. The gable walls and also the low walls beneath the dormer windows had been white-washed and the ceiling was of plaster.

They walked over to the corner where Dick had suggested making the entrance.

"Yes," he said, "I think this corner will do nicely. There's some plaster already fallen down on to the floor here. That makes the job easier. Jack," he said, turning to Best, "I'll arrange for Lucy Lockett and Andy to make the trap-door. You'll have to help. But they'll do the actual trap; they're experts. Fit it so that the laths are cut behind the plaster and show nothing from below. You can support the plaster from above. I'll give you some cement for it. That hole where the plaster's down already will do nicely. It's near enough to the gable wall to lean a short ladder against and a man can climb up, get through and take the ladder with him. You must be damn careful always about this loose plaster lying on the floor. See that it's always left dusty and no footmarks must be left around."

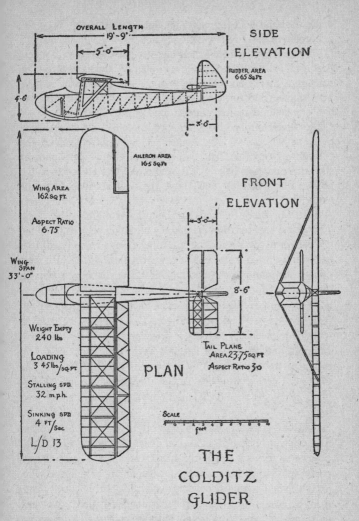

OVERALL LENGTH
19'-9"

5'-0"

SIDE
ELEVATION

RUDDER AREA
6·65 Sq.Ft.

4·6

3'-0"

AILERON AREA
16·5 Sq.Fts

WING AREA
162 SQ. FT.

ASPECT RATIO
6·75

FRONT
ELEVATION

3'-0"

WING
SPAN
33'-0"

8'-6"

WEIGHT EMPTY
240 lbs

LOADING
3·45 lbs/SQ.FT.

TAIL PLANE
AREA 23·75 Sq.Ft.
ASPECT RATIO 3·0

PLAN

STALLING SPD.
32 m.p.h.

SINKING SPD
4 FT/Sec

L/D 13

SCALE

feet

THE
COLDITZ
GLIDER

THE GLIDER PLANS HAVE BEEN COPIED FROM THE ORIGINAL DRAWING MADE
AT COLDITZ AND NOW IN THE POSSESSION OF JACK BEST IN KENYA

A stooge put his head round the door of the attic:

"Jerries in the yard," was all he said.

The four men retraced their steps to the door. As they left, Jack Best, the last in line, spread a heavy dust mixture over suspicious marks on the floor with the aid of a small bellows which he carried for the purpose. It looked like a small bee-hive smoker and was effective in action.

In the dormitory below, Dick continued, "If you need any paint or whitewash, I've got some. You can collect all the cobweb mixture you like yourselves and also a few pounds of soot and dust will help. We'll need a hell of a lot to cover the false wall. When do you think the wall sections could be ready?"

"We can produce them in about a fortnight," said Jack. "There's a big area to cover and it's all got to be prefab."

"All right then," said Dick, "other things being equal let's prepare for to-day fortnight—after the last *Appell*. I'll produce a sample of the plaster beforehand. Then you can get weaving on producing it in bulk. I can lend you five volunteers and Lulu and myself, making seven for the building operation; you'll collect the rest between you. Don't forget the stooges, Tony, I guess you'll see to that. Provided the design—the calculations and so on—are checked again and found O.K., the escape is on, as far as I'm concerned. I wouldn't dream of taking off with you, of course, but then I was brought up in a Tank and I get scared moving in anything weighing less than ten tons."

A fortnight later, all through the night, a dozen men worked furiously with shaded lights to assemble the dummy wall! Screws were used to fix the framework to the existing roof truss. All had been carefully measured up beforehand. The prefabricated sections, covered with a layer of canvas, were then screwed into their predetermined positions. Towards morning, the plastering began, with the thick puddle prepared according to Lulu's prescription. It stuck well to the canvas but the droppings created a problem for the camouflage men who followed. Damp marks on the floor at the foot of the wall could not be covered easily.

By dawn the wall was finished and professional touches had been applied. But, as the morning light pierced through the chinks in the tiles, they showed up a wall which did not look in the least like the original. The colour stuck out like a sore thumb. It was dark brown, uneven, and patchy with sooty streaks. Too late to do anything now; the team departed to clean up and rest for an hour before the 7 a.m. *Appell*. They were depressed.

Dick felt badly about the result of the night's work but he was sure the cause of the trouble was the moisture. If only the Jerries would keep away for twenty-four hours, he thought—the crisis would be past. He watched the Germans all day with apprehension. Towards evening he breathed more freely and together with Lulu Lawton he paid a visit to the wall. It was already much better in appearance but still damp. Another day would improve it out of all recognition.

During the next day the Germans paid a routine visit to the attics. They must have flashed their torches cursorily. There were no alarms. All that day, Tony Rolt and Jack Best paced the courtyard nervously, longing to mount the stairs every hour to register any toning down in the colour of the wall. But they had to possess their souls in patience—no good could come of too frequent visits. It was wiser to keep away.

Towards the evening, just before dark, Dick and Lulu went to the attic along with the glider team. Stooge Wardle (the submarine lieutenant), recently added fourth member of the team, who had helped in the wall construction, was there. As they opened the door a broad smile showed on Dick's face. The change in the colour of the wall was remarkable. The tint was not yet perfect, but, to anyone who had seen it twenty-four hours before, it was clear that it would be perfect in a matter of another twelve hours. The stucco had now turned an old sandy grey, like Sussex or Cotswold stone, and would be a lighter colour by the morning. It was almost indistinguishable from the surrounding walls even to those who had worked on it.

Dick turned to Jack Best and said wryly:

"Jack, you'd better think about fitting that trap-door mighty quick. The ball's over to you and you're holding up the proceedings. Get on to Andy and Lucy. Thanks, Lulu," he added, turning to him, "you've got a better eye for colour than I thought a few hours ago."

"Don't be a damn fool," said Lulu, "anyone in the wool trade knows about allowances for moisture. It's a question of judgment. There's nowt to be afraid of."

"So you concocted that b—— awful mixture!" said Stooge, turning to Lulu. "I thought we'd all been having our legs pulled. Now I must say"—he looked at the wall critically— "it's not bad; not bad at all for an amateur job."

"Any more cock from you and I'll make you walk the plank," retorted Lulu cheerfully.

A load had been lifted from their minds. They locked the attic door and returned to their quarters talking animatedly of the next stage in the venture.

The attic was vacated entirely for a week in order to watch Jerry reactions. Patrols unlocked the doors and inspected the attics almost every day. They noticed nothing unusual. After the week had elapsed Best completed his trap-door and the team took possession of their workshop. The construction of the glider began in earnest.

A work-bench was set up, and tables for the jigs and templets. There were no windows in the workshop, but Dick and Lulu produced electric light. Dick also provided the glue which was melted on a stove, using as fuel a mixture of any kind of fat that could be found, including boot polish. The glue came, mostly, through the channels of Checko's black market. Racks for the tools soon made their appearance. The four men spent the greater part of every day at their work and continued, sometimes, late into the night. Then they had to use heavily shaded lamps to prevent light showing through cracks between the roof tiles. The myriad component parts of the glider piled higher and higher upon the floor and hung festooned from long pegs on the beams awaiting the final assembly.

Their carpenter's kit consisted of the following principal tools:

A side-framed saw, the handle of beech bed-board, the frame of iron window bars and the blade of gramophone spring with eight teeth to the inch.

A minute saw for very fine work, with gramophone spring blade, twenty-five teeth to the inch.

A square, made of beech and gramophone spring.

A gauge, made of beech, with a cupboard bolt and a gramophone needle.

A large plane, fourteen and a half inches long with a two-inch blade, bribed from the Goons, the wooden box made of four pieces of beech screwed together.

A small plane, eight and a half inches long, with a blade made from a table knife.

Another plane, five inches long.

Drills for making holes in wood were made of nails; a five-eighths-inch drill for metal was obtained by bribery.

And lastly there was a set of keys, including a universal door pick, forged from a bucket handle.

The two wings of the glider were each made up of seventeen aerofoil section frames or ribs, manufactured out of deal and beech bed-boards, which were cut into long strips of cross-section, half an inch by three-eighths of an inch. The ribs were put together in jigs, dovetailed, glued and gussetted where necessary, using three-ply wood stripped down to two-ply, nailed in position. The underside of the wing was flat. The curve on the upper leading edge was reproduced on the aerofoil sections partly by bending the wood strips and partly by making a series of small saw nicks along the outer edge to give pliability.

The aerofoil sections were assembled by threading on to the spars and tacking into position. The main spar of each wing was a solid floor-board eighteen feet long of section five inches by three-quarters of an inch. A secondary spar at the trailing edge of the wing, of section two and a half inches by three-quarters of an inch, provided the surface on to which the ailerons were hinged.

The aileron ribs were of uniform construction from one end to the other; they were fourteen inches wide. Ten ribs and two spars, smaller than those of the main wings, were required for the tail wing, made in one piece, to fix above the rear end of the fuselage.

The fuselage itself was constructed from floor-boards cut into strips of section one and a quarter inches by three-quarters of an inch. The two side trusses were curved in both the vertical and horizontal planes and were strapped together at the bottom by short, straight ties and at the top by longer hooped ties, all gussetted where necessary. A raised head-rest, behind the pilot's seat, provided the pillar which supported the wings. Light wooden struts nine feet long were also used underneath the wings. A wide skid of well-planed board shaped like a ski was hinged to the fuselage at the front end. It was also highly polished with french chalk and lead. The top of the fuselage bellied upwards, which gave it a streamlined, airworthy appearance. It was not unlike the body of a Spitfire. The controls—stick, rudder-bar and rudder—were of conventional pattern, lightly constructed. The control wires were made from field telephone wire which the Goons had used for electric lighting in certain rooms.

Prison sleeping-bags of blue and white check cotton were employed for the 'skinning' of the glider. Wrapped around the leading edge of the wings, they were stretched tightly back to the trailing edge, where they were sewn together. Doping was the next process and, for this, German ration millet was ground fine and boiled in water for four hours, forming a paste. This was applied hot to the skin. When cool and dry, it produced a smooth, glossy surface, shrinking the fabric at the same time, so that it became as taut as a drum.

Apart from the light two-ply gussets and thin sheet-metal capping-pieces used all over the machine, parts requiring greater strength and solidity were made from straps and bars taken from some of the iron bedsteads used by senior officers in the *Saalhaus*. Such parts were the root fittings, stout metal straps with steel dowels, two at the inside end of each wing-spar, which linked the wings together through the fuselage immediately behind the cockpit.

The four members of the glider team knew that only two of them would eventually take off in it. They agreed not to make the selection until the machine was ready, thereby ensuring that all four would continue to put their whole effort into the labour of construction.

Normally all four of them were in the workshop together: three at work and one stooging. The stooge sat on a cross-beam in the apex of the roof above the heads of those below. He raised a tile, propping it up with a wedge. Through the slot provided he could see a window in the British quarters on the third floor in which a second stooge was posted. The second stooge surveyed the courtyard and the entrance to it. He employed four signals: a white towel which, placed prominently in the window, meant 'all clear', a blue towel, which meant 'Silence—Goons in the building—stop smoking', a green mustard-pot, which meant 'stand by for danger—silence—take precautionary measures to quit workshop', and a larger red-painted metal jar containing salt which meant, 'quit workshop at once'.

The safety of the team depended greatly on the common sense of the window stooge. To quit the workshop, camouflage the entrance and conceal the ladder took a good five minutes. The stooge had to divine when the Germans really meant business such as a snap *Appell* and when they were just snooping, for which the green signal would suffice.

The above stooging system was not enough. Circumstances might arise in which the stooge might not be able to give his signals. This would occur, for instance, if the Germans raided his room and prevented him from acting. A secondary system —another electric stooge—was brought into play if the window stooge failed.

Germans, entering the room in which the stooge worked, had to pass through an ante-chamber. In this lobby sat another stooge. As soon as a Goon entered the lobby he lifted a small piece of iron mostly covered with rubber which lay at his hand, against a corner of the window-sill. The action broke an electric circuit. Upstairs, a long way off, in the glider workshop, a light promptly went out. In case this was not noticed (with other lights on) a long nail fell at the same time from an electromagnet into a tin basin which acted like a gong.

The complete stooging system, organised for work over an extended period of time, involved a personnel, consisting of twelve principal stooges, known as 'the disciples', with forty assistant stooges.

During the ten months which it took to construct the glider, there were some thirty red alarms—wearing on the nerves, and every day's work included at least one or two 'greens'. The most nerve-wracking 'green' alarm the team experienced occurred when three German N.C.O.s spent over an hour in the attic. They remained motionless while the Jerries probed the floors and even sounded the false wall, but discovered nothing. Old plaster on walls often sounds hollow! That fact probably saved them. The Jerries were after the hidden wireless-set.

Work continued on the components and on the assembly of wings, fuselage, rudder and controls and on the runway saddle boards, pulleys and ropes through the winter of 1944–5. Construction had started seriously in May. The take-off was scheduled for the spring of 1945. By that time, it was estimated that air-raids over the Berlin and Leipzig areas of Germany would be sufficiently intensified to provide ample black-out cover at night in which to break out the hole in the outside wall, set up the launching-ramp, and take off without being heard by the sentries below or seen by observers farther afield in the village. By the spring, too, the winter floods on the meadows flanking the far side of the river below the Castle should have subsided. They would provide an excellent landing-ground for the glider, over three hundred feet below the launching-ramp and two hundred yards away.

The stage was being set for the greatest escape in history. Would the spring of 1945 see its fruition?

PART IV: 1945

CHAPTER XXII

THE END APPROACHES

IN January 1945 the camp held about three hundred British officers from England and every part of the Commonwealth. A recent arrival was Brigadier Davis of the Ulster Rifles, who had been parachuted into Albania. There were the three Americans, the twelve Czech airmen in the R.A.F., some Yugoslav officers, a company of de Gaullist paratroopers from North Africa, and a number, growing daily, of other Free French officers.

Early in February, *Prominente* began to collect in Colditz from different parts of Germany. Five French Generals arrived from the east led by General Denny. A sixth should have arrived, but was detained and 'Klim-tinned'—never heard of again.

General Bor Komorowski, the head of that courageous, almost suicidal band of Polish patriots who kept the heart of Poland beating throughout the blackest years of the war, arrived, accompanied by five Polish Generals and other staff officers. The Warsaw insurrection was the culminating point in the General's underground career. He survived, though war, treachery and murder had threatened to engulf him each day. He possessed hostage value in the eyes of the German leaders, which fact undoubtedly saved his head.

A man of infinite courage and resource, he won the hearts of all who knew him by his simplicity and cheerful friendliness. He was every inch a hero, yet with the modesty of an æsthete, saintly in his detached outlook upon life. His head was partly bald and reminded one of a tonsured monk. Of slender physique, medium in height but wiry, he had direct, searching, hazel eyes under dark eyebrows. A neatly trimmed moustache, beneath an aquiline nose, set off his sensitive nostrils.

In March twelve hundred French officers were dumped into the prison, six hundred more parked in the village. They had been marched eighty-five miles from their camp east of the Elbe in the face of the Russian advance. Overnight, Colditz became a crowded refugee centre. Men slept everywhere, on straw laid out on the floors. The Castle theatre became a large dormitory choked with human beings. It was calculated that if everybody assembled in the courtyard at once there would be three officers per square yard of cobbles. The invasion heralded the end of an era—the end of normal camp life. The closing days of the war were at hand.

The French, many of them old friends from the early days of Colditz, were starving and there were a large number of sick and dying hospital cases amongst them. They had had no nourishing food for months. The British took them gradually in hand, sharing food and clothing, while the S.B.O. and the French Generals fought with the German Camp Commandant for extra medical attention, which was produced, and for medicines, which never materialised.

Heavy air-raids, centred on the Leuna oil refineries south of Leipzig, became a nightly performance. By day, the tactical Allied air force began to make its appearance.

The tempo of events quickened and the daily wireless news bulletins issued in the camp showed that the end was approaching.

The race was nearly finished.

It had been described in a German propaganda leaflet, distributed in English to British prisoners and others in Germany, in the following terms, as early as September 1944:

In 1944 they [the Allies] started a grand offensive, and at the same time Stalin, in the east, threw in all he had. It was certainly impressive. But why was this sudden terrific outburst of energy necessary? Why all the hurry?

Because Churchill knew something. A year and more ago he knew something which most of the Germans at that time had no idea of. Mr. Herbert Morrison knows something about it, too. Remember how he warned the House of Commons recently about the 'Frightful things' which Germany had in store for Britain.

This vast Allied onslaught against Germany is not a sign of strength. It has been caused by their deadly anxiety and intense panic. They must get to Germany and defeat her before she can use her new weapons.

Think of a race between two motor-cars. The Allied motor-car, although it has been fitted up with a reserve petrol tank, has now got to go all out. The German machine, which had been left far behind as its juice ran out, has in the meantime filled up again. And it is racing ahead. Its tanks are full with special fuel.

Germany's victory, the final victory, is not so very far away. . . .

The German V1's were well known by September 1944, when this article was published. The V2's were about to start their work of indiscriminate destruction. But Hitler had another secret weapon nearing completion. His scientists were working frantically on the heavy-water bomb—the hydrogen bomb.

Lieutenant John Winant, Junior, of the U.S. Army Air Force, arrived in April. Being the son of the American Ambassador to the United Kingdom, the Germans treated him as a *Prominente*. He had been shot down in a Flying Fortress raid over Münster. A fair-haired young man with steel-blue eyes, and a strong, though sensitive, character, he went to war straight from his university.

Early in April, Dick Howe's wireless communiqués began to speak of General Patton's and General Hodge's armoured spearheads, moving like shafts of lightning and driving deep into enemy territory.

Colonel "Willie" Tod, the S.B.O. of the camp, came into his own as the man to be relied upon in a crisis. He was recognised as the senior officer of the whole camp and represented all nationalities in the routine dealings with the Germans. He watched the mounting tide of chaos around the Castle with cool detachment, and, having the confidence of his own officers, he was able to handle the Germans with skill. He was all that a soldier should be.

Aged about fifty-four, Willie Tod was a regular officer of the Royal Scots Fusiliers, tall, grey-haired and good-looking, with strong features and bright blue eyes.

Dick Howe always remembered a short conversation he had had with him; it must have occurred in 1943. He had lost his son—killed fighting. The news had come to him, a helpless prisoner in Colditz. Dick had said, sympathetically, after some casual conversation:

"I'm sorry, Colonel, about the news you've just had."

Tod replied simply, "It happens to soldiers." There was a moment's pause, then they had continued their discussion.

Almost forgotten, as the tornado of world events swept across the globe and the Allied armies from West and East dashed headlong to meet each other in the heart of the German Reich, the Colditz glider was made ready for flight. Discussion centred around the use to be made of it. Dick had recently been criticised for allowing the building of the glider to proceed. Some senior officers criticised it on the grounds that it was completed too late for use, saying that a better estimate of the time required to build it should have been made. They were correct in that the glider was finished too late to be of use for an escape, but they were speaking after the event. Others maintained it was a waste of good time and material from the very beginning. The answer to this was a simple one. None of the men even remotely connected with its production regretted what they had done. As for others, did it concern them?

Nobody could foresee when the climax and conclusion of the war would occur. If it had not occurred in the spring of 1945, but months, perhaps even a year later, which was by no means impossible, then the glider would have undoubtedly been launched. Those who built it were prepared to fly in it. They were certain it would take off.

Colonel Tod did not criticise. Even if he had wanted to, the discipline of a soldier forbade the criticism of junior officers who had been allowed to build the glider with the help of his own staff and with his own knowledge. On the contrary, Tod foresaw the possibility of a last and desperate use for the glider and issued his instructions accordingly: "The glider is to be held in reserve in strict secrecy until the Castle is liberated, or until you have further prior instructions from myself or my successor in command."

On Tuesday, April 10th, came a new sound; quite different to the familiar 'whoof' of bombs which had been falling every night on Leipzig and the Leuna synthetic oil plant not twenty-five miles away. There was the distinct crump of shell bursts, and the evening clouds glowed on the horizon with vivid infected spots as the dusk came down.

Dick found it difficult to throw off the feeling of unreality that surrounded the events taking place. This untoward intrusion into the normality of the camp was deeply upsetting. Here was a routine that it had been sacrilegeous to break during five years, now going overboard in a day. *Appells* almost ceased. The S.B.O. was repeatedly in conference with the German Camp Commandant, and not inside the prison, but outside, in the Kommandantur. A world was coming to an end. It was an eerie feeling and unsettling.

There were maniacs at the helm in Berlin. The prisoners of Colditz were hostages. They had known it for a long time. There were so many imponderables in the atmosphere surrounding them and in the kaleidoscopic nightmare of events taking place in Germany. Anything might happen. "Thank God," Dick thought, "there's a cool head looking after our interests. Tod will handle the situation if anyone can." The same thought was in the minds of many. Their lives were literally in his hands.

Tod had their confidence because their discipline showed it. His responsibility was so much the greater. He must save their lives at all costs, and in these hours life was being held cheaply by the Germans. An S.S. Division had moved into the village of Colditz overnight. He had information that the remnants

287

(those who had not died of starvation or illness) of four hundred Jewish slave prisoners, in a camp three miles from the town, had been murdered already by the newcomers. Four only survived to tell the tale, having remained hidden under piles of dead until nightfall.

Tod saw clearly that he had to temporise, yet show no weakness. The German Commandant was terrified. His own *Wehrmacht* High Command had moved to Dresden. Underneath his window were the S.S. and the Gestapo. The mention of the Russians, who were closing in from the east, made him shiver. Hodge's Task Forces from the west were advancing quickly—but how quickly would they reach Colditz? They might be checked. The Commandant would run with the hare and hunt with the hounds as long as he possibly could.

The murder of prisoners on the spot was the first danger. A time might come when it would be advisable for them to make a mass break-out and run for the Allied lines. But there was no front line, properly speaking, at the moment, within two hundred miles. Over that distance, the *Sturmabteilungen*—stormtroopers—and the Hitler Youth were running amok, well-armed and merciless. Tod was not going to lose half his men that way if he could help it. Then, close at hand, was the S.S. Division in the village and in the surrounding district. The prisoners might not make their escape quick enough to pass even this initial obstacle, and their break-out might precipitate the very mass murder from which they were trying to escape.

The second danger which the S.B.O. had to combat was the removal of the prisoners to the redoubts in which the Nazi fanatics would make their last stand. Hitler's own redoubt was known to be in Bavaria around his beloved Berchtesgaden. Here he would bargain for his life and those of his immediate entourage, employing as many *Prominente* prisoners as he could muster as his hostages. His minions, the S.S. and the Gestapo, would similarly use officer prisoners and even the rank and file, wherever they could seize and hold them in last-ditch defences and mountain fortresses.

Tod's strategy, therefore, was to turn to the best account

the value of his men to the Germans as live prisoners; while, at the same time, stalling and delaying any attempt to move them away from the advancing Allied columns.

There was a third danger which Tod had to envisage, in connection with which he issued his orders concerning the glider. It was to be a standby in case the Commander of the S.S. troops in the surrounding district had a dangerous brain-wave. He might take over the Castle itself and use it as a stronghold for a last stand on the lines of the siege of the Alcazar in the Spanish Civil War of the thirties. The prisoners would not, in that case, be compelled to move from Colditz, which was the order expected and which Tod was prepared to resist. There was a danger that the Germans, in desperate straits, might turn upon him and say, "All right, if you will not move for us and with us, then we shall move into the Castle and you will remain, too, as you so wish it, and as our hostages!"

In this event, the glider could come into its own, to send emissaries from the prisoners, like carrier pigeons, in the hope that they would reach the Allied lines, conveying perhaps vital information at a crucial stage in the siege, or even the plans for a combined assault, from outside and from within.

In the early afternoon of April 10th a messenger arrived at Colditz from the Wilhelmstrasse, in Berlin, carrying an offer to General Bor Komorowski. The Commandant conveyed to him the instructions of Hitler, to the effect that he should be freed at once along with his staff, who included General Petczynski, his Chief of Staff, and General Chrusciel, Com-mander of the Warsaw garrison, on condition that they helped Germany to form an underground army to fight against the Russians. It was the third time the offer had been made, and for the third time the General rejected it.

Wednesday, April 11th, passed quietly within the Castle. The sentries around the perimeter remained at their posts. In the distance the thunder of battle continued. Ominously, in the foreground beneath the Castle, could be seen feverish preparations for the defence of the town. The bridge across the River Mulde was mined, ready for detonating. Tanks and motorised artillery rattled through the streets to positions in the woods around. Houses on the outskirts were taken over by troops and barricaded for defence.

The unreality of it all continued to obsess the minds of men like Dick, who had looked down upon the quiet town without ever noticing a change during five and a half weary years. The scene had become so permanent, so indestructible, that nothing could change it; only in their dreams and reveries had the scene ever altered. When they awoke it was always there, the same as before, unchanged.

They had imagined bombs falling on the houses; Allied artillery flashing and shells raining into the town; the rattle of machine-guns; then the advance into the streets; British Tommies, armed with hand-grenades and tommy-guns, creeping stealthily or dashing forward from doorway to doorway in the wake of Mark IV tanks. The dreams of years had never materialised. Could it be different now? Why should it be different? The sound of the guns in the distance might fade to-morrow. The Germans would bring up reserves. They would drive wedges into Hodge's advance. The wireless news would alter, at first subtly, letting the listener down very gently, then the Allied retreat would begin. The S.S. would leave Colditz once more . . . to its former peace. The distant rumble of bombing in the great cities would alone remain a reality. That had gone on for so long now, it was part of their lives, but it altered nothing. 'To its former peace . . . !' A quiet, like that of the solitary confinement cell, where the thud of the heart, beating in futility, is the loudest noise, would descend again.

Dick shivered at the prospect and his skin crept. If the guns were to retire, now that they were so near, perhaps real after all; if the 'crumps' of exploding shells died away now, it would be much harder for him to live and bear the silence. To raise the hopes of a despairing prisoner, then to drop him back into the slough of despondency, is one of the more refined tortures that mankind has invented.

Dick dared not hope. He lived a suspended existence, numbing his virile senses with a self-imposed stupor.

He slept feverishly that night. The gunfire had ceased and he asked himself repeatedly, "Will it begin again in the morning?" It was always at night that thoughts took their own course and the will was at its weakest. He longed for the reassuring sound of the guns.

Thursday, April 12th, dawned. As the prisoners sat at their tables over a breakfast of acorn coffee and German bread, news came through from the wireless-room, which was continuously manned, that the Americans were at Leuna. They were only twenty-five miles away. A cheer went up at the announcement, and the fears of the night gave way to a reassurance which buoyed the spirit through the daylight hours.

The defence preparations continued around the village more furiously. Slit trenches could be seen everywhere, thrown up, like mushrooms during the night, in the fields on the higher slopes and bordering the woods. Boys and girls of all ages could be seen at work with spades and pickaxes alongside their elders in uniform. The Germans looked as if they were going to make a serious stand in the country around the Castle.

Keith Milne, the 'City Slicker', known also as 'the Breed' because he came from Saskatoon, had, in the course of the years, manufactured a couple of good telescopes, making use of spectacle lenses. They were in high demand, more so than Rex Harrison's telescope, the lenses of which had been made by grinding down glass marbles. Scarlet O'Hara swore the Castle would not be relieved until the pearl handles on General Patton's own pair of pistols could be seen through a telescope.

Towards evening, Colonel Tod was called to the Kommandantur. Lance Pope, of Franz Josef fame, accompanied him to interpret in case of difficulty. Oberst Prawitt, tall and emaciated, standing beside his desk in the plainly furnished office, looked at the commander of his prisoners. There was no softness in the answering glance. Tod stepped forward over the soft pile carpet and took from Prawitt's hand the letter which he held out. It was a letter from Himmler's headquarters, addressed from Himmler personally, but unsigned. It contained the marching orders for the *Prominente*. They were to be removed that night to an unknown destination. Two buses would be waiting at the Kommandantur entrance at midnight. Oberst Prawitt would be answerable with his life if any of them escaped.

"This is an outrage, Herr Oberst. The order must be disobeyed," said Tod.

"I cannot. I am under orders, even though I might wish to disobey them," was the reply.

"Our guns are on the horizon and you still have the temerity to dare to carry out this act? Herr Oberst, you must reflect. You will have to answer for the lives of every one of the men on this list which I see attached to the order," said Tod, flinging the papers on the desk.

"You must also reflect," said Prawitt. He looked very old, tired and haggard, and his white hair was bedraggled. He was no longer master of the situation. He was merely a tool in the hands of men who used the blackmail of life or death to impose their will. "If I overrule this order which has come through the local S.S. Headquarters, they will enter the Castle and see that it is carried out. I shall not even live to see it done. There will be many deaths throughout the camp and still the *Prominente* will depart. What will you have achieved?"

"Have you no sense of justice, Herr Oberst? If you will not face matters now, you will have to face them later, before an Allied court-martial."

"I would far rather face an Allied court-martial," said the Commandant with a sign of infinite weariness. He was played out. The future that he saw before him was a violent death, sooner or later, and he preferred it later. The thin thread which held him to life was still precious, old as he was. Time was his only hope and a poor hope at that, but he would try the course that gave him time.

The dangers of the situation presented themselves clearly enough to Tod. If the Commandant would not act, the S.S. would, with bloodshed that might end anywhere. It was not the moment for heroics by unarmed men—unless—and he thought of the last resort, but, looking at the Commandant he could see, almost before he said what was in his mind, that it was useless.

"Will you either hand over the garrison inside the Castle and the armoury to me, or will you, at least, help me to hide or get away the *Prominente* from here?" he asked.

"It is more than my life is worth. If the men escape, they will not get far. It is better to temporise."

"You are certainly not a hero, Herr Oberst!"

"I am old but not yet ready to die in a suicidal attempt to save the enemies of Germany. In fact, any such attempt by me will merely precipitate their end."

Tod saw the relentless logic behind his words. They were both confronted with a vicious enemy who valued life at nothing. He too, must play for time. Time alone could save the *Prominente*.

"What is their destination?" he asked.

"I do not know."

Tod was not sure that he was not lying.

"I insist on knowing their destination," he reiterated.

"I can only do one thing," said the Commandant. "As some of my personnel will accompany them, I can instruct that they bring back here a message from your men. From that, you should know where they have gone."

The conversation was at an end.

The S.B.O. was escorted back to the prison, where he found that extra guards had already been mounted over the quarters of the *Prominente*. An *Appell* was held just before dusk and the *Prominente* were then locked into their cells.

Colonel Tod was allowed to speak to them. He told their senior, Captain the Master of Elphinstone, of his conversation with the Commandant, of the position with regard to the Castle and warned him, at all costs, to fight for time, wherever they might find themselves. "The situation is changing hourly and in our favour," he concluded, and then gave them a final word to cheer them, saying, "I've foreseen this eventuality for some time. You will not be deserted. The Swiss Protecting Power Authorities have had specific warning and requests to watch this camp and to follow the movement of any prisoners. They are in close contact with German authorities in Berlin, who are in the know. You will probably be followed by a representative in person or, if not, your movements will be known in their Legation. You are being carefully watched. Good-bye and good luck to all of you."

Nobody else was allowed near them. At 11.30 p.m. the order came for them to move. They were roused from their beds and given two hours to dress, pack and make ready. At 1.30 a.m. they were escorted through a lane of guards to two waiting buses. Bor Komorowski was there with twelve of his most senior officers. John Winant appeared. There were seven British: Captain the Master of Elphinstone, Lieutenant Lord Lascelles, Giles Romilly, Captains the Earl of Hopetoun, Michael Alexander, and Earl Haig, and Lieutenant Max de Hamel. The prison windows were crowded with faces. There was a chorus of good-byes! and good lucks! The twenty-one men filed through the gate. Outside two buses were waiting to take them to an unknown destination. . . .

There was really not much difference between those who left and those who remained. They were all going to be hostages; only the Nazi *Herrenrasse* believed in classifying them, under the delusion that the Allies would bargain for the lives of men as if they were cattle; pedigree cattle being worth more than others.

As the buses, escorted by a light-armoured vehicle, tore out of Colditz and into the night, Giles Romilly, in the British bus, said suddenly, breaking the silence:

"I thought you'd all like to know to-day is Friday the thirteenth."

CHAPTER XXIII

HITLER'S LAST REDOUBT

DURING the course of Friday there was a lull within the Castle. Two important items of news only came into the camp: one, from the guards returning after taking the *Prominente* to their destination, the second from the secret wireless receiver. In their wake, the story of Colditz divides naturally into two separate trails, which it were better the reader followed separately to avoid becoming lost. The first trail leads away from the Castle.

A written message was handed to Colonel Tod, signed by Elphinstone, saying the party had arrived safely at the Castle of Königstein on the River Elbe; the same from which General Giraud had escaped to rejoin the Allies earlier in the war. Two of them, he added, Hopetoun and Haig, were seriously ill. They had been ill before they left, as the authorities knew well, and the journey had made their condition worse.

On Saturday, the 14th, in the afternoon, the *Prominente* were moved, under heavy guard as before, from Königstein, through Czechoslovakia, to Klattau on the borders of Bavaria. There they spent the night. Hopetoun and Haig were left behind at Königstein being too ill to move. The German Commandant had to obtain permission from Berlin to leave them.[1] The sound of Allied guns could be heard as the two buses and the armoured car left Königstein heading for Hitler's redoubt in the Bavarian mountains.

Sunday morning, in bright spring sunshine, the *Prominente*

[1] See Author's note on page 320.

were moved again. Now they headed towards Austria. As evening drew on, they arrived at Laufen on the River Salzach that divides Austria from Bavaria. They stopped outside the barracks, once the palace of the Archbishops of Salzburg, and also the prison where the story of Colditz began. The barracks, which, at the beginning of the war, had been Oflag VII C, was now a civilian internee camp.

Elphinstone as head of the British party refused to disembark. He was suspicious. The camp was not under *Wehrmacht* control, and responsibility for any outrage might be difficult to trace. Where he was, he was definitely under *Wehrmacht* control, facing an Army Colonel who would pay with his head under Himmler's orders if his prisoners escaped, and who would also pay with his head under Allied retribution if they disappeared by other means.

The German Colonel in charge agreed to take them to another camp at Tittmoning, ten miles away, occupied by Dutch officers.

It was nearly dark when they reached Tittmoning. They were marched into the prison, another castle perched on a hill, and in the presence of the German Commandant, were introduced to the senior Dutch officers. Giles Romilly could hardly contain himself. Who should he see in the group standing before them but Vandy, grinning all over his face and with the usual devilish twinkle in his eye. Giles was the only one in the British group who had been a contemporary of Vandy in Colditz. The others had all arrived after his departure.

The Commandant of the camp commended the party to the care of the Dutch officers and left them together in order to organise extra precautions amongst the guards. Himmler's orders were clear: German officers responsible for the prisoners would pay with their lives if any of the prisoners escaped.

As soon as they were by themselves, Giles approached Vandy and the two men shook hands warmly.

"I am zo glad you haf come here. Ve vill look after you," said Vandy ubiquitously. "How strange to meet you again in such circumstances."

"Tell me how you got to this camp," said Romilly, "and then I'll give you all the news from Colditz."

Vandy looked at him.

"Come with me. Virst you must haf a hot coffee and something to eat."

He led Romilly through the echoing corridors, to a mess-room where a meal was in full swing. They sat down together and as Romilly ate hungrily, Vandy went on:

"I vas sent here in January because the Germans thought to get rid off me. I vas a damn nuisance, they said. I vas *Deutsch-feindlich*. They knew I organised all the Dutch escapes and zo they sent me here where there are only old officers and many sick ones—none who vish to escape. Zo they thought, but again they are wrong, vor I haf now some men here ready to escape!" Vandy chuckled with glee. He was looking older and his face was deeply lined, but his eye had not lost its sparkle.

Vandy introduced Giles to the officers in the refectory and they talked for some time. Then he escorted him to a dormitory prepared for the five British and the one American *Prominente*, John Winant. The Polish Generals were entertained by another Dutch officers' mess in a different part of the Castle and slept in a separate dormitory.

The *Prominente* stayed at Tittmoning for several days.

On Thursday, April 19th, Vandy had news through the German guards, some of whom were in his pay, that Goebbels and Himmler had been seen in cars, passing through Tittmoning at high speed, in a whirlwind of dust, taking the road to the redoubt built near Hitler's Berchtesgaden. On the same day the *Prominente* were informed they were to be moved to Laufen. There was little doubt as to the implications of this move. At Laufen, out of the control of the Army, Himmler's thugs would take charge of them.

A secret conference was held at which Vandy produced a plan of campaign. He was nothing if not resourceful, but he was not only resourceful, he was far-sighted. He had a method of escape prepared for two of his own officers which could be used in an emergency such as this. This escape could take place the next day, the 20th. He proposed that three officers, of whom one should be Romilly, who spoke German fluently, and the other two his Dutchmen, should escape by his projected route. But he had not finished. He proposed to wall up the other five (including Winant) in a secret radio room which he had prepared for a clandestine wireless-set. They would have food and water for a week, and the Germans would think they had escaped with the three.

The *Prominente* had only to listen to Vandy for ten minutes, after which they placed themselves entirely in his hands.

April 20th was Hitler's birthday. The escape was planned for the evening. Romilly was equipped along with Lieutenant André Tieleman and a young officer cadet, both of whom had come to Tittmoning by mistake, as they were neither elderly nor decrepit, nor sick, nor dangerous like Vandy.

First of all, the five men were walled into the secret radio room with their food reserves. Then, as the moon rose, Vandy and his assistant for the escape, Captain van den Wall Bake, escorted the three escapers to a doorway in the castle from which, one at a time and with suitable distraction of the sentries by helpers in the castle windows, they were able to make a quick dash into the shadows immediately underneath a pagoda sentry-box inside the prison perimeter and beside an eight-foot wall bounding the castle. On the other side of the wall was a seventy-foot drop to a water meadow. Vandy had the rope. He climbed carefully up the pagoda framework to the top of the wall and secured the rope firmly to a timber strut. The sentry was ten feet above him, on the platform, inside a glass shelter with a veranda around it. Vandy helped Tieleman to mount and then eased him over the edge for the long descent. Dutchmen, in their mess-rooms close by, were playing musical instruments and keeping up a continuous cacophony of laughter, music and singing. Romilly and the Dutch cadet came next. Romilly lay flat on the top of the wall and gripped the rope. As he lifted one leg to drop over, he hit one of the timber stanchions a resounding whack with his boot. The sentry came out of his pagoda and leaned over the balustrade. He saw two men standing on the wall and a third lying along it. He had left his rifle inside the pagoda. He yelled "Halt!" and ran to fetch it. In that instant Romilly disappeared over the edge and Vandy whispered to van den Wall Bake, "Quick! Quick! on to the wall." Van den Wall Bake had not been seen in the shadows. The next moment he was lying on the top beside Vandy.

The sentry had rung the alarm bell and now dashed on to the veranda again, aiming his rifle over the side at the three men and shouting: *"Hände hoch! Hände hoch!"* The Dutchmen complied as best they could without going over the edge down the seventy-foot drop. The guard was turned out, arrived at the double and arrested the three men. The sentry reported he had caught them in the act and had spotted them in time, before anyone had escaped.

They were led before the Commandant, who treated them jocosely, in conformity with the state of the war at that moment.

"How silly of you to try to escape now! What is the point? The war is nearly over. You will be home soon. I have told you that General Eisenhower has issued strict orders by wireless that prisoners are to remain in their camps. They run excessive dangers of being killed by moving about alone in the open country at this time. I suppose you just wished more quickly to see your wives and sweethearts?"

The Commandant was elderly, grey-haired and formerly a retired senior ranking army officer. He was not an arrogant personality.

Vandy replied in German.

"Of course, the Commandant has divined our intentions correctly."

"Very well, the matter is closed. I must, according to regulations, hold an *Appell*. I am sorry, but, please remember, it is you who have caused this trouble and not me."

The whistles blew and the floodlights were switched on. The Dutch officers assembled, and the Polish *Prominente* assembled. . . . There was a pause as the German officers, with horror-stricken incredulity, surveyed the ranks before them. Hurriedly and nervously the count was taken. Six *Prominente* and one Dutch officer were missing. A second count was taken. The result was the same. It was reported to the Commandant in his office. The elderly soldier's hair rose from his scalp. He had thought he would spend the last years of his life quietly and peacefully. Now, in a moment, all had changed and he saw his head in the noose, the gallows below him and felt the sickening drop. No! he thought, as his eyes started from his head, it would not be like that. Instead, he felt the handkerchief round his eyes, he could hear the fire orders and then one rending crackle. . . .

He sat up in his chair behind his desk. His junior officers were awaiting orders. He would have to give them. He would be signing his own death warrant. He must stall. It was his only hope. He ordered his officers to search the camp at once and to continue until he issued further orders.

Searching continued for two days in the camp. Nothing was found. The Commandant had to report and give himself up. He was arrested, summarily court-martialled and sentenced to death. The order of execution remained only to be signed by Himmler, as being the head of the organisation which, under Hitler's authority, had issued the original commands. Himmler was not easily accessible. He was already in hiding in the mountains. In the meantime, the search continued desperately, outside the camp. Three thousand Germans scoured the countryside without avail. The Polish *Prominente* were removed to Laufen. On the fifth day—perhaps information had leaked out, nobody could tell—they began to search inside the camp again, knocking down walls, removing floors and attacking ceilings. Eventually, they came upon the secret hide and unearthed four British officers and John Winant.

This discovery occurred on Tuesday, April 24th. What followed is best told by the Master of Elphinstone himself in a report which was published in *The Times*:

Under very heavy escort we were taken to the internee

camp at Laufen. Here the German general commanding the Munich area visited the camp, and in the course of an interview finally gave me his word of honour that we should remain there until the end of the war—a promise repeated in the presence of the Swiss Minister by the German Kommandant next day. The latter, however, could, or would, give no information as to the reason for our detention apart from all other officer-prisoners, except that it was ordered by Himmler.

All remained quiet until the fall of Munich, and then, with the Americans once more rapidly approaching, the orders were given that we were to move at once—in spite of promises given—into the mountains of the Austrian Tyrol. Two officers, an S.S. colonel and a *Luftwaffe* major, were sent by Obergruppenführer and General of S.S. Berger to conduct us. At 6.30 a.m. we entered the transport, with the colonel fingering his revolver, watching us, together with a somewhat sinister-looking blonde woman who accompanied him in his car. This was possibly the most trying of all the moves, as the whole scene had a gangster-like atmosphere. We drove through Salzburg, past Berchtesgaden, and finally stopped at a Stalag in a remote valley in the Tyrol. We were allowed no contact with the prisoners, who included representatives of most of the Allied nations, but were isolated in the German part of the camp.

The representative of the Swiss Legation (Protecting Power), with admirable and very reassuring promptitude, followed us and visited the Kommandant within a very few hours of our arrival. Later the Swiss Minister and his staff started on the series of interviews and discussions with the leading German Government figures who were in the neighbourhood. This work, which they carried out with such wonderful patience and success, was of the utmost difficulty, as the leaders were scattered in remote mountain hamlets, and all roads were choked with army vehicles and personnel.

Finally, S.S. Obergruppenführer Berger, chief, among other things, of all prisoner-of-war affairs, agreed to hand us over to the Swiss and allow them to conduct us through the lines. He did this on his own responsibility, and warned the Swiss that other elements in the Government would, if they

301

knew, resist his orders and lay hands on us. He therefore sent to the camp a special guard under an S.S. colonel, armed with every type of weapon, to guard us against the "other German elements" during this final night of our captivity.

Berger himself came to visit us and in a long and theatrically declaimed speech reiterated, probably for the last time, many of the well-worn phrases of German propaganda together with several revelations of the complete break-up of the German Government and people. He then informed us that owing to this break-up he felt he was no longer in a position to safeguard us properly and had agreed to hand us over to Swiss protection. On leaving, he turned, theatrical to the end, to the German officers in charge of us and, having given his final commands, said: "Gentlemen, these are probably the last orders I shall give as a high official of the Third German Reich." We were due to leave at eleven next morning. The Swiss Legation attaché who was to accompany us in his car arrived early, but for more than three rather tantalising hours there was no sign of the German trucks which were to take the party, a fact which caused some anxiety in view of Berger's warnings. At length, however, two other trucks were secured locally, thanks once again to the perseverance of the Swiss attaché, and finally at about 5 p.m. we set off, each vehicle draped with the Swiss flag, along the densely packed roads. Accompanying us was an S.S. medical officer as personal representative of General Berger.

At about 11.30 p.m. this officer stopped the convoy in a small village in the mountains, saying he had orders from Obergruppenführer Berger to see that we had food and drink in his headquarters here. We entered a house filled with S.S. troops, many of them intoxicated, and were shown into an upstairs room where some food and much drink were laid out. In the middle of the meal the Obergruppenführer himself once more made a theatrical entry, played the expansive if somewhat nerve-strained host, and again poured out a flood of propaganda and explanation. After some time he gave an order to an S.S. adjutant, who handed him a scarlet leather case. After yet another speech he turned to me, as senior of the British-American party, and handed me the case, as "proof of his good feelings." Inside was an elaborately ornamented pistol of

302

ivory, brass and enamel, with his own signature engraved across the butt.

After this strange interlude we set off once more. At dawn we passed successfully through the last German post, and shortly afterwards were halted, to our joy and relief, by American tanks. A few hours later we were most kindly and hospitably welcomed by an American Divisional Head-quarters at Innsbruck. It would be difficult indeed 'for our party adequately to express our gratitude to the Swiss Minister and his staff for all that they did to make this release possible.

The Polish *Prominente* were released in the same convoy.

It is interesting to note that Colonel Tod's last cheering words to the *Prominente* before they left Colditz were not said without avail. The Swiss Minister to Germany was on their trail and caught up with them at Laufen on April 25th.

Giles Romilly takes up the thread of his own last escape from the castle at Tittmoning in an article he wrote for the *Sunday Express* of May 6th, 1945. He says:

My legs were dangling over the wall. The drop was seventy feet down to the moon-whitened grass, and it looked terrify-ing.

I gripped the rope, let myself forward and began to go down faster than expected.

I knew I should grip with my feet, but never once managed it. And the rope was tearing my fingers. About half-way I remember thinking, "This parachute should open soon".

At the bottom, already down, was the Dutch officer, Lieu-tenant André Tieleman.

We tramped down lonely sideroads, star-guided. It was a grand night. And it was Hitler's birthday. And we were free; precariously free—but still free.

That was eleven days ago.

We were *Prominente,* and I heard the word in Dachau horror-camp.

In Dachau there were thirty-two thousand prisoners—and

forty *Prominente*. Two of the "Proms" were English. One was Lieutenant-Colonel McGrath, brought there for refusing to form a "Free Irish" corps.

The other, I believe, was Major Stevens, captured on the Dutch frontier by a trick in the first months of the war.

A few days before the U.S. troops moved in the "Proms" were moved to Schloss Ita, near Innsbruck in the Tyrol.

The *Prominente* were, indeed, all moving in the same direction. From camps all over Germany, the great trek had begun to bring Hitler's hostages into his spider's web, cast in the Austrian mountains.

Romilly and Tieleman managed to reach Munich in three days, after some adventures. On one occasion, they were held for questioning at a police station, but their papers, prepared by Vandy, were found to be in order. The officer in charge received an urgent telephone message while they were standing in his office, concerning the escape of important prisoners from Tittmoning. He hurried them out of the office immediately, saying he had an urgent assignment, and politely wished them a pleasant journey.

In Munich, the two men lived as Germans, quietly and inconspicuously in a cheap hotel, awaiting the American advance. They reported themselves to American Army Headquarters as soon as the latter entered the city during the last week of April. Romilly was back in England by May 2nd.

Vandy had not completed his duty as a soldier and an ally. Not satisfied with having delayed for five days the execution of Himmler's orders, perhaps saving the lives of the *Prominente* thereby, he risked his life by leaving the camp in the dead of night as soon as the Americans had entered Tittmoning, and contrary to American Army orders. There was a severe curfew in operation. Anyone seen on the streets was liable to be shot on sight. He appeared at American Headquarters where he reported the transfer of the *Prominente* including John Winant and was able, moreover, through his own German sources of information to give details as to the route they had taken into the Tyrol from Laufen.

The cataclysm that swept over Germany and Austria in April saved many lives. Communications were severed, the roads were clogged with refugee traffic, and the precious signatures of Hitler's hierarchy were not forthcoming. Hitler committed suicide in the Berlin bunker on April 30th; many executions were stayed and many a happy man to-day owes his continuing life on this globe to a missing black scrawl on a sheet of white paper; among them is the German Commandant of the Dutch camp at Tittmoning.

CHAPTER XXIV

FINALE: THE RELIEF OF COLDITZ

BACK in the Castle: Friday, April 13th, an unlucky day for the
Prominente, brought good news to Colditz through the secret
wireless receiver. Hodge's spearhead, south of Leipzig, was
advancing again after a slight check during the day of the 12th.
The Americans were twenty miles away at dawn and, by the
evening, they were in the Colditz area, invisible but there,
nevertheless. Shells fell in the town as the dusk approached
and in the distance machine-gun fire could be heard. Desultory
firing continued through the night.

The next morning, Saturday, the 14th, at dawn, the battle
for Colditz began. The Allied Air Forces had possession of the
sky. An American reconnaissance plane zoomed overhead. A
few shells followed, dropping into various parts of the town.
The artillery were ranging.

Colonel Tod was called again to the Kommandantur, where
Prawitt faced him.

"You are to move the British out of the Castle towards the
east under guard. I have orders from Dresden."

This was Tod's chance. Twenty-four hours had just made
the difference. The S.S. had their hands full. To-day they were
under attack fighting a battle, and they could not possibly deal
with three hundred British prisoners not to mention a thousand
Frenchmen. They could not even spare the time to come into
the camp and shoot them all. Tod seized the opportunity.

"The British refuse to move," he said. "You will have to
turn them out with the bayonet and the British will fight. This
is not mutiny. It is self-defence. You are sending them out to
their death. Tell Dresden we shall not move."

Tod was recalling another occasion, a long time ago, when the Commandant had shown he was less fearful of his superiors when they were a long way off. Those nearby were heavily engaged which came to the same thing.

The Commandant weakened.

"I shall 'phone my Headquarters," he said, sitting down at his desk and picking up the army field telephone. He spoke to a couple of exchanges in turn, using German code names. Then he was speaking to the General. He reported the position at Colditz, leading up to his interview with Tod; ending with, "and the British refuse to move."

There was an explosion from the other end. A guttural German voice was yelling blue murder at the Commandant who held the receiver far away from his ear. Gradually the rasping died down. Oberst Prawitt was at last showing signs of courage. With remarkable calm he addressed his senior:

"I cannot move the prisoners without shooting them and they will then resist. Their Commander will disclaim mutiny on grounds of self-defence. Will you take the responsibility if I use my weapons and prisoners are killed?"

"No!" came the answer, shouted down the telephone.

"Neither will I!" said the Commandant and banged down the receiver . . .

Even the few marker shells dropped into Colditz by the American artillery were having a surprisingly salutary effect on the conduct of affairs within the Castle walls.

The prisoners did not move.

Heavy shelling started in the afternoon and buildings were soon on fire in many quarters. The noise of gunfire increased to a crescendo. To the onlookers in the Castle, no orderly plan appeared to be unfolding. There was only destruction, smoke, flames and noise, the tearing scrunch of shells, the whine of splinters, the acrid smell of burnt explosive and chaos.

Half a dozen shells landed in the Castle, splintering glass everywhere and leaving ragged holes in the roof. Nobody was seriously hurt. Duggie Bader was knocked off his tin legs. The prisoners were ordered to the ground-floor.

The Kommandantur fared worse and a dozen shells tore large gaps in the building, wounding several Germans. Nevertheless, the general shelling appeared to be avoiding the Castle.

In the early afternoon, Colonel Tod had another session with Oberst Prawitt. The Commandant, judging by his appearance, had probably received information, though he did not say so, that the S.S. would not retreat into the Castle and make a stand in it. His face showed immense relief. He was wreathed in smiles and almost fawning on Tod as he told him that he would surrender to him the inside of the Castle on certain conditions: the S.S. were still in the town, and no sign must be given to them that the Castle had been surrendered; no national or other coloured flags to be in evidence! no white flags of surrender to be visible at the windows; appearances to be kept up by leaving the sentries at their posts around the exterior; a guarantee to be given by the S.B.O. that he, Oberst Prawitt, would not be handed over to the Russians.

Tod refused to give any guarantees. He thought for a moment, realising the value and importance of access to the armoury in case of need. He decided to take a risk. He compromised on one point, making a counter proposal. If the interior of the whole Castle were handed over to him, including the armoury if and when he so desired, so that he could move his officers freely within the Kommandantur area, he would instruct them not to show signs of surrender outside the Castle. He added that he would see the Commandant was treated with justice, that was as far as he could go. Tod was becoming master of the situation. He would move his officers about and would obtain arms if he wanted them though already he felt the danger from the S.S. receding. He ran the risk that the Americans might take it into their heads to blow up the Castle not knowing who was inside. He would like to have put out flags. He used his judgment. The shells, he considered, which had entered the Castle were 'off target'. The Americans were now pouring high explosive into the town. He was sure that they were avoiding the Castle and for no other reason than that they knew there were prisoners inside. Finally, Tod considered it wiser to keep his men within the inner courtyard, unless the situation deteriorated. If the S.S. decided to move into the Castle he was to be informed in time. The Commandant was not treacherous. He himself with a small staff would keep their eye on developments from the Kommandantur.

The Commandant accepted the terms with some alacrity. As Colonel Tod walked back to the prisoners' courtyard to assemble his staff officers, the first American tanks were spotted on the horizon through Keith Milne's telescope.

All through the night of the 14th–15th the battle for Colditz continued. There was an electric power cut in the whole district, and the slave gang was hard put to it to keep the wireless receiver in action. The searchlights went out. Instead, a pale moon suffused the Castle with ghostly luminosity. Its belfries, buttresses and towering walls stood out grimly against the skyline. Unearthly lights and shadows flickered across the surface, cast up from the flames and the smoke in the valley. Like an evil witch, it hovered over the steaming cauldron of the town, applying fuel to the fire underneath as the bright flashes of exploding shells sent dark clouds into the air and new fires licked around the bowl.

Nobody slept much during the night. The moon cast a grey light into the dormitories and the very air seemed feverish. Men tossed and turned, straw palliasses rustled interminably. Explosions shook the buildings and air blast whoofed through the wide-open windows, tinkling the panes of glass. The rasp of machine-guns increased as the moonlight faded, giving place to a dawn that streaked layers of grey and gold across the sky from the east. The rattle of muskets drew nearer. American light bombers droned overhead and dropped their shattering loads on the railway lines and the roads.

Sunday, April 15th, saw the culmination of the attack. The weather was fine and the sun shone in a translucent spring sky. American shellfire was heavy all through the morning, yet the Castle was not hit. It was now obviously being carefully preserved. The town was being reduced to a mass of burning timber, rubble and twisted steel.

One of the five French Generals who had recently arrived, General de Boisse, of the French 62nd Division, chose this morning to have his portrait painted in pastels by the camp artist, John Watton. A jagged white chalk streak on the picture, underneath the General's chin, which he would not allow to be removed, records to this day the moment when the Germans tried to blow up Colditz bridge.

It was their last despairing effort to delay the Americans before retreating with their tanks, a beaten enemy, towards the south-east.

The blown bridge did not collapse. Piers were damaged but the roadway held, and the Americans were not stopped. By eleven o'clock in the morning their tanks were seen in the town. One after the other, with long intervals between, they trundled carefully into the main street, splaying out fanwise into secondary roads and lanes as they reached them. Moving warily in front and around the tanks could be seen the mine-removal squads and the infantry. The latter, covered by the tanks, advanced from house to house amongst the ruins, breaking in the front doors where they remained standing, and disappearing inside. From the windows, white sheets would appear, one after the other, in token of surrender.

Underneath the walls of the Castle, a tank rounded a street corner. Lying in the gutter, not fifty yards away, a fair-haired Hitler Youth, of scarcely fifteen years, opened up on it with a machine-gun. A woman, probably his mother, screamed at him from an upper window in the house nearby. Another machine-gun crackled angrily, and the boy rolled over. American G.I.s appeared from behind the tank, and began taking over the houses, one by one, on either side of the street.

Half an hour later, the gate into the prisoners' courtyard opened and an American soldier stepped into the spring sunshine in the middle of the yard. A tall, broad-chested G.I. with an open, weather-beaten countenance, his belt and straps festooned with ammunition clips and grenades, a sub-machine gun in his hand, he stood and, looking upwards, slowly turned around. His gaze toured the full circle of the steep roofs above him, the massive walls, the barred windows and, finally, the cobbles at his feet.

There were many officers in the courtyard at the time. For fully a minute they watched him, incredulously. Some were walking around the yard. They stopped and stared at him blankly. Some were chatting in groups. They ceased talking and looked, quizzically, in his direction. A few, unperturbed by the march of events, were sitting on benches, reading. The sudden silence made them raise their heads. They stared with mouths agape at the strange intruder standing in the sunlight. Faces at the windows remained motionless like wax masks without expression.

Dick Howe saw the G.I. enter. A brainstorm momentarily paralysed the normal currents of his mind. His memory played tricks upon him, and switched, suddenly, to a scene which floated past his inward eye. He saw himself standing on a dusty road outside Calais in 1940, unarmed and a prisoner. A German soldier was passing and he shouted, *"Für Sie ist der Krieg zu Ende. Wir fahren gegen England. Sie gehen nach Deutschland."* Now the irony of the words struck him. "For you the war is over." That was five years ago. And the German? He was probably dead long ago.

An officer, standing near the gate, advanced with outstretched hand and shook the hand extended by the American, who grinned at him and said, cheerfully, "Any doughboys here?" The spell was broken.

Suddenly, a mob was rushing towards him, shouting and cheering and struggling madly to reach him, to make sure that he was alive, to touch him, and from the touch to know again the miracle of living, to be men in their own right, freed from bondage, outcast no more, liberated by their Allies and their friends, their faith in God's mercy justified, their patience rewarded, the nobility of mankind vindicated, justice at last accomplished and tyranny once more overcome.

Men wept, unable to restrain themselves. It was not enough

that the body was free once more to roam the earth. Feelings, pent up and dammed behind the mounting walls of five successive torturing, introverted years, had to erupt.

They welled up like gushing springs, they overflowed, they burst their banks, they tumbled unhindered and uncontrolled. Frenchmen with tears streaming down their faces kissed each other on both cheeks—the salute of brothers. They kissed the G.I., they kissed everyone within range. The storm of emotion burst. The merciful rain descended. The grey clouds drifted from the horizon of the mind, borne on fresh salt- and moisture-laden breezes across the unchained oceans of memory from the far-off shores of love. Home and country beckoned, loved ones were waiting. Wives and sweethearts, mothers, fathers, and children never seen, were calling across the gulf of the absent years.

Man was at his finest amidst the grandeur of this moment of liberation. A noble symphony arranged by the Great Composer had reached its thunderous finale and, as the last triumphal chord swelled into the Hymn of Nations, man looked into the face of his Creator turned towards him, a vision of tenderness, mirrored for an instant by the purity of his own unrepressed torrent of joy and thankfulness. At such a moment, mountains move at the behest of man, he has such power in the sight of God.

CHAPTER XXV

CODA: THE CLIFFS OF DOVER

THE celebrations upon the relief of the Castle began in earnest on Sunday afternoon, April 15th. Food reserves, laid in for a siege, were broken into and the Americans brought wine and beer from the town. Colonel Tod wisely kept the prisoners inside the Castle until the first exuberance at their deliverance had worn off. It was better they should become accustomed in their minds to the idea that they were free before they were actually let loose upon the world. They were, be it remembered, 'the men of spirit'.

Tod had already organised officers into squads with specific duties and instructions, varying according to the different eventualities that he could foresee. In the circumstances, as no fighting was required of his men, only the squads with technical duties came into action. Before they did so, however, he held a conference with the American officer commanding the troops who had captured the town.

Lieutenant-Colonel Shaughnessy came from Carolina. He spoke with a slow drawl and acted with lightning rapidity. He was not, after all, in command of one of Hodge's most daring spearheads, driving hundreds of miles into enemy territory in advance of the main forces, for nothing. Tried in battle, full of initiative and daring, he was one of the men who shortened the war and saved thousands of lives.

A Colonel, he was at the head of a force from Combat Command 'R' of the 9th Armoured Division (Fifth Corps) of the U.S. First Army. He had under him the 3rd Battalion of the 273rd Infantry Regiment, 69th Infantry Division, and detachments of tanks and mobile artillery taken from the 9th Armoured Division. These together constituted his task force.

By this time, incidentally, it is worth recording that the 9th Armoured Division had been nicknamed by the Germans the 'Phantom Division' because it seemed to be everywhere there was action. Among Shaughnessy's junior officers was Lieutenant Kenny Dodson, the efficient young artillery officer who had commanded the shoot against Colditz. The first American squad actually to set foot in the Castle consisted of an Intelligence and Reconnaissance section of four men from H.Q. Company, 3rd Battalion, 273rd Infantry Regiment. They had entered the village in the early morning and were gradually driven up the hill to the Castle by American shell-fire. Seeing no guards they forced open the moat gateway and found themselves in the German Kommandantur courtyard. Two groups of men faced them. On one side were senior Allied officers led by Colonel Tod. On the other was a disconsolate body of German officers. The four young men promptly disarmed the Germans, and one of them, Private First-class Walter V. Burrows, of Pennsylvania, volunteered to escort them back to Shaughnessy's Headquarters. Private First-class Alan H. Murphey, Bronze Star Medal, of New York State, led the section. The other two were Privates First-class Francis A. Giegnas, Junior, of New Jersey, and Robert B. Miller of Pennsylvania.

At the conference, held in the German Kommandantur, Shaughnessy accepted the surrender of the Castle and its garrison. The Commandant and Hauptmann Eggers, the Security Officer, were arrested. Tod proposed that the P.O.W.s, other than those on special duties, should be kept within the Castle precincts until Tuesday the 17th. Shaughnessy agreed this was wise and warned that German suicide parties were still dotted all over the countryside. Tod offered the services of his organised squads to keep the water and electricity supply of Colditz functioning, to look after other essential town services, and to see that repairs were effected as quickly as possible. Shaughnessy accepted, and the British Technical Squads came into action.

Gordon Rolfe left the camp with a party within the hour, to

take over the Colditz power station and start it running again. Dick set off with another party to look after the water-pumping station. On the way he commandeered a powerful B.M.W. German Army motor-cycle which became his 'transport' until he boarded a plane for England. He found the pumping station had not suffered badly from the bombardment. Buildings had been damaged but the sturdy machinery was in working order. Debris alone had to be cleared and the pumps could be started again on power from the heavy oil engines. German staff were already back at the station when he arrived. The Teutonic passion for work and order could not be denied. Dick found they needed no goading and no supervision, although they did not know how, where or when their next pay packet would materialise. They cleared and cleaned and repaired. The pumps were working again by Sunday evening, supplying water to the town. Water pipes were burst and leaking everywhere. The task of repairing them was tackled by another squad of Royal Engineers.

In the Castle, Americans came and went and stories of the latter days went the rounds. Lieutenant Dodson confessed that the Castle was within an ace of being bombarded by his mobile artillery detachment with high explosive shells followed by phosphorous, when the task force approached Colditz. Standing orders were to flatten anything that showed resistance. Colditz showed resistance, and the best target in the town was the Castle. Dodson's artillery was fanned out and ranging on it when a spotter noticed a flag in one of the windows through his binoculars. It was a French flag. He scanned the Castle more closely and saw a Union Jack. He immediately telephoned Dodson who held his fire and sent word back to headquarters at Hohnbach, a village they had just captured, asking for confirmation as to the nature of the Castle. The answer came through: "Do not repeat not shell Castle which contains P.O.W."

The prison was, in fact, within an ace of being shelled. As far as can be ascertained, Hohnbach received the order to preserve the Castle from Hodge's headquarters at about the same time as Dodson asked for confirmation. Be it noted that this occurred some twelve hours before Colonel Tod agreed with the German Commandant not to hang out flags. By then there was evidence indicating that the shelling was deliberately directed away from the Castle.

On Sunday afternoon, the glider was taken from its hiding-place. The trap-door in the floor of the workshop was carefully enlarged and the glider parts were lowered into the big attic with the dormer windows. In this empty room the four builders assembled the glider. By five o'clock it was ready. They sealed the trap-door up to the workshop and then opened the main door of the lower attic. Dick experienced the pleasure of sitting in the cockpit and manipulating the controls. "It's a perfect little bird," he said as he waggled the rudder. "I believe I'd be as safe in this as in my old Matilda."

And Lulu Lawton commented sadly, "I'd have given a lot to see the Jerries' reaction when the bathful of concrete landed on the floor after falling sixty feet."

News of the existence of the glider had spread like wild-fire. The camp had been advised that the glider would be on view, and there was a queue already waiting that stretched to the bottom of the spiral staircase. When the door opened the crowd surged forward.

As there were thirteen hundred officers in the camp at the time, the queue continued late into the evening. An American girl, a newspaper correspondent—Lee Carson was her name—had found her way to Colditz and she was escorted to the attic by Duggie Bader. She took photographs. (The glider builders and the author would give much to be able to trace them.)

The glider reposed on its polished skid, a symphony in blue and white check; its wings glossy and taut; its controls sensitive, balanced, easy to the touch; a tropical bird, it looked as if it needed only a gentle breeze to float it easily off the ground. It filled the attic. Its total span from wing-tip to wing-tip was thirty-three feet. It was a beautiful piece of craftsmanship and astounded all who saw it. Men gasped with wonder and appreciation as they toured around it. The Americans asked:

"Where has it come from? How was it possible to build it under the Germans' noses?" They were told.

Germans, remaining in the camp under Allied orders to keep it functioning, who saw it, also asked the same questions. The answer was, "You were our guards. You ought to know without being told."

Before the prisoners vacated the Castle the attic was locked up again. Both the glider and the secret workshop may still be there to this day. . . .

Monday the 16th was a dog-day in which prisoners recovered from the celebrations of Sunday and began to regain their perspective, looking towards new horizons.

On Tuesday they were allowed the freedom of Colditz, but warned not to venture into the surrounding country which was placed out-of-bounds. Three Frenchmen who disobeyed the order were recaptured by the Germans and disappeared.

Colonel Shaughnessy was busy, with British and French help, organising preparations for the evacuation of the prisoners. Dick Howe recalls two vivid impressions of that day. The first was that of the Weasel, the City Slicker and Mac (MacColm) holding open house in a villa near the Castle in which three beautiful blonde German girls acted as their hostesses serving tea, coffee, drinks and meals throughout the day to all visitors The second was that of the Distillery Monopoly Directors, Charlie Goonstein van Rood, Bush Parker and Bag Dickenson, driving around the town in a huge Mercedes-Benz touring car.

The town was found to be full of slave workers of both sexes: Poles, French, Czechs, Russians, Rumanians, Yugoslavs, Hungarians and Jews.

On Wednesday, April 18th, the evacuation began.

American trucks, driven by Negro drivers, carried the British contingent a hundred miles to the south-west.

Dick, on his B.M.W., acted as outrider to one of the

columns. The convoy was widely spread out for safety, and on the move, the Negroes drove the trucks at full throttle all the time. The leading fifteen-hundredweight truck contained the American officer in charge and Hauptmann Püpcke, one of the German officers of Colditz. He knew the roads of the district. The going was dangerous at times, especially through the woods, where German *Sturmgeschütze* nests—S.S. storm-troopers—still lurked in ambush. Dick, at the behest of the American officer, had the nasty job of reconnoitring a road-block which loomed ahead at one stage of the journey. He rode flat out up to it, weaving as he approached. He found it un-manned. Not once, through thirty miles of no-man's land, was the column shot at, though shadows flitted about amongst the trees in the surrounding woods. Strength in numbers seemed to be the explanation.

They arrived, in the late afternoon, at a captured airfield near Chemnitz, called Kaledar, were given a hot meal of American Army rations and bedded down on clean straw for the night.

Early next morning, as Dick stepped out of the hut where they had been sleeping, he was accosted by the Major in charge of the airfield.

"I hear you boys are back from five years in prison?" he questioned.

"That's correct," said Dick.

"I guess you're keen to get back home then. I'll see what I can do." He hailed the leading crew of a flight of Dakotas that had just landed.

"Where're you going back to?" he shouted.

The leading officer replied, approaching,

"We're due for Rolle."

"No, you're not," said the Major, "you're going to England."

"Suits me!" came the answer.

Within two hours they were boarding the planes. There must have been ten of them, because they took the whole British contingent, thirty to a plane. Dick tried to take his B.M.W. with him—it was a beautiful machine. There was nothing doing, he had to leave it behind. He rode around the hutted camp at the edge of the airfield until he saw a G.I. coming out of a workshop. With a roar he rode up behind him, stopped and said,

"Hey! can you ride a motor-bike?"

"Yea."

"Well," said Dick dismounting, "you've got one."

He hurried off to join his plane and, looking back, saw the G.I., arms akimbo, slowly walking around the machine, with his eyes agog, like an art connoisseur who had just been presented with an old master out of the sky.

The weather was bad and the ceiling was practically zero. In Dick's plane were many of the 'Old Contemptibles'—men who had been in Colditz from the very early days: Guy German, Rupert Barry, Scarlet O'Hara, Cyril Lewthwaite, Padre Platt, Don Donaldson, Peter Storie Pugh, Stooge Wardle, Keith Milne and Jim Rogers. The plane cavorted about the sky. Everybody except Don Donaldson was sick. They landed to refuel at Rouen, and then crossed the Channel amongst the clouds, almost dropping into the sea at times.

Jim Rogers, who was not as ill as some of the others, went forward to the cockpit and looked ahead into the blank wall of vapour. He asked the pilot,

"Are we anywhere near Dover?" The plane lurched and sank a hundred feet. The green spuming sea appeared just below them.

"Don't know!" was the reply, "I'm following the guy in front."

Jim scanned the clouds in front without seeing anything. He was rubbing his head ruefully where something hard had hit him when the aircraft bumped.

"Visibility yesterday was nil," said the pilot. "One of our planes flew head on into the cliffs. It's better to-day."

Jim went back to the others, seated facing each other on the floor, backs propped up against the bulwarks. They were looking green. The smell of sick was overpowering. Jim was terrified. After five years, to come to a sticky end in the Channel!

He longed to see the cliffs of Dover but he did not want to meet them head on. He could see the crash coming. In a daze he heard his own voice,

"We're nearly home, boys. The pilot's terrific. Gives you confidence. He says he's sorry about the weather, but he wants you to see the cliffs of Dover. That's why he's flying low—so you don't miss them." He suddenly halted in his speech as he realised what he had said. Then another thought struck him. "About time I stopped this morale boosting," he said to himself. "The chaps'll have to look after themselves now."

Don Donaldson, the R.A.F. veteran, wedged in a corner near the tail, had been dozing peacefully. He looked up at Jim and then at the rows of green faces around him and said, "Tell 'em a story, Old Horse. They look as if they need cheering up. Tell 'em about the Mandarin's daughter you met in Hong Kong. They've got to get accustomed to having women-folk around again."

AUTHOR'S NOTE
(see page 295)

When Admiral Doenitz surrendered on May 2nd after the death of Hitler, the Russians, by Allied agreement, occupied Königstein. A week later, the prisoners, including senior staff officers, Dutch, Belgian, French, British and American, were still confined in the Castle. Two Americans escaped to the American lines, forty miles away, and within hours a U.S. armed convoy entered the town and removed the whole prisoner contingent. Hopetoun and Haig were promptly flown to Britain in an ambulance plane. Both men recovered their health slowly.